HOOP ROOTS

Books by John Edgar Wideman

A GLANCE AWAY

HURRY HOME

THE LYNCHERS

DAMBALLAH

HIDING PLACE

SENT FOR YOU YESTERDAY

BROTHERS AND KEEPERS

REUBEN

FEVER

PHILADELPHIA FIRE

THE COLLECTED STORIES OF
JOHN EDGAR WIDEMAN

FATHERALONG

THE CATTLE KILLING

TWO CITIES: A LOVE STORY

HOOP ROOTS

HOOP ROOTS

John Edgar Wideman

Houghton Mifflin Company

BOSTON   NEW YORK   2001

For information about permission to reproduce
selections from this book, write to Permissions,
Houghton Mifflin Company, 215 Park Avenue South,
New York, New York 10003.

Visit our Web site: www.houghtonmifflinbooks.com.

Library of Congress Cataloging-in-Publication Data
Wideman, John Edgar.
Hoop roots / John Edgar Wideman.
    p.   cm.
    ISBN 0-395-85731-7
    1. Wideman, John Edgar—Childhood and youth.
2. Authors, American—20th century—Biography.
3. African American authors—Biography. 4. Basketball.
I. Title.
    PS3573.I26 Z467   2001
    813'.54—dc21
    [B]   2001026455

Book design by Melissa Lotfy
Typefaces: Sabon, Akzidenz Grotesk

Printed in the United States of America
QUM 10 9 8 7 6 5 4 3 2 1

Hoop stories—
in homage to W. E. B. Du Bois and *The Souls
of Black Folk*—model, guide, beacon

For Catherine

Many bead artists, discussing . . . what happens to them during the beading process, describe transformations not unlike altered states of consciousness. The act of beading requires intense concentration and small-scale, delicate repetitive action—something that makes time pass without notice and causes the eyes to go out of focus, blurring one's vision and creating a dreamlike state. The gestures of beading begin to take over, to have their own momentum, life, and energy with which the beader is in synchrony. Beading is thus both a physical as well as a metaphysical experience in which artists become both masters of and mastered by their medium.

—Henry John Drewal and John Mason,
Beads, Body, and Soul

CONTENTS

More

*We went to the playground court to find our missing fa-
thers. We didn't find them but we found a game and the
game served us as a daddy of sorts. We formed families
of men and boys, male clans ruled and disciplined by the
game's demands, its hard, distant, implacable gaze, its
rare, maybe loving embrace of us: the game taught us to
respect it and respect ourselves and other players. Playing
the game provided sanctuary, refuge from a hostile world,
and also toughened us by instructing us in styles for cop-
ing with that world. Only trouble was, to reach the court
we had left our women behind. Even though we'd found
the game and it allowed us, if not to become our own
fathers, at least to glimpse their faces, hear their voices,
the family we'd run away from home to restore would
remain broken until we returned to share the tales of
our wandering, listen to the women tell theirs.*

No book. Only a wish I can make something like a book about a game I've played for most of my life, the game of playground basketball I love and now must stop playing. At fifty-nine I'm well past the age most people would consider the natural, inevitable time to give up what's clearly a young person's sport. According to this conventional wisdom I've been stealing for years, decades, stretching unreasonably my time on the court, lacing on sneakers, abusing my body, running up and down as if it never has to end. My three kids are grown and I have a granddaughter in North Carolina old enough to chatter with me on the phone and as I write these words a horrifically bloody century has just ended, my marriage of thirty-plus years has unraveled, and each morning my body requires more coaxing, more warming up to maneuver through the thicket of old aches and pains that settle in during sleep. Still, for some reason basketball feels important. I'm not giving it up willingly. I dream about it. I'm devoting passion and energy to writing a basketball book. Writing something like a book, anyway, because for me what's more important than any product this project achieves is for the process to feel something like playing the game I can't let go.

So this writing is for me, first. A way of holding on. Letting go. Starting a story so a story can end. Telling playground basketball stories, and if I tell them well they will be more about basketball than about me. Because the game rules. The game will assert its primacy. I need the game more than it needs me. You learn that simple truth as a neophyte, an unskilled beginner enthralled, intimidated by the unlikely prospect that you'll ever become as good as those you watch. Learn this truth again, differently, the same truth and a different truth as a veteran observing the action you can barely keep up with anymore and shouldn't even be trying to keep up with anymore. You play for yourself, but the game's never for you or about you. Even at your best, in those charmed instants when the ball leaves your hand and you know that what's going to happen next will be exactly what you want to happen, not maybe or wishing or hoping, just the thrill coursing through your body of being in the flow, in synch, no fear of missing or losing or falling out of time—even in those split seconds which are one form of grace the game delivers, the game is larger than you, it's simply permitting you to experience a glimmer, a shimmer of how large it is, how just a smidgen of it can fill you almost to bursting. When you were born the game was here waiting, and the beat will go on without you.

I think of this game and see my first son, Dan, best ten-year-old free-throw shooter in Wyoming, slowly bowing his head, his knees nearly buckling, eyes filling with tears, looking suddenly so tiny out there alone on the foul line in a cavernous Nebraska high school gym when he realizes his best is not going to be good enough that particular day to win the eleven-and-under regional-free throw contest. His brother, Jake, at thirteen sinking two sweet, all-net jumpers in a row from the corner to win a tough, tight pickup game in the university gym when finally both my sons are old enough to hold their own and play with me on the same team against college kids. See their sister, my daughter, Jamila, leading her Stanford University women's team, number one in the country, into an arena packed with 14,000 fans, a huge roar of rooting for and against them greeting her and her teammates as they trot onto the court, then the eerie quiet two and a half hours later, two and a half hours of some of the most riveting hoop I've ever watched, as Jamila, totally exhausted, collapses into her mother's arms after performing heroically and losing in overtime her final college game.

Whatever you make of this book, I need it. Need it the way I've needed the playground game. Need it like I needed this rain softly falling now, finally, after a whole day so close to rain I found myself holding my breath till dark in expectation of the first large, cooling drops. A sweltering June day I climbed a steep trail up a mountain and hiked through woods surrounding two small reservoirs where people skinny-dip and sunbathe naked, as if the summer of love never ended. Rain in the air, in the sky, on my mind all day. Gray heaps of clouds drifting in, gradually trumping what's been mainly blue. Then the sky scrubs itself stark blue again. The threat of rain never going away, however, even in the brightest streaming down of sunshine, and I can't stop needing it, daydreaming cool rain breaking through. Need to write something like a book because last week back home in Pittsburgh, in the morning I visited my brother Robby who's serving a life term in Western Penitentiary and in the afternoon of the same day visited in a VA hospital the body of my father whose mind has been erased by the disease Robby and the other prisoners call *old-timers*. Need it in this season of losses, losses already recorded in stone and imminent losses, virtual losses, dues paid and dues still to pay heavy on my mind, never far from my thoughts whatever else I might find myself doing in this transitional time, season to season, epoch to epoch, century to century, young to old, life to dying, giving up things, losing things I never believed I'd have to relinquish.

Playground basketball only a game. Why, given my constant struggling and juggling to fit a busy schedule into days without enough hours, does basketball sit there, above the fray, a true and unblemished exception to the rules, the countless hours committed to it unregretted. Why was basketball untouchable over the years as I devised and revised blueprints for making the most profitable use of my time. Why am I missing the playground game, yearning for it now even before it quite slips away. Why when I know good and well it's time to stop playing hoop, time to reconcile myself to the idea of moving on, why do I continue to treat these ideas as unacceptable. Why can't I shake the thought that this break from the game can't be final. If I'm patient, hang around, give myself a little time to heal, to get right, I'll be back out on the court again, won't I.

If I knew the answers, I probably wouldn't need to write the book, or the something like a book I'm pushing for, would settle for, anxious it may be less but also hoping for more than a book. No answers sought here. No book. My need enough. My desire to lose myself in doing something like playing the game.

Growing up, I needed basketball because my family was poor and colored, hemmed in by material circumstances none of us knew how to control, and if I wanted more, a larger, different portion than other poor colored folks in Homewood, I had to single myself out. I say *if I wanted more* because *if* was a real question, a stumbling block many kids in Homewood couldn't get past. It's probably accurate to say that anybody, everybody wants more. But how strong is the desire. How long does it last. What forms does it take. How many young people are convinced they deserve more or believe they possess the strength required to obtain more or believe they actually have a chance for more. The idea of race and the practice of racism in our country work against African-American kids forming and sustaining belief in themselves. Wanting more doesn't teach you there are ways to get there. Nor does it create the self-image of a deserving recipient, a worthwhile person worth striving for. You need the plausibility, the possibility of imagining a different life for yourself, other than the meager portion doled out by the imperatives of race and racism, the negative prospects impressed continuously upon a black kid's consciousness, stifling, stunting the self-awareness of far too many. Including black kids not poor. Imagining a different portion is the first step, the door cracking between known and unknown. A door on alternative possibilities. If you want more and you're lucky enough, as I was, to choose or be chosen by some sort of game, you may then begin to forge a game plan. If you believe you're in the game, you may be willing to learn the game's ABCs. Learn what it costs to play. Begin making yourself a player.

I figured out early that hard, solo work the only way to get certain things about hoop right. Every chance I got I practiced alone the shooting, dribbling skills other kids had somehow mastered. Fear part of it. Fear of failure. Of humiliation. Love just as important as fear. Unconditional love from my family. A sense someone cared, someone rooted for me, someone expected me to do well. I didn't want to let those folks down nor behave on the court in a fashion they might be ashamed of. If I wanted more, I must risk failing, and it helped immeasurably to know that somebody somewhere supported my effort to play well. Would support me if I didn't play well. If no one cared, why bother. Why beat myself up. Set myself up for disappointment. Love helped me imagine I possessed the power to invent myself, make more of myself, become a player.

Fear and love, love and fear raised the stakes of the game. Engendered the beginnings of a hunger, the hunger driving the serious players I admire most, who never seem satisfied no matter how well they perform, players who consistently push themselves as if more hustle, more speed, more brawling competitiveness is never too much. Players who refuse to settle into a comfort zone, who won't accept limits, who attack the game with the same unstinting voraciousness as the game when it attacks them, consuming the best of their bodies and spirits.

The pampering and privileges I received because I was male and the oldest child in the various households of our extended clan certified love in abundance and also stimulated my desire for more. The slightly larger share my mother sometimes tried to slip me when she divided a cake or pie under the hawk eyes of my siblings I took not only as a sign of love and eldest status, as they did. The tiny bit extra also reinforced a sense of entitlement. Without exactly knowing it, I was beginning to single myself out, practicing in the interior world of daydream and fantasy, where no one could eavesdrop, how it might feel to exercise power and authority, fire and a voice I had almost no reason to anticipate my material circumstances—colored and poor in Homewood—would ever grant me.

Growing up in a world where adults heaped love on kids in any and every fashion they could manage, the women lavishing daily, close-up care and attention, the men leaving the house at dawn to line up on the corner where work might or might not arrive, men gone from can to caint, splicing multiple, piecemeal jobs into a precarious living wage, where delicious meals were scraped together from cheap cuts beaten and boiled to tenderness, from government-surplus cheese, powdered milk, and canned, ground, jellied, mystery meat, from chicken's feet, necks, gizzards, beef neckbones, pig's feet, a world in which piles of shiny new toys appeared miraculously once a year at Christmas, the holiday when grownups spent themselves silly, diving deeper, more hopelessly into debt as if one morning of glittering extravagance could erase all the empty-handed ones, in this world of abrupt change, boom and bust, feast and famine where love on one hand acted as a steadying, stabilizing force and on the other hand could exert no control whatsoever over the oppressive economic environment in which both kids and adults were trapped, without that love I would have been a lost soul, but love also created a desperate hunger for more, far more than the people who loved me could provide. Love bred a dark fear of its absence. Because if love disappeared, what would remain. Wouldn't the point be I didn't measure up, didn't deserve love.

As a kid, did I think about my life in terms of wanting more. More of what. Where would I find it. Did I actually pose similar questions to myself. When. How. Why. Looking back, I'm pretty sure about love, an awakening hunger for the game, and not too sure of much else. The act of looking back, the action of writing down what I think I see/saw, destroys certainty. The past presents itself fluidly, changeably, at least as much a work in progress as the present or future.

No scorebook. No reliable witnesses or too many witnesses. Too much time. No time. One beauty of playground hoop is how relentlessly, scrupulously it encloses and defines moments. Playing the game well requires all your attention. When you're working to stay in the game, the game works to keep you there. None of the mind's subtle, complex operations are shut down when you play, they're just intently harnessed, focused to serve the game's complex demands. In the heat of the game you may conceive of yourself playing the game, an aspect of yourself watching another aspect perform, but the speed of the game, its continuous go and flow, doesn't allow a player to indulge this conscious splitting-off and self-reflection, common, perhaps necessary, to writing autobiography. Whatever advantages such self-division confers are swiftly overridden when you're playing hoop by the compelling necessity *to be,* to be acutely alert to what you're experiencing as play, the consuming reality of the game's immediate demands. You are the experience. Or it thumps you in the face like a teammate's pass you weren't expecting when you should have been expecting.

Writing autobiography, looking back, trying to recall and represent yourself at some point in the past, you are playing many games simultaneously. There are many selves, many sets of rules jostling for position. None offers the clarifying, cleansing unity of playing hoop. The ball court provides a frame, boundaries, the fun and challenge of call and response that forces you to concentrate your boundless energy within a defined yet seemingly unlimited space. The past is not forgotten when you walk onto the court to play. It lives in the Great Time of the game's flow, incorporating past present and future, time passing as you work to bring to bear all you've ever learned about the game, your educated instincts, conditioned responses, experience accumulated from however many years you've played and watched the game played, a past that's irrelevant baggage unless you can access it instantaneously. Second thoughts useless. Opportunities knock once. And if you think about missing the previous shot when you're attempting the next one, most likely you'll miss it, too. And on and on, you lose, until, unless you get your head back into the game. Into what's next and next and next. The past is crucial, though not in the usual sense. Means everything or nothing depending on how it's employed and how you should employ it strictly, ruthlessly dictated by the flow, the moment. Yes. You can sit back and ponder your performance later, learn from your mistakes, maybe, or spin good stories and shapeshift mistakes into spectacular plays, but none of that's playing ball.

If playground hoop is about the once and only go and flow of time, its unbroken continuity, about time's thick, immersing, perpetual presence, writing foregrounds the alienating disconnect among competing selves, competing, often antagonistic voices within the writer, voices with separate agendas, voices occupying discrete, unbridgeable islands of time and space. Writing, whether it settles into a traditional formulaic set of conventions to govern the relationship between writer and reader or experiments with these borders, relies on some mode of narrative sequencing or "story line" to function as the game's spine of action functions to keep everybody's attention through a linear duration of time. The problem for writers is that story must be invented anew for each narrative. A story interesting to one person may bore another. Writing describes ball games the reader can never be sure anybody has ever played. The only access to them is through the writer's creation. You can't go there or know there, just accept someone's words they exist.

While playing the game is everything in playground hoop, in writing, if there ever was a game, it's finished before the reader arrives. The written text happens only after the action it describes, real action or imaginary, is over. Everybody's dead in a way before the story begins. The writer may be dead too, even though the text also and always enacts itself in a timeless, eternally present tense of composition. Pity the poor writer. He or she's a benchwarmer, a kind of made-up spectator who may or not be spectating the game in front of his face, or other games, other places, other times, or a mixture of the actual, of memory, wishes, dreams of game, a fictitious fan like those created in press releases by promoters who claim the arena's empty stands are full of adoring, paying customers so other paying customers will be attracted. Though the writer seems to be in charge, he's more like a coach who can't insert himself in the lineup. The closest he can come to the action is sending in a substitute for himself and reflecting the action from the sub's point of view. He can lend the sub his uniform, name, number, but the writer remains stuck on the pine.

In the early days of sports broadcasting, announcers at small-town, local radio stations would receive a tickertape summary of a baseball game occurring far away in a major league city. Based on the tape's skeletal account, the announcer (President Ronald Reagan labored as this kind of fabulator) would narrate the game to his listening audience as if he were sitting behind home plate, observing play by play what he was saying. Depending on the announcer's skill (deception) in manufacturing details, filling in background, elaborating in a colorful, dramatic fashion on the bare-bones info of a scanty script, the fiction of a ball game would become satisfyingly real or not for listeners. The writer's voice, like the voice of this remote, radio, play-by-play announcer, pitches itself to the reader from a site distanced from the action words describe—by many kinds of distance, many kinds of remove, many layers of art and artifice, illusion and lies that also keep the reader at a distance, multiple removes from the action, many forms of remove the reader can choose to think about or not (is this report fiction or documentary, true or false, is the tale-teller reliable, am I listening to a real person or a made-up person pretending to be a person, etc., etc.), but removes always there, built into the circumstances, conditioned by the nature of narrative construction.

Here's the paradox: hoop frees you to play by putting you into a real cage. Writing cages the writer with the illusion of freedom. Playing ball, you submit for a time to certain narrow arbitrary rules, certain circumscribed choices. But once in, there's no script, no narrative line you must follow. Writing lets you imagine you're outside time, freely generating rules and choices, but as you tell your story you're bound tighter and tighter, word by word, following the script you narrate. No logical reason a playground game can't go on forever. In a sense that's exactly what Great Time, the vast, all-encompassing ocean of nonlinear time, allows the game to do. A piece of writing without the unfolding drama of closure promised or implicit can feel shapeless, like it might go on forever, and probably loses its audience at that point.

Fortunately, graciously, the unpredictability of language, its stubborn self-referentiality, its mysterious capacity to mutate, assert a will of its own no matter how hard you struggle to enslave it, bend it, coerce it to express your bidding, language, with its shadowy, imminent resources and magical emergent properties, sometimes approximates a hoop game's freedom. The writer feels what it's like to be a player when the medium rules, when its constraints are also a free ride to unforeseen, unexpected, surprising destinations, to breaks and zones offering the chance to do something, be somebody, somewhere, somehow new. As if the tape the remote baseball announcer depends upon suddenly stops transmitting and he improvises a home-run riff to fill dead air, then discovers when the tape resumes ticking that some batter has knocked a ball out of the park.

Given all the above, I still want more from writing. More than a sense of being stuck on the sidelines. More than the puppetmaster's invisibility. Something besides the defeated, slump-shouldered dejection of seeing my team lose a game before I get a chance to enter it. Not because I expect more from writing, I just need more. Want to share the immediate excitement of process, of invention, of play. (Maybe that's why I teach writing.) Need more in the same way I needed more as I was growing up in Homewood. Let me be clear. The more I'm talking about then and now is not simply an extra slice of pie or cake. Seeking more means self-discovery. Means redefining the art I practice. In the present instance, wanting to compose and share a piece of writing that won't fail because it might not fit someone else's notion of what a book should be.

One of the worst trials for Americans of visible African descent (and maybe for invisible crossovers too) is the perpetual fear of not measuring up to standards established by so-called white people who imagine themselves the standard issue and also presume themselves to be the issuers of standards. We're plagued, even when we have every reason to know better, by deep-seated anxieties—are we doomed because we are not these "white" other people, are we fated, because we are who we are, never to be good enough. I need writing because it can extend the measure of what's possible, allow me to engage in defining standards. In my chosen field I can strive to accomplish what Michael Jordan has achieved in playing hoop—become a standard for others to measure themselves against.

So playground basketball and writing, alike and unlike, both start there—ways to single myself out. Seeking qualities in myself worth saving, something others might appreciate and reward, qualities, above all, I can count on to prove a point to myself, to change myself for better or worse. Hoop and writing may result in the most basic sort of self-knowledge, but none of that's guaranteed. They're about the seeking, the inquiry, process not destination. Hoop and writing intrigue me because no matter how many answers I articulate, how gaudy my stat sheet appears, hoop and writing keep asking the same questions. Is anybody home in there. Who. If I take a chance and turn the sucker out, will he be worth a hot damn, worth the trouble. Or shame me. Embarrass me. Or represent. Shine forth.

But before basketball and writing came music. All music but especially music performed by people who sounded like me, like the voices of Homewood. Music informing me how much more there was to being a black boy growing up than I'd ever have suspected without music's intimations. Music carved space. Music spoke a language of emotion, literally moved me, excited my mind and spirit, set my body parts dancing. A language half understood, brimming with much more than I could comprehend, but a language addressed to me, language belonging to me because it described me. Even when I didn't know exactly what a beat or rhythm or deep bass riff or falsetto trill were saying, I was seized. I could recognize what amounted to ideas, new information, trains of thought, revelations in Sam Cooke and the Soul Stirrers or the Swan Silvertones or Dixie Hummingbirds or Hank Ballard and the Midnighters. Though I couldn't translate the lucid, shimmering counterpoint of quartet close harmony into words, part of the magic, the freedom of music meant that I didn't need to turn it into words. And I guess I was lucky or smart because I didn't try to translate. Music escaped the net of familiar, everyday language, the official, standard register of speech, the standardized sound and sense that too regularly felt as if they weren't addressed to me, didn't belong to me. In various degrees Homewood folks resisted the dominant vernacular of the language, our speech played against it, or you could say fought, since our ways of talking were intended to detoxify certain features of the common language we felt unfairly raised some people (not us) up because they pronounced particular words in a specific fashion, people who, to our ears, flattened, depersonalized the rhythm of their English. Put other people (us) down who elided or decorated the pronunciation of individual words, who foregrounded the musical possibilities of their talk, speakers for whom cadence, repetition, tone, beat, metaphor, silence expressed a range of meanings and messages others might pursue by expanding and elaborating their vocabularies. The dominant language culture disrespected us, employed the arbitrary authority of its speech habits to mock our culturally inherited difference. Music assured me there was more out there to experience than a world already wrapped up tight in somebody else's words, words tangling me up in them while they also perversely excluded me. Long before I met Caliban, I experienced his ambivalence toward Prospero's tongue.

Good African-American music said once upon a time I'd been fluent in tongues the music spoke, and becoming an adult would surely involve relearning, needing to master these tongues again. Music promised more. It named me, stole my name, changed the names of familiar things around me, imbued ordinary situations with drama the way Hollywood soundtracks pump up the ante of mundane scenes. *Transcendent* is a word that comes to mind when I consider the capacity of music to expand the parameters of experience upward, elevating the spirit, extending the range of what's possible. Music ushers in a transcendent reality. Yes, it did and does rise, did inform my spirit, but music's messages just as consistently took dead aim at my flesh. Penetrated down to the body's visceral core. Even gospel, with its drumbeat and holler and dance roots, worked down to the gut, groin, ground. Transcendent, okay, but better to say music opened me—up and down and all around. Many years after leaving Homewood I encountered a Byzantine icon in a Cypriot church, a portrait of an angel with eyes all over, eyes on bosom, chin, wings, hands, arms, hundreds of all-seeing eyes, eyes all seen once the artist painted his vision. Pierced and transfigured by light, light entering, light going forth from the angel's eyes, a nimbus of light crowning her, and I think that's a picture of how music transformed me as I learned to listen and began dreaming of making my own songs.

No, not transformed or transfigured. Those ideas a little too easy. Just like the angel picture's a little too pretty. But I'm working. Working to help you see what I mean because that helps me see better. More. We're still on the more. Music said there's much more to life than meets the eye and said you were born with a gift, a faculty something like an eye or ear, and if you learn how to make it pay attention, it will reveal much more about the more there is to life, the more there is to you. You'll become different, you are different when you pay attention. Everything's larger than if you don't. Today I say to myself a gift was planted long, long ago deep inside the music by wise people wishing the best for you, wishing something extra for you—transfiguration, transformation—more for you infused in African-American music by beleaguered people who foresaw your coming and understood how desperately you'd need what they'd sown in the music. People who'd used music to single themselves out, to save themselves, music tattooing invisible markings on their skin (like those electronic dots stamped on your palm, unseeable except in a beam of infrared light you must pass your hand through before exiting from the prison visiting room). Hands clapping, feet stomping, a sway, beat, and keening moan, tribal markings aglow when the music's present, identifying your ancestors to each other, to you and yours in a vicious world that strips you and mocks your nakedness. African people who honored something precious in themselves worth too much to let anybody crush and found a means to pass on this knowledge, this more, this other inalienable part of themselves in the songs they sang, the rhythms thumped on drums or flesh with hands, sticks, feet, the whole body's bump and glide, lift and fall through air.

Finally, along with the music, also coming before and informing hoop, there were stories. They were out there. An oral history, so to speak, our version of who when what why. In somebody's mouth. Somebody's ear. Staying alive.

The thing was, since they were out there, being told and retold, you didn't have to think about them. Like money in the bank. You could count on them. There when you needed them.

All kinds of stories for different occasions, to be told in particular places, at particular times, and as I hung around the court more and more, I heard the ball-playing ones. About hoop. About the playground game I can look back and say, yes, it's something I truly loved, one of the few things truly loved. Of course, I love my children, my blood relatives, but that's a different love. I didn't have to fall in love to love them, because I can't fall out of love with them. They were here before I got here and will be here long after I'm gone. They are who I am, all of us pieces of a larger thing each of us would be worth less without. The larger thing running through the blood we share and keep alive simply by living, by staying alive.

Playground hoop's something like that only it's not there first time you open your eyes, open your mouth to breathe. Hoop's like the people not blood kin you meet and love. You learn hoop. Then you fall in love. Learn the game and play the game a certain way and what you feel about it can turn to more than you ever dreamed a game could be, a game that starts out as messing around, trying to accomplish something vaguely challenging and fun, throw a ball through a hoop, a fun, silly kind of trick at first till you decide you want to do it better, shoot and never miss, pass and always deliver the ball where it's supposed to go, jump up and never come down. The more you think about getting better, getting to be the best, the harder it is to play without dreaming about a perfect game. Funny thing is, it's not exactly about being the one who achieves the perfect game. You might be the one for a hot minute or in your mind sometimes and that's enough to keep you working, trying, make you turn up day after day on the hot asphalt so when the perfect game happens, even if it ain't you out there playing, you'll be around to see it. If you're real lucky and real good, maybe you will be on the court every minute the perfect game's going. The hours and hours practicing alone, just you and the announcer's voice and the cheering fans you imagine as you attempt the game-winning shot, the missing and misfiring and coming close and dragging home cause you got your ass thoroughly whipped, the hot streak, the sweet, slick move to the hoop so fine that if anybody had really been paying attention they would have snipped it out of the jive game in which you pulled it off and spliced it into the highlight reel of the perfect game, all of this prepares you to fall for playground hoop. Then love of the game rises like the ball from a shooter's hand, rising and you hope his aim is true cause you know just as sure as you're up, you're also coming down. You're not the shooter and not the ball and not the goal either but you carry a little bit of each inside you once you start dreaming of the perfect game, perfect shot, the arc, the wrist flick, the net's sigh, how it flips up like the tail end of a skirt in the wind when the ball drops through clean.

But before the hoop stories I heard lots of Homewood stories told by the older folks in Pittsburgh and a few stories from other places—stories, for instance, about Promised Land, South Carolina, where my grandfather Harry Wideman was raised.

One of these precious few goes something like this.

When my grandfather was a little, little dusty-butt boy, he said, too young to trudge off in the dark with the men and work the fields from can to caint, from dawn's first light when you can barely see what your hands are doing, John Edgar, he said, till dark again when you cain't see nothing he said they'd leave him behind with the women and him not fit for women's work neither so his job looking after Charlie Rackett, his old, old grandfather some called the African because he came over on the last boat and talked the African talk, John Edgar, my grandfather told me, pausing in his story, tilting back his head, cocking it to one side and closing his old eyes that were becoming the color of his yellowing fingernails, Harry Wideman leaving me a minute so he could hear one more time, maybe, those old, sung African words before he told me more about his job, about keeping an eye on Charlie Rackett, fetching him water from the barrel, feeding him dinner from the pot the women left behind on the stove when they trucked to the fields to feed the men on them hot-as-a-furnace afternoons like it always was John Edgar a hotter heat than youall gets up north here, youall don't know nothing bout heat, huh-uh, nosiree, heat crackling the air, heat keep them hot salty prickles all up in your nose, funny how being little sometimes you don't pay heat no mind, you ain't sweating under no heavy, itchy sack of something slung over your sore shoulder, ain't thinking bout how many loads you got to make fore caint and that be why heat ain't so bad sometimes if you little and why heat ain't so mean up here neither, John Edgar.

After I gets old Charlie Rackett watered and fed and him sat up dozing in his bed at the head of the cabin, smack in the middle so he could see everybody come in or go out and everybody could see him napping with one eye spooky open like he did, sleep or wake, soon's everything's quiet, even old Charlie Rackett snoring quiet and nothing, not a breath of air moving in that cabin, I'd slip outdoors and commence to getting into whatever I'm spozed not to be getting into, digging like I been told a thousand times not to dig in the chink mud what hold them logs, them walls together, hold together that little cabin where all us lives, from the newest born riding on they mama's hip out in the fields to old man Charlie Rackett hisself laid up in bed too old to work, it's my job to watch him all day but soon's he's sleep I'm outdoors, digging like a groundhog where I know better than be digging, John Edgar, and don't you know I found up in there tween them logs a big piece of shiny money once I spit on it and rub and rubbed a corner of it on my shirttail gold money somebody musta hid a long time ago in the olden days I bet, one them African slaves they say work round here before I was born he musta found it or stole it and saved it for a running-away day or just saved it for a rainy day what never come or come so rainy and quick it washed away the poor African what stuck a piece of money in that hole tween two logs so it was forgot till the afternoon I found it and laid it in my hand, heavy and one corner shiny like I said after I spit on it and rubbed it good. Thinking for a minute I'm rich. Think, boy oh boy. Caint wait to spend it. I'm one happy little dusty-butt rascal. Next time they carries us to town gon buy me everything in sight. Rock candy and soda pop and chocolate peanuts and I'm spending up that big piece of money fast as I can think of things to buy till I opens up my fist and looks again at the piece of money laid crosst my crusty palm. Ain't hardly going in my holey pocket, huh-uh, nosir. I'ma tuck it right back in that chink where I found it and scrape up some chink mud hide it again. No way if I keeps it I'ma get to spend it up. Little as I was I knows better. Way too big a piece of money for some little dusty-butt fella like me. Where you get that, boy. Say you found it. Uh-huh. Where you been to find a piece of gold, boy. And don't be wetting up your lips to tell no lie, neither. What you been into you ain't spozed to be into. Give it here, boy. This not boy money, boy. Hand it right here.

Now maybe they woulda let me keep it. Maybe I coulda spent it any ole way I wanted to spend it, but what I did was take no chances and slide it back in there twixt the logs and patch up the chink all nice and kept my secret. Said one day I'ma come back and get you, money. One day need you bad and come dig you out again, but don't you know John Edgar your granddaddy never did, not to this day. Often wondered if you and your mama'd let me carry you down home to Promiseland one them summers when you was a boy, wondered if that gold piece of money still be hiding there. Wonder now if the walls still standing. If anything left standing of that cabin used to hold us all man woman and child packed in way back when. Heap of people living there when I was a boy and not a single soul I know of all them folks still living anywhere. Your granddaddy most likely the last one John Edgar and I'm getting so I can hardly remember anybody, anything from back in them days and times. Last trip musta been fifteen, twenty years now.

Didn't think to go looking for no old cabin, no old wall, no old money. Past the day and season be traipsing through them briary woods looking for nothing. Too late now. You a grown man with children of your own now, but when you was a boy, sometimes I think we mighta walked back in there together and found it.

I've heard just a few of my South Carolina grandfather Harry Wideman's tales, and because there are only a few, each is a little sad—sad because one of a few, sad because I never accompanied him to the home place in Promised Land and now he's gone, it's too late now, and this story particularly sad because his good luck frightened him and he hid it from himself and sad because it's mostly about missing him, missing a chance, but telling it here and now in this fashion, trying to put his spin on it, trying to find written words for his telling and of course not coming close to getting his voice right, it's sad but not sad, too, because missing a last second shot, losing a basketball game you would have won if the shot went in, though it feels like the worst, the saddest possible moment and you die a little, as awful as you feel, the world doesn't end, there's more time and if you're lucky another game, and even if no more games for you, there's the game itself and its undiminished power to present such excruciating moments like the one you don't believe you'll survive as it's happening, while you watch your shot fall short off the front of the rim. On the other hand the moment, shot made or shot missed, lets you feel as if your fate's in your hands, lets you decide with a flick of your wrist whether something grand or devastating will befall you, a moment of power, a chance to try, a chance to put your signature on the moment, win or lose, and what could be better than this rare, privileged moment served up to you by the playground game, what could be more like living large.

More in my grandfather's story. A chance to imagine myself different. Missing an opportunity refines hunger, extenuates it. The hunger, in spite of missed chances, to play, to try again, to appreciate what didn't, doesn't happen as well as what does, and probably there's no other road to get there, to find yourself open and the ball in your hands. Pen in your hands. Music, stories, love singling me out and scaring me half to death because I couldn't abide the thought of losing love. Needing more, always more and looking for things I could do well, somebody special I could be in the music, the stories, the game of playground basketball on its way next.

First Shot

Shining has to do with completeness: didan. *Something that is completed and ready for use is often described as shining in Yoruba.*

—Rowland Abiodun, "Beads"

I COULD TAKE YOU THERE . . . show you the exact place on Finance Street in Homewood, Pittsburgh, Pennsylvania, where fifty years ago playground basketball began for me, and what would you see. Stand with you on the vacant side of Finance where nobody lives and look through a rusty fence that separates the unpaved sidewalk from a steep hillside overgrown with weeds and stubby trees, whose flat crest bedded railroad tracks when I was a kid and trains still run there and a busway too now, ferrying Homewood people back and forth from downtown Pittsburgh, point through the rusty webbing of twisted wire to a level expanse of ground along the foot of the hillside where no trace remains of a building that once occupied the empty space you see there today, the only structure on this side then, no fence, just this big shedlike building on our negro street where white men arrived to work every weekday, cramming their cars and pickups helter-skelter on the hillside, the bottom row's wheels straddling the curb.

Standing here, we are not far from the T-junction terminating Finance Street at Braddock, an avenue named for a Revolutionary War general, a dead white man as much a stranger to me once upon a time as the white strangers who worked in the factory or warehouse or bottling plant doing whatever they did in the only building on the track side of Finance, a block and a half from Braddock Avenue, three and a half from Homewood, the other avenue bracketing our short street backed flush against a jungly hillside. Finance a street easy to miss if you blinked after the dark, echoing underpasses on Braddock and Homewood below the train tracks, delivering you here to a community most Pittsburgh people thought of as the wrong side of the tracks, this street marking the beginning and end of the neighborhood in which I was raised, where I used to look for trains in the sky, a street dividing so-called black people from so-called white people, where basketball began for me.

My grandmother's house, 7415, and everybody else's on Finance — Smiths, Conleys, Colberts, Betts, Clarks, etc. — faced the tracks. With my chest pressed into the back of the sofa beneath the front room window, just tall enough on my knees to see out, I'd daydream away hours, waiting for the next train's rumble to fill the house, rattle the window glass I liked to frost in winter with my warm breath and draw on, airplanes, horses, moon faces with slits for eyes, crying eyes that shed real tears when I stroked them right, rivers of tears dripping all the way down the pane, ghost eyes and streaks still visible when the women did their spring cleaning and my grandmother hollered, Look at all this mess, boy. Better stop that scribble-scrabbling on my windows.

No matter how far forward you leaned over the sofa's back, you couldn't see the building farther up the block, on the opposite side of Finance, I could lead you to today and show you where it all began, where fifty-some years ago at a hoop nailed to its outside wall I touched a basketball first time and launched my first shot. And because it couldn't be seen from 7415's front window, the wall, the building were out of bounds. In those days with everybody in the house on edge, a little shaky, a little unhappy because my parents had split up for the first time and we'd moved back to Homewood without my father to live in my mother's mother's house, sometimes it seemed the whole world might be coming apart, especially at 2 or 3 A.M., startled awake by a train crashing through the bedroom walls, me lying eyes wide open for hours worrying about how, piece by piece, anybody could ever put things back together again.

I guess it was easy in that crowded house for everybody to get on everybody else's nerves and I heard a lot of G'wan away from here and play, boy. The words sounding like a prison sentence since going out to play meant occupying myself in the fenced-in back yard or on the porch or sidewalk in front of 7415 so if any adult wanted to check on my whereabouts a loud shout would be enough to get my attention. Just to be sure I wasn't into any mischief, the adult in charge could spy through the front room picture window or the little square window at the back of the house above the kitchen sink. Playing outdoors meant staying close enough so no one ever needed to step out of 7415 to keep an eye on you.

On a good day my mom, grandmother, or one of my aunts might take me by the hand across Finance and let me roam the hillside. Don't you dare try and cross the street till I come back for you. And don't you dare march yourself up near those tracks. Whoever escorted me repeated these commandments and a few others, usually ending with the rule, Better stay where I can see you, young man, or I'll snatch your narrow hips home.

I tried never to be busted for breaking rules because getting caught brought more rules, tighter lockdown, but even in a household of loving, attentive women, an only child, particularly a male child, could slip away. In Homewood boys need to think they can get away with things. And sometimes women encourage boys to believe they can. How else keep alive in their male children the cute, mischievous twinkle racial oppression strives to extinguish. To cut slack for their men, the women made allowance for the fact that boys will be boys. Created space, a license for their men to bend rules, a hedge against demeaning rules. The women required this slack as much as the boys if they didn't want to be nailed down too tightly themselves. But the women also had learned from bitter experience that they could be accomplices in crimes against themselves, setting themselves up to be sideswiped or demolished by the first and last rule: you can't trust people, especially men and boys wounded by rules, to respect rules.

As a kid I thought women made up the rules and I resented them for it. I also couldn't help noticing that women were more restricted by rules than men. The rule for instance that kept women home all day and night with us kids. Females (though I'd never have dreamed of calling them *females* or *women* then), my grandmother, aunts, and mother, seemed embodiments of rules and I began to treat them as I treated rules — obstacles to be circumvented, deceived, ignored when I could. If I got caught straying too far out of line, my mother would threaten, Wait till your father gets home. And if and when he did arrive home that day, he might punish me with his hard hand for breaking rules I knew he didn't follow. It seemed to me my father came and went as he pleased. Said whatever to whomever. Closed himself off in the bedroom and nobody better disturb him. Clearly, if I ever grew big enough, strong enough, no one could punish me. I'd be a man, on top like my father, privileged to make my own rules, to slam people for busting rules I wasn't obliged to honor. Men could, perhaps should, I believed, go about their business as if women's rules didn't exist.

I learned I could slip outside the frame of 7415's front window, just so I didn't stay away too long, just so I wasn't invisible when somebody in a bad mood or a big hurry came looking for me. On a tight leash, yes, but it stretched far enough so I could pretend no leash tethered me to the center of the space whose edges I roamed. Part of me, even then, understood that pain-in-the-butt restrictions were linked to being loved and indulged in my grandmother's house and that I couldn't have one without the other. The dread of losing 7415's special sense of well-being, even for a short cloudburst of frowns or fussing or tighter rules, of losing the kisses, smiles, and mostly sweet, untroubled rhythm of my days, usually was enough to persuade me to police myself.

Abiding by the women's rules paid off, but some days, boy, you know what I mean, slipping away exerted an irresistible pull. Whatever sensible purposes the rules served—my safety, the convenience and peace of mind of the adults—they were also a challenge, a dare. They existed to be broken. The afternoon I fired my first shot at a hoop, I was testing as I did daily in a hundred secret games how much I could get away with. In this instance, how long could I remain out of sight of 7415's front window. Visible within the frame a minute, then gone for two, visible again, then absent five minutes, sneaking farther up Finance with each foray and on each trip away longer. I knew whoever was in charge of me would get busy with one thing or another inside the house. Plus, I figured out three facts I could count on. First, I wouldn't be allowed to play on the hillside unless they trusted me. Second, the more I appeared to cooperate, the more trust and less surveillance there would be. Third, the eyes constantly on duty at the window scanning the hillside existed only in my mind. Except for unusual circumstances—my mom maybe, on one of those days when her eyes were red and puffy, her nose sniffling, a glazed-look day when she might sit at the front window or the kitchen table and stare for hours at nothing, silent, a force field of hurt so palpable around her you bumped into the sting of its barbed wire if you stepped too close—no adult would plant herself on the couch under the window with nothing better to do than maintain unbroken vigilance on the empty hillside where I was playing.

Once I understood that my imagination endowed the eyes with more power than they deserved, I was ready to begin imagining their absence, begin preparing myself for the great escape, the moment when I could convince myself I had nothing to fear from the patrolling eyes. Minute by minute, day by day, I stretched my leash a little farther. Coached myself to stay away a little longer. No one's watching all the time. Even if Aunt Sis or Aunt Geral or Grandma Freed peeks out and doesn't see you she'll figure you'll be right back in a second, you're a good boy, they trust you and boys will be boys, so she'll go on about her business and when she checks again, sure enough, there you'll be, or at worst, if she's having a worry-wart day, she'll stand at the window a minute or two till you reappear, back safe inside the arc where you're supposed to be. No problem. If she grumbles or cuts her eye at you later—Better stay where I can see you, mister. Don't be getting too big for your britches—a bit of a smile probably in her sideways glance. Boys will be boys.

No problem as long as the scenarios I constructed inside my boy's pea-brained skull more or less matched what actually transpired inside the house. Of course once I ventured out of sight of 7415, anybody behind the glass was as invisible to me as I was to them. I remember thinking yes, it's a window and through it you're able to watch rain and snow, trains shake-rattle-and-rolling past up on the hilltop, see Freed's roses blooming pink and bloody purple on bushes the neighbors begged her for cuttings from each spring, check out odd-looking grownups walking to and from stores on Homewood Avenue, but seeing through a window is also being blind as far as it doesn't allow you to look at what it hides beyond the view it commands. I wouldn't have thought the word *commands* then, probably wouldn't have formulated my idea in words at all, but I know I intuited something very precise about how brick walls and windows could function in the same fashion when it comes to keeping you unaware.

I wanted to explore what might be happening farther up Finance Street so I wished away the watching eyes. Pretended I controlled the appearance and disappearance of adult faces in the rectangle of glass, just as I once believed the moon followed me when I ran up and down the street, believed the moon vacated the sky when I paid it no mind, believed, in the darkness of the Bellmawr show, I could entice June Allyson's blue, blue eyes to glance down from the screen and smile at the brown boy curled in his seat, shyly in love with her.

After my Aunt Geral had deposited me on the hillside I'd stare at her back as she recrossed Finance to my grandmother's house, to see whether or not she looked in both directions for oncoming traffic before she stepped into the street. *Stop, look, and listen,* the rule she recited to me each time she took my hand and crossed me to play on the hillside. I was always a little worried and maybe slightly disappointed when she didn't get hit by a car those times she didn't bother to stop look and listen. Once she'd made it safely to the paved side of Finance, I'd turn away, hang around at the foot of the hillside as if I needed time to get my bearings. I might even shuffle a couple fake steps away from the direction I intended to scoot in as fast as I could the instant I decided she'd had time to reenter the house, take a peek at me through the window. I knew better than to turn around like a dumbbell and stare at 7415. Why in the world would I need to know what was happening behind my back. Weren't the dirt, weeds, stones, trees, bushes, and insects of the hillside more than enough to keep my hands busy, my mind occupied.

I pretended, then came to believe, that I didn't need to turn around to see what transpired in the window behind me. I depended on a picture in my mind, my ability to sense the weight of eyes on my shoulders. I drew a square in the empty air in front of me, and it mirrored what hovered behind my back. I could see Aunt Geral's face, see her eyes, unaware that I watched them, gazing at me, then at the scruffy, overgrown hillside, at parcels of cloud in the sky, the emptiness of gleaming rails waiting for a train. My aunt gazing till what's in front of her eyes mingles with what's not there and she stares through it all, past it to the story of whatever she's deciding to do next. I could feel myself becoming transparent, disappearing as her mind fixed on something besides the nephew playing on the hill. As I think back, I can't help comparing my fake view of her in a made-up mirror in the air to her fading view of me, to this view of a fifty-year-old moment flickering on and off in my head while I attempt to represent it for the you — *mirror, mirror on the wall* — I'm imagining reading these words. The you I promised to take by the hand to where it all started, the place basketball began for me.

If I'd sprinted full speed from the spot on Finance opposite my grandmother's house, I bet I could have reached the building where white men were shooting baskets before my Aunt Geraldine could clomp through the house to a sinkful of dishes in the kitchen. Clomp, clomp, clomp, in her mashed-back houseshoes, glancing at the silent phone, running her finger along the grooved edge of the china cabinet with the cut-glass bowl on top. Sometimes she'd sigh, Wish you were a nice sugar-and-spice girl instead of all snips and snails and puppy tails, you nasty rascal, you. Old enough to stick your arms down in these soapsuds and help your auntie with this mess if you were a sweet little girl child.

From my perspective, an eight- or nine-year-old black boy on stolen time who seldom had much to do with white people, the men up the street in a pool of sunshine in front of the only building on the track side of Finance, launching shots at a hang-dog, netless hoop, seemed huge and old, but it's likely they were in their twenties and thirties, some probably teenagers. A few had stripped off their shirts. I remember pale flesh, hairy chests and armpits, bony rib cages and shoulders, long, lanky arms. They blend into the faces and bodies of guys I played with on mostly white teams in high school and college. For some reason one wears in my memory a full beard like the fair-haired Jesus on a calendar, his blue eyes following you around the Sunday school room of Homewood AME Zion Church.

The men didn't talk much as they took turns shooting, rebounding. Some lounged in the shade smoking, ignoring the ball and basket. Seven or eight guys total, I think, probably on lunch break. Somebody had nailed a rusty hoop to a board above truck-size double doors adjacent to the building's entrance. A bright summer day but the interior beyond the partly open double doors in deep shadow. Boxes stacked inside. Machinery too. What little I could see, unfamiliar. Nothing I recognized then nor learned later gave me a clue what work the white men who showed up each weekday performed when they weren't outside shooting baskets.

Once or twice as I watched from the curb the basketball bounced toward me and I retrieved it, rolled it back. Can't tell you whether it was a good, tight, regulation-size ball or some scuffed, lopsided, balloony thing they might kick around or clobber with a bat when they didn't feel like shooting. I don't remember anyone speaking to me. And that was fine because it saved me having to answer. I definitely didn't want to say *yessir* or *nosir* to men without shirts throwing a ball at a basket. I'd been taught at home to be polite to all grownups, especially polite, and as close to silent as I could manage without being impolite, if the grownups happened to be white male strangers. Whether these men shooting hoops spoke or not, I knew I'd better be ready with an appropriate form of address, so I was searching my mind for one. Wonder now if one existed. Or was the point to keep boys like me guessing.

Being unnoticed or ignored allowed me to continue observing them from my spot at the edge of Finance where there could have been a sidewalk if anybody had bothered to pave the no-houses side of the street. Since my presence seemed not to matter, I felt comfortably invisible, a ghost who glided into view once or twice, only intruding enough to keep the ball out of the street, guide it back into the circle.

I must have been watching longer than I realized or maybe till that moment I really had been invisible shuttling back and forth from the safety zone opposite 7415's front window because one of them said, Kid's not going to leave till he gets a shot. Here, kid. C'mon. Try one. I wish I could describe the man who called me over because remembering him might demonstrate how conscious we made ourselves of white people as individuals, aware of their particular features, character, the threat or advantage a specific person posed. In a way, the last great campaign for civil rights, commencing in the southern states in the early fifties, during the same period this scene on Finance Street occurs, was a demand, a concerted political movement to secure, among other things, the same attentive, circumspect recognition of us as individuals that I was compelled, at my peril, to afford to this white guy who handed or passed me a ball.

I could say the ball felt enormous in my hands, because it probably did. I could say I was suddenly shy, timid, and they had to coax me from the margin where I'd been silently watching. Say once I stepped onto the smooth driveway in front of the hoop with the ball in my hands and the basket a mile high poking out from a board fastened on the brick wall, I could tell you how great it felt then to pat the ball for the first time, feel it rise off the asphalt back to my hand, the thrill of lifting the ball with both hands, sighting over it at the hoop, trying to get all my small weight under it and do what I'd watched the bigger, stronger, pale bodies do. No doubt all the above is true. I could also say the men laughed at the air ball I bricked up or encouraged me and gave me more shots or I heaved the ball high and straight and true that first time so it banked off the board through the rim, *Two*, and everybody whooped and hollered. Could say any damned thing because I don't recall what happened, only that it happened, my first shot in that exact place under the circumstances I'm relating, me AWOL from 7415's front window, suddenly scared I'd lost track of time, shooting and hauling ass back down the track side of Finance because I'd probably been out of sight way too long. The story enlarging, fact, fiction, and something in between, till I become who I am today, the story growing truer and less true as I make it up and it makes me up, but one thing's sure, the spot's still there on Finance and I've never forgotten my first shot.

If you stood with me today on the unpaved side of Finance, our backs to the emptiness where I once watched a bunch of guys tossing a ball at a hoop, you'd see that the house side of Finance is now a classic example of urban decay, the movable famine that can descend on any section of a city and gradually render it unfit for human habitation. Blighted stretches, small or vast, with the look of postwar bombed-out desolation are a ubiquitous feature of American cityscapes, monuments dramatizing our failed experiment in democracy, as symbolic of the nation's character and the way we govern ourselves as the installation on Pennsylvania Avenue, and just as familiar, as unreal, to most citizens as that big white castle. Small, battered houses crammed together, desperately in need of paint, repairs, the wrecking ball. Busted sidewalks, broken windows, boarded-up, deserted shells next to occupied dwellings, vacant lots like the toothless gaps in a rotting mouth. Trash and clutter collect here. The street a bin for wrappers, plastic bottles, Styrofoam boxes, the indestructible fag ends of products manufactured to die here, products not worth a damn when they were freshly conceived, minted, and cynically routed here. Finance a cliché example of a cliché, almost too good to be true. The street could be a simulation like the impossibly rich, ripe meals on fast-food billboards, but real people must subsist on this fake portion we see.

By studying a brick in the wall of a Finance house, you might understand better what you're seeing, what I want to say about what's over there, so close to where we stand, *surprise, surprise,* watching us as we watch it. A single, filthy brick, face cracked and pitted, mortar around its edges eroded, crumbling, weakening the wall the brick is part of, a wall intended to enclose and protect, a wall that's a promise of security for a family, one of many walls raised on this street in Homewood, a community bearing the name and aspirations of the estate an early settler erected here, *Homewood,* the borrowed name itself a promise of protection, a European immigrant's dream of private space carved from the forest, civilized space for carrying on work, rearing a family, enjoying leisure, a collective vision that draws people together into cities of brickmakers and bricklayers and poets and teachers and bakers, and that vision of civic interdependence and productivity and safety and common ground a bulwark against chaos, against the nightmare jungle of bloody tooth and claw with every creature out for itself, the anarchic violence of deadly competition that only the biggest, strongest survive and they survive only as long as chaos sees fit because chaos always wins, the chaos you see in that solitary brick if you study the evidence of its untended decay in a wall on its way to falling down and taking other bricks, the wall, the neighborhood, the whole city down with it. Any city, regardless of scale, wealth, power, and majesty, always as fragile as a house of cards, and the hopeless, doomed brick I'm endowing with life, a history as we examine it, this brick one of the cards, perhaps the very card working loose that will doom a nation.

Not much farther down Finance, less than twenty yards from where we're positioned, there among the shabby little shallow-porched row houses, is the one Ed Fleming, a former NBA player, used to visit back when these small houses were neatly, proudly maintained—flower gardens, white picket fences, vine-laced trellises, green awnings—his mother's house, Ed Fleming told me when I was grown enough to tell him I often saw him cruise by 7415 in his two-tone Buick Roadmaster years ago when I was a kid staying on Finance. By the time this conversation with Ed Fleming occurred, I'd played four years of college ball, three years in Europe, had started teaching at the University of Pennsylvania in Philadelphia, only returned to Pittsburgh to visit family and friends for holidays or a few days each summer, always if possible squeezing in a couple hot tussles with the fellows from the old days on the outdoor courts.

On the court it can be easy to pretend nothing has changed, ever changes. So what Craig Copeland and Cato spend much more time on the sidelines now, play-by-playing the action rather than playing ball. They were old heads when I was coming up and talked a whole lot of smack then too. To them I would always be an up-and-comer, the next green, shaky generation, a youngblood who could play, who had those young, powerful legs that allow you to get away with much foolishness on the court, but a long, long way to go, they'd whisper to anybody listening, before I'd really understand what the game's about. If ever. Craig and Cato and Delton and Jay schooled me decades ago and would school me again, off and on the court, each time I returned to Pittsburgh.

From some players in these summer runs, the younger, flashy, promising ones who'd come up right behind me, from these players, old themselves now, I would receive the respect reserved for old heads. An elder for them no matter their age, and usually they'd find a spot for me when they picked a squad. Then there were the new reigning court monarchs, *the king is dead, long live the king,* who wouldn't want to be stuck with an old head on their team if the opposing team didn't have a used-to-be to match him up against. Already got my five, old-timer, they'd say. Didn't need to say the court belonged to them. In their high-flying prime and the game their stage and didn't want to give up one glory minute in the spotlight if they could help it. Winning games the only way to stay out there and show your stuff and even if you were a star you needed as foolproof a supporting cast as possible. A king would let you know your role real quick in no uncertain terms. Maybe old heads knew the game, maybe once upon a time they could play, but today's today, old-timer. Damn, man, you got to get me the rock. Didn't you see me way head of everybody. You got to rebound and kick it out, home. And stay wit your man, bro. Foul the motherfucker if you can't stop him no other way. Or send his ass down the paint to me. No way these chumps beat us you pass me the ball.

You'd always hear the fast ones, the ones full of themselves and the rush of their skills, who hadn't figured out the game might be about more than improvising highlight reel moments when they would operate, dominate, you'd hear these newest, fastest ones who didn't know you from before grumbling when you couldn't keep up with the way they played the game, the only way they thought it should be played. Leg ball. One on one. Or one on two or one on three or five or one on the universe. The bigger the odds, the better. Whoever gets his hands on the ball keeps it, dribbles and shoots and goes for the rebound if he misses. Pass the pill only if all other options exhausted. Unless it's a pass executed as spectacularly, as show-stoppingly and oh la-la and signature as a slam dunk. Players taking turns in a way so the action's rudely, crudely democratic, live and let live. What the white boys and coaches and some of us call jungle ball. Youngblood leg ball. Signifying you don't need a brain to play it. Signifying the absence of a brain if leg ball's your style.

Old heads, usta-bes and wannabes and never-wases on the sidelines, whoop and point fingers when the strong legs they'd lost or possessed only in their dreams power some college star or precocious high school hotshot or just a local street-ball pogo-stick brother up and up to throw down *blam* in whoever's face. Whoop even louder when the same thoroughbred legs put a trash-talking, skywalking neophyte in a jam, a mile high up in the stratosphere and no place to go but down, down, the ball lost off his knee or a dribble fumbled by his no-handle hands and the other team scores while he's still hanging up there in thin air, mouth open, wondering what happened. *My bad.* Damn right, chump. *Game.* G'wan over there and sit down, chump. *Next.* Who got next. Sit on down, boy, and take your weak shit wit you.

See. Didn't I tell you, man. Brother can jump to the moon but can't play a lick. Never could, never will. A hard head, you hear what I'm saying . . . hardheaded like you used to be till we schooled your youngblood ass . . . and I find myself back in the middle of a sentence that hasn't ended since the last time I blew into town, kicking back on Saturday morning with Cato and Gary and Craig and Jay and all the absent others summoned by the talk, in the bleachers, in Westinghouse Park or Mellon or East Liberty, gearing up, taping up ankles, bracing knees, binding hamstrings, Ace bandages, spandex, Ben Gay, Advil, eyeglasses secured by Croakies, waiting our turn to trot out for winners, our turn to hobble back after absorbing a beating, winners again on the sidelines as we fire up healing patter right where we left it simmering.

Nothing changes except not long ago I ran into Ed Fleming not on the playground but in a funeral parlor. How long since I'd seen him last the first question in my mind after I almost didn't recognize the broad-shouldered man in a dark suit surrounded by a cluster of mourners just inside the entrance of a viewing parlor down the hall from the one in which my brother's son Omar, victim of a gang killing, was laid out in Warden's. Ed Fleming a wee bit heavier, thicker than I remembered, but sure enough him, the big eyes, round face, dark skin, small, trim mustache, the intimidating poise and quiet reserve of his expression, a stern mask that disappears in a second when he recognizes an old acquaintance and beams. Bigger, yes, but definitely Ed Fleming. Solid, compact, that gliding, effortless go and flow in his movements. Cat quick. Cat eyes mobile, always scanning his surroundings. Sounding his options. Alert for whatever might be required next, fighting through a pick, planting an elbow in somebody's chest, tensing himself for a collision with a two-hundred-fifty-pound body hurtling toward him full speed. Hand fighting, chest bumping. Punishing in his own swift, sure way the beefy, six-foot-seven opposing forward, a cheap-shot bully who's been hissing nigger this and nigger that just loud enough to be heard above his bad kielbasa breath the whole first half.

Ed Fleming's body type and color a stigma, a danger to the bearer for five hundred years in racist America. Convict body, field hand body, too unadulterated African, too raw, too black, too powerful and quick and assertive for most whites and some colored folks to feel comfortable around until Michael Jordan arrived and legitimated Ed Fleming's complexion and physique, mainstreaming them, blunting the threatening edge, commodifying the Jordan look, as if the physical, sexual potency of a dark, streamlined, muscular body could be purchased, as if anybody, everybody—Swede, Korean, Peruvian, Croat, New Englander—could be like Mike.

Before Renoir painted them, Marcel Proust said, there were no Renoir women in Paris. But after Renoir painted them, you saw them everywhere. In his novel *Remembrance of Things Past,* Proust goes on to compare the great artist to an oculist who teaches his patients to see in a new fashion. Until a ubiquitous, saturating ad campaign established Michael Jordan as a paragon of male beauty, male style, male potency and achievement, a dark body like his was not deemed particularly attractive by most Americans. If acknowledged at all by either blacks or whites, Jordan's physical type usually was cast in a negative light, served as a sort of grown-up Sambo caricature or a dark blot on a mug shot. Like a stealth bomber, a body like Jordan's carried out its business below the cultural radar. Then, thanks to Nike among others, you began to see MJ everywhere. Suddenly everybody wanted to look like him. Ad after ad cashed in on the paradox of white fascination with blackness: the obdurate otherness, invisibility, and mandated inaccessibility of blackness versus its transparency, seductiveness, and omnipresence.

Though chattel slavery a thing of the past, black bodies still occupy the auction block. And not just any old negro body, but bionic miracle machines like Michael Jordan's. This news brought customers from across the globe running. Anybody with the price of the ticket could become a shareholder. Buy the pleasure of watching the value of your stock and yourself in your MJ cap or sneakers or sweatsuit skyrocket as MJ leads the Chicago Bulls to another NBA world championship. This modern, media-driven, vicarious, virtual possession of a black body better than buying a slave, with all the attendant burdens of ownership. By simply copping certain trademarked booty, you could choose if and when you wished to be like Mike. Or, to be more precise, you could choose to appropriate and identify with only those black body parts you desired (dismember and reconfigure the black body) and leave the rest, the negative, bad parts, alone. Unless you found a little touch of the gangster rap, drug, hoodlum deviancy nice; then you could turn your cap backward, droop your baggy, hip-hop trousers below the crack of your ass, represent some of that outlaw stuff too. Represent "bad" without worrying about paying dues bad black boys pay —poverty, jail, apartheid, early graves. Or so the deal seemed to promise.

Then somebody noticed that the black body's power to stir desire and sell things transcended any individual black pitchperson. If even the historically despised, abused black male body, the threatening, agile stereotype of rapist, runaway slave, athlete, criminal, could exert a fatal attraction, let's see what we can sell with other black bodies, light and dark, male and female, fat and slim, the beige ones you have to look at twice to decide their *race*. Highlighted and showcased in the Africanized entertainment subculture of contemporary American popular music, dance, fashion, and sport, where black body pleasure, black body performance, black body perfection are deployed to stand for those magical transformations certain products promise their consumers, it's no wonder the black body is irresistible, unforgettable.

Just as centuries ago the commerce in black bodies fostered a new worldwide economic order, the commerce in images of blackness during the last decade has accelerated globalization of the marketplace. Nike, to cite one obvious example, piled up enormous profits by building an international network of factories and outlets to exploit the allure of blackness, its status as contraband, as a primal site of guilt and pleasure, of longing and dread. In spite of or perhaps because of the shameful history of what we call "race relations," our collective imagination carries forward both the empathetic image of the long-suffering black Christ on the cross of white oppression and the black body as a field of dreams where whites can play out erotic fantasies. Again, is it in spite of or because of a reigning Christian ethos proclaiming such oppression, such desires, to be unacceptable. Today, given its proven track record as a desired commodity spawning other desirable commodities, the black body is too hot to touch, too hot not to touch. Perhaps the old African-American folk saying is as relevant for cultures as for individuals: *Go black and you never go back.*

Ed Fleming's wide, sloping shoulders are exaggerated by a fashionable suit jacket tailored so any wearer of the style appears constructed the way Ed Fleming actually is under the rich fabric. He's a bit more rounded now, his shoulders thick from years of keeping opponents boxed out beneath the backboards, years of tensing his upper torso, especially the ridge of muscle across the top of his back, to receive blows, weight, or coiled for a leap—quick, high, balanced—when the basketball rebounds off the glass. Head held high, long arms poised comfortably at his sides, he appears taller than he is. With what would be in today's NBA a guard-size body, Ed Fleming in the fifties had mastered a big man's game. Three inches shorter, less elongated than Michael Jordan, Ed Fleming at about six-foot-three was a forward, an inside player his entire college and professional career. The sort of smart banger, hustler, who contests every free ball. Persistent, fearless, he picks up the loose change most players treat as below their notice, chump change floating around at unspectacular moments in a game. He earns small victories in pitched skirmishes peripheral to the main action, battles unrecorded on stat sheets or in scorebooks, relentless because he understands that the little stuff accumulates and determines who wins or loses close games, who winds up winning championships.

He played for very white teams in very white cities—Niagara University, Rochester Royals, Syracuse Nats—in very white leagues during an era when color as much as any other physical attribute decided the position—guard, forward, center—you'd play, determined, in most cases, if you were dark and not seven feet tall, that you wouldn't play at all in college or the pros.

How long. How long had it been since we'd seen each other last the question I decided not to ask Ed Fleming in Warden's because Warden's Funeral Home already steeped in lost chances, lost causes, lost time, time nobody gets back, those heartrending, thuggish truths about time you don't need to waste more precious time bemoaning in Warden's. Warden's where everybody winds up when time's up. So I told myself, Forget about how long. Go on and enjoy your little chat with this man while there's still time. Leave time alone and maybe it will leave you alone a bit longer till you get past this season of dying. Sons dying before their fathers. Nephews gone before their uncles. A country dying before it grows past its adolescent bluster, selfishness, callousness, and cruelty.

Time already dreary and topsy-turvy enough with my twenty-one-year-old nephew down the hall in a casket. He should have outlived me. Survived to mourn me. If he's gone, why am I still here. In the room with Omar's body, I'd been hit with a pounding urge to run. Flee far away. Flee the stuffy room, sweetly disinfected air, the cloying, piped-in organ moan, the oppressively tacky furniture, the finality of opportunities forever missed. I couldn't muster a sense of closure, couldn't begin composing my goodbyes to the more than man-size boy in the casket who'd never grow into adulthood, never discover he possessed within himself all he needed to become a man. Omar wasn't going to be one of the lucky ones who survived the terrible winnowing, who might evolve terms less self-destructive than those he and his peers had invented to love themselves.

For Omar and his crew, the only way to be a man, to own themselves, was to loom larger than life in made-for-TV mini-dramas playing out each day on the screen of Homewood's streets. Homewood's streets comprised the known universe, the only world mattering in their eyes. Gang loyalty, protecting turf, copping pussy, buying and selling the drugs that fueled an underground economy were the salient facts of life, the responsibilities of manhood. To perform those duties you maintained an unforgiving, uncompromising code of violence—tit for tat, eye for an eye, two or three eyes for one even better. Manhood and self-respect gauged by quick, simple measures. Could you handle what was out there in the streets. *Whatever.* Were you *whatever,* meaning were you capable of doing anything, responding with all the cold-blooded force necessary in whatever situation arises. Were you *locs,* as in loco—crazy, unpredictable. Could you *hold it down,* handle the reality of danger, violence, anarchy, whatever, in a fashion that manifests both cool and locs. Could you stay focused on what's *real, be real,* deal with what's out there, the material conditions staring you in the face every day—poverty, no way out, firefights, crooked cops, the dog-eat-dog bottom line, the absolute separation of your everyday world from the Disneyland dream white people walked around in. *Real,* the obvious, violent, down and dirty, risky, minute-by-minute clinging and scheming to get along truth of street life, ghetto immurement for young men. No future, no plans, no prospects beyond the present moment. Were you prepared, as anybody real or locs or whatever must be, to *jack,* to violently snatch what you needed—a car, money, sex, pride, status—from anybody, man, woman, child, who possessed what you wanted.

Guns the final arbiter of manhood. Cold, unbiased, on point. Computer logic of the trigger, the hot button. On or off. Yes or no. Alive or dead. No further questions necessary. No teenage angst. No adolescent anxiety. Somebody pulls a gun and you're dead or he's dead if you shoot first and shoot truer. Bang. Bang. Are you live or dead. Wiped off the set or still around to play another day. Get it on. Deal another twenty-four. Hold it down. Stay real, locs, whatever.

I'd excused myself from a half-whispered conversation with a stunned family member or friend and slipped out of the room where Omar's murdered body lay in state, exited like a thief from the scene of a crime, hoping the grief, frustration, and anger throbbing in my skull would stay in goddamned Parlor D.

After I recognized Ed Fleming among the mourners in Parlor A, I recalled hearing that he had been badly beaten in a fight at the high school where he taught history and coached basketball. Instead of trying to recollect how long it had been since I'd seen him last, I let the scanty details I'd picked up about the fight trickle through my mind and realized I knew next to nothing about the incident. Probably wouldn't learn more now. Unless Ed Fleming carried visible scars or the invisible ones had left their mark. Curious as I was, I wouldn't bring up the fight, and why would he. Here. Now. The years between us a mountain we'd been scrambling up from opposite sides. Lost to each other till this moment in Warden's.

I'd heard various rumors, different stories—a gang of outlaw students had jumped Ed Fleming and fucked him up good, or Coach Ed Fleming had challenged some giant tough-guy kid and found out too late, the hard way, he was no longer an undersized NBA forward who night after night could take on taller guys in higher weight classes and hold his own. Whichever story true, or partly true, all the versions I'd heard had ended the same. Ed Fleming beaten down, serious hurts put on his tough old pro's body. Hard for me to believe any of the stories; a platoon of kids or one as big as King Kong his gorilla-ass self wouldn't stand a chance against the Ed Fleming who had roughed me up when I was coming up to teach me rough, the Ed Fleming who'd been cop, jury, and judge when it came to establishing how roughly the game would be played on Homewood court.

Remember, beneath what might seem to be cutthroat anarchy, the one-on-one individualism and crudeness of playground basketball, there is a core of shared assumptions, tacit agreements among the participants or a game couldn't, wouldn't exist. A player must learn, then respect the unspoken rules, respect opponents, himself, his teammates, the sanctity and fragility of the shared enterprise. The learning is direct, immediate, hands-on, face to face. Like the lore of an oral culture, if one generation neglects to transmit it to the next, the game disappears.

Rather than a set of rules for playing the game, there is an instrument, the court, and the point of playground hoop is to coax music from it. Metal backboards or wooden or fiberglass or none, half court or full, cramped or unbound dimensions, iron hoops ten feet or nine and a half or eight feet tall, two players or twenty, the game accommodates itself, the instrument's exquisitely responsive to good-faith efforts. Think of the infinite possibilities for expression sleeping in a drum or story. Neither drum nor story is a fixed form, and every new player, every new writer or teller of tales may expand the definition of drum or story, employ the instrument in an original fashion, change our notions of what constitutes a story or drum. Drumming, storytelling, playing hoop are actions, practices, processes, manifestations of invisible imaginaries—revelations of what players are thinking and feeling, their desires as much as or more than what a casual observer sees materialized in performance. How would you know someone conceives of his body, its hollows, fat, bones, and solid meat as a drum until he starts the percussive, rhythmic patting and striking of his hands on his flesh. *Hambone, Hambone, where you been.* Or know until the words appear on the page that a woman's stream of silent thought could be represented to tell a story. Or understand that the barely visible scribbles of foul line, key, half-court line, out-of-bounds act as powerfully as the veve floor drawings of Vodun to organize and sacralize court space. Or know until you've watched enough and played enough that the court not only runs horizontally along the flat ground but also extends itself backward and forward in time, extends vertically above and below the surface of the earth, and those hoop-crowned poles at either end of the court, like the Christian cross, identify and honor the intersection of what humans can and can't comprehend, symbolize the simultaneous ritual presence of sky place and earth place and mirroring waters between, and know that the player who climbs air up, up toward the rim is entering for a charmed instant another mysterious dimension, his spirit as well as body rising like a ball arcing toward the hoop, like the souls of believers, of the unborn, undead, the ancestors who are raised and glide along a stick planted in combed, threshed soil to summon the loa.

Nearly everything essential to the playground game resides in players' heads. The game's as portable as a belief. Fluid, flexible, and as open to interpretation as a song. Basketball on the playground requires no referee, coach, clock, scoreboard, rulebook. Players call fouls, keep score, mediate disputes, police out-of-bounds, decide case by case, mano a mano how close to mugging and mayhem the pushing and shoving and jockeying for position are allowed to escalate. They agree to seriously challenge each other physically but not maim one another in this game where everybody is constantly moving and extremely vulnerable, unprotected by helmets or pads as they fly through the air, sprint full speed, set picks and screens within the relatively small scale of a court's dimensions, a court that shrinks precipitously, dangerously, the bigger, stronger, and faster the players are, the more both teams want to win.

The playground game is generated by desire. The desire to play. In this sense also it's truly a player's game. It exists nowhere except where and when the players' minds and bodies construct it. If I hadn't watched the game and listened to the stories, how would I have discovered its existence. How could I play it. The game's pure because it's a product of the players' will and imagination. If the players' desire cools, there is no game. Or at best some sloppy substitute of game not worth bothering with.

On the other hand the game's also sensitive to the call and response of its physical environment, the nature of the play mediated by location, the condition and size of the playing surface, weather, the skill and numbers of players. Some courts draw players from all over a city. Other spots gain their rep from the players who reside near enough to be summoned by the drum of action. The history of a court, the roll call of greats who once competed there, the vagaries of urban renewal (removal), the official posture of the city, the welcome or rejection extended by the court's residential neighbors all leach into the game's soil.

To be worthwhile in any venue, the action must be improvised on the spot. You got to go there to know there. Like classic African-American jazz, playground hoop is a one-time, one-more-time thing. Every note, move, solo, pat of the ball happens only once. Unique. Gone as soon as it gets here. Like a river you can't enter twice in the same spot. Each performance created for/within an unrepeatable context, a specific, concrete situation that hasn't appeared before or since. The hoop moves, the notes materialize in the flow of playing, then disappear instantly, preserved only in memory or word of mouth. Performance is all. The present tense presides. Films of playground hoop, recordings of jazz may achieve their own variety of art, repeatable, portable, stopping time, outside time in their frozen fashion, but the action is always long gone as soon as the players step off the court, off the bandstand. Gone in the limbo of fine lost things where lyric poetry seeks its subject.

Playground hoop is doing it. Participating in the action. *Being there.* The chance to be out there flying up and down the court. Its duration finite. Its time the only time, yet so intimate, inalienable, saturated, whole, it's all time, Great Time. Each isolated moment briefer than brief (was I there, did it happen to me, tell me about it) also provides continuity, the novel, constantly evolving, improvised context allowing the solo, the move to happen one more time because the players share lore—assumptions, standards, common memories (an aesthetic) about making music, playing the game. These understandings persist. Are the ground against which the figures become visible.

You can pick up in the playing if you listen hard, listen easy enough, the chorus saying, We are doing this together and it's just us out here but the game has been here before, other players have found themselves in the middle of this same deep, good shit and figured out how to deal. Similar moments set in transient yet abiding structures registered in the minds of players who are also the truest fans. The medium the message. Fragments of performance suggestive of a forever unfinished whole, the perfect whole tantalizingly close to now and also forever receding, each fleeting segment vital, absolutely necessary and equal and right if the show's going to go on. The context that provides possibilities for the unexpected, the unknown, does not compromise or bully the moments. Playground hoop invented to offer room, become room, to bust open and disappear except as invisible frame for what's in the break. For what's next, for what no one's ever done, ever seen before. Maybe the primary reason the game exists and persists is because it reliably supplies *breaks,* moments a player dreams of seizing and making his or her own when he or she thinks *music* or thinks *basketball*. Moments when weight, the everyday dominoes collapsing one after the other of linear time, is shed. When the player's free to play.

If urban blight indeed a movable famine, playground ball the city's movable feast. Thesis and antithesis. Blight a sign of material decay, ball a sign of spiritual health rising from the rubble. One embodying apartheid, denial, and exclusion, the other in-your-face, finding, jacking what it needs to energize an independent space. The so-called mainstream stigmatizes the "ghetto" while it also celebrates and emulates hoop spawned in the "ghetto," discovering in playground basketball a fount of contemporary style and values. Feast and famine connected, disconnected, merging, conflicting in confounding ways, both equally, frustratingly expressive in their separate modes of the conundrum of "race."

Homewood the location of my first court. I learned to play there the serious way the big guys played, learned to take a beating and bounce up again, to hold my spot against all comers. Learned to arrive early to watch the big guys filing in slowly, regally, me always hoping they'd be a player short and need me for a while till somebody real arrived. The court straight up Finance Street, then cross Homewood Avenue, duck under the billboard that shielded the weedy hollow at the foot of the hillside where my grandfather and his dago red–swilling cronies shot crap and told lies. Sneak past them, hump through the Bum's Forest on a worn foot trail paralleling the railroad tracks to the baseball field and park. Or walk the tracks the whole way there. Or maybe go the longer, respectable way. Stay on Finance Street's sidewalk till the intersection of Finance and Homewood, turn right down Homewood a few blocks to Hamilton and left on Hamilton to the school, then left again up the steep slope along the iron schoolyard fence, and the court's just past the swimming pool behind the school. Either way, the out-of-bounds short cuts or the by-the-rules route, the hoop court in Westinghouse Park just a quick minute from my grand-mother's house.

Bleak and unpromising as it sits today, abandoned for other, more glamorous sites, Westinghouse Park the place. That dinky, runty rectangular patch of asphalt and other courts like it incubated playground hoop, birthed the game still contested in countless varied venues across America and the world, a creation that is a compelling, vigorous assertion of human individuality and community embodied in a contest this simple: you try to throw a ball, usually but not necessarily a round, bouncing ball, through an elevated hoop more times than your opponent, disciplining the action's flow by a set of mutually agreed-upon rules, some inherited, learned, some improvised on the spot.

Ed Fleming whom I'd seen last . . . when . . . where . . . now here in Warden's in his charcoal gray, fashionable, gangster-shouldered suit in the midst of a crowd of mourners congregated just inside the entrance of Parlor A.

After we'd talked a minute or so and he had to go back inside and I needed to return to Omar, he said, Uh-huh. My mom lived on Finance. For a good long while before she passed. Heard her speak highly of Mrs. French. And Mrs. French your grandmother, huh. Hmmm. I never knew that. Heard my mother praise Mrs. French many times. Good to see you, man. You take care of yourself now, John. Don't be a stranger. Holler next time you're in town.

John. I don't believe I'd ever heard Ed Fleming say my first name. A baptism of sorts, in Warden's of all places. He'd always called me Wideman on the court. The surname detached, objectified, like when it's entered in a scorebook. *Wideman.* A clean slate for each new game. Every game you're obligated, challenged to fill the line of empty slots following your name with field goals attempted and made, foul shots hit or missed, personal fouls, rebounds, steals, turnovers, assists, blocked shots. Who Wideman *is* is drastically simplified. You are the numbers, period. Nothing else matters — where you came from, who your daddy or grandmammy might be — you're just a player. *Wideman.* The numbers — over the course of a game, over the course of a season, a career — accumulate or not, may resonate or not when another player says your name, an announcer or fan says your name. You get used to people observing the last-name-only convention until *Wideman*'s a tag that doesn't exactly belong to you anymore. *Wideman* only signifies the numbers racked up, then wiped clean so your name's a question mark each time a game begins. And unfair though it may be, the sole numbers really mattering always the ones in progress — when they're skimpy, they peg you as a chump, forget how you kicked ass the game before or the last dozen games.

On the playground no uniforms and numbers identify you. A single name's enough on Homewood court, and if it's your surname, *Wideman,* it's said with a little intentional chill of de-personalization, the way a referee calls you by your uniform number, foul on *Ten,* in high school or college games. Strictly business on the playground too, when somebody chooses you in the meat-market picking of teams for the first serious run of the day. Alternating choices till a limit of ten spots filled, the two guys choosing — they earn the privilege by being the first two to hit a foul shot — call you by your last name or maybe a nickname: Got Smith — Gimme Pooky — Got Jones — Take Sky. You can go years, a lifetime, playing alongside guys and know them only by their court handles. Read something in a newspaper about one of your basketball buddies and never know it's him, *Snobs,* inside the disguise of a whole, proper name. You'll have to hear the good news or bad news over again on the sidelines from somebody who tells the story with the court name in place. *D'you hear about Snobs, man.*

Ed Fleming had always called me Wideman in my coming-up days. For him to acknowledge a life for me off the court would have been highly improbable back then. Why would he care who I was. Or who I thought I was. He was a legend. He ruled. He was a grown man, born into a different age set, with different running buddies who'd come up hooping together, getting in and out of trouble together, and obviously no outsider could enter that cohort, just like nobody could leave it. Because I was precocious on the court, my age-group friends seldom accompanied me when I played ball. In some ways it meant I stuck out like a sore thumb. I didn't mind being a special case, didn't like the loneliness. No crew to hang with on walks to the court or back home again. No chance to replay games in our words, from our rookies' perspective. No opportunity to boast or tease each other or badmouth some old head turkey who thought he was god's gift. Over time I'd discover half the fun of playground ball resided in these rituals that extended the game, the imagined recreations like a good preacher retelling Adam and Eve, jazzing up his version with parables and homilies and metaphor not only to stitch together a way to live in the world but exemplify a style of doing it with his words. No crew meant I had no one to watch my back unless an older player chose to look out for me. Literally a look. One look all it took to dissuade a bully from coming down too hard on the youngblood. Rules, consequences communicated in a single glance from one of the enforcers like Ed Fleming nobody's hardly going to the mat to challenge.

To some of his peers he was *Ed* or *Fleming*. Always *Ed Fleming* in my mind. Both names necessary, three inseparable syllables, more incantation or open-sesame mantra than a name. A mini–sound bite like those heroic epithets identifying characters —Ox-eyed Hera, Swift-heeled Achilles—whose adventures I followed in the *Golden Book of Greek Myth* or in Classics Illustrated comic versions of the *Iliad* and *Odyssey*. See the guy down low, backing into the key, *pat, pat, pat,* demanding inch by inch the space he needs. That's not just any old Ed or Fleming. He's *the* Ed Fleming. Implacable. Irresistible. Each dribble a hammerstroke staking out his claim. *Pát. Pat.* Both names, all three syllables spoken internally, honored, even when I don't say them aloud. Even now, forty years later in Warden's, when I call him *Ed,* the single, naked sound coming out of my mouth almost as surprising for me to hear as hearing *John* pass through Ed Fleming's lips.

To my father, Edgar, he would have been *Fleming,* one of a vintage crop of good young players rising up behind him. Fleming, Stokes, and their teammates, winners at Homewood's Westinghouse High of the state title, kids good enough to groom and be wary of simultaneously, especially the Fleming boy since one day soon he might also encroach upon *Eddie,* my father's court name. My father, Edgar Wideman, would have taken a prodigy like Ed Fleming under his wing, tested him, whipped on him unmercifully, protected him with hard stares if anybody got too close to actually damaging the precious talent, the fragile ego and vulnerable physique of a large, scrappy, tough kid just about but not quite ready to handle the weight and anger of adult males who used the court to certify their deepest resources of skill, determination, heart, resources they could publicly exhibit and hone few other places in a Jim Crow society. Homewood court a threshing ground, and the weak better not stray too close to the blades. The men could find release for some of the best things in themselves, and of course that included dangerous stuff too. Play not exactly play. No-no-no. Winning and losing cut deep. Very, very deep. Yet ability, a refined repertoire of hoop skill enabling you to win more often than lose, not the thing that gave you a passing or failing grade on the court. The real examination results, the score that counts so much it keeps the play, for all its ferocity, about more than winning or losing, registers inside each player. When you step on or off the court, how do other players look at you and you at them. What name do they call you by, how is the saying of your name inflected. Among the infinitely nuanced possibilities a particular pronunciation might suggest, which one is communicated to you, to others when you're greeted, when you are picked for a squad, when players talk about you and you're not around, when they are not around and you talk to yourself about the court, about the game, replaying the action in your mind on that private, private screen at home, at night, in bed, recalling a whole hot afternoon and you have to fill in the slots, the blanks, where your name goes into the imagining. What is it, how is it said.

To Ed Fleming, *Wideman* would be the respected name of one of the old heads who broke him in and also the name of a kid coming up behind him. Wideman *père*. Wideman *fils*. Did he ever have trouble distinguishing us, keeping us straight. Did he concern himself with policing such a fine line. Something he once said to me indicated he didn't always differentiate. In Great Time what goes round comes round. After hip-checking me *blam* into the fence just behind the poles and backboard when we were both after a loose ball, or maybe it was when he lifted me off my feet and tossed me a yard or so from the sweet spot I thought I was strong enough to deny him, bodying him away from it for a couple of seconds till he decided to show me that day what he could bring to bear if he really needed a spot as much as I needed him out of it, Ed Fleming whispered words to this effect: Your daddy was extra rough on me, and boy, I'm sure gonna return the favor. Gonna give you a hard row to hoe, son, and don't start crybabying or calling fouls neither, not today, youngblood. If you can't stand the heat, get out the kitchen.

So Ed Fleming's hoop war with my father not over in one generation. He revisited it through me. Hard truths imprinted on Edgar Wideman's will and flesh by some anonymous bunch of old guys hooping, then imprinted by my father on Ed Fleming, coming home to roost in my bruised feelings and meat, in the knobby-boned body I prayed daily would hurry up and get padded by muscle like Ed Fleming's.

What my father had reaped and sown would sprout up

again when the weather turned warm enough for outdoor runs to commence at Homewood court. The game, its lore and lessons. For instance, *Never forget*—not where you came from nor what's coming up behind you, a lesson concretely applied when you're dribbling the ball, leading a fast break attack on the opponent's basket, when it's a matter of peripheral vision, of the Janus look backward and forward so you're aware of who's in front of you and behind, also mapping 360 degrees all the other players' positions on the court, the kaleidoscoping shifts, the evolving opportunities and hazards your rush to the hoop engenders. More abstractly applied, the lesson reminds you to take seriously your place in time, in tradition, within the community of players. Ed Fleming and the other vets teaching me to take my time, no matter the speed I'm traveling. Teaching me to be, not to underreach or overreach myself. Either way you cheated the game, cheated your name, the name in progress, the unfolding narrative, told and retold, backward, forward, sideways, inside out, of who you would turn out to be as you played.

I learned, among other things, to recognize and be grateful for a helping hand, learned it might not be exactly the kind of hand I thought I wanted, maybe it would be a rough hand, a bitter pill, but I was learning to appreciate different hands on their different terms. Above all learning not to be so intent on moving forward I turned my back on the ones behind who might need my hand or have one to offer.

Learned about time as I was learning the game. Because the game is time. Not time out from the real business of life. Not simply play time. Time. Like good gospel music, the game brings time, tells time, announces the good news that there is Great Time beyond clock time and this superabundance, this sphere where you can be larger than you are, belongs to nobody. It's too vast. Everlasting. *Elsewhere.* Yet you can go there. It's in your hands. White people nor nobody else owns it. It's waiting for you to claim it. The game conjures Great Time, gives it and takes it away. Clock time, linear time irrelevant while the game's on—two teams might battle fifteen minutes to complete a run or twice as long or till dark hides the court forever if neither side pushes ahead by two baskets in a deuce (win by two) contest. The game trumps time, supersedes it. Good hoop, like good rhythm-and-blues music, alerts you to what's always there, abiding, presiding, master of ceremonies ready to empower your spirit and body, the beat lurking, dancing in all things whether you're conscious of its presence or not. Great Time your chance to be. To get down. Out. To do it right. Right on time. The game, again like gospel music, propagates rhythm, a flow and go, a back beat you can tune into so time's lonely, featureless stretch feels as charged, as sensuous, as accessible a medium as wind or water. You don't really own game time, but the fit feels so close to perfect you can't help believing on occasion it belongs to you.

Playing the game is not counting time nor translating, reducing, calculating it in arbitrary material measures, not turning it into something else, possessing it or hoarding it or exchanging it for money. In other words not alienating time, not following the dictates of the workaday world that would orphan our bodies from time. In the game nothing counts about time except its nonstop, swift passing and the way that passage beating inside you is so deep, so sweet and quick like a longed-for, unexpected kiss over before you know you've been kissed but the thrill isn't gone, gets stronger and stronger when time allows you to stand back from it, remember it, it lingers because you're still there as well as here, riding Great Time, what you were and are and will be as long as you're in the air, the game.

Synchronicity. You and time in synch. In touch. Rhythm one name for how the touch feels, how it registers, how you can let go and find yourself part of time's flow. Dancing with an invisible partner who's so good at dancing you forget who's leading, who's following, aware instead only of the rhythm, on time, stepping, and your body free, mind free, dancing the steps.

You're large, large and tiny too. Time a co-conspirator as you *break* from clock time. Everything happening simultaneously so you don't have to hurry or slow down. The game in its own good time comes to you as you come to understand its rhythms. You're not counting but the count's inside you, heard and unheard. Disciplined by years of experiencing the action, your body responds to the internalized measures, frees your playing mind. You let yourself go where the game flows. Gametime opens like your mouth when you drew your first breath.

A flash in the corner of your eye and you remember to look instantly forward and backward, scan all 360 degrees of the court with the extra eyes in the rear of your skull to include the many, many directions and dimensions in which time flies. You punch up all previous occasions, all those unfolding, particular scenes similar to this one, recall doing something like this before, and begin to picture how it happened before and how you want it to happen now. You rise off the ground with the ball gripped in both hands, up into the air where you can't stay long. Just long enough to forget how fast you must return to the hard ground, because you have business to take care of before the inevitable crash landing. Occupy yourself while you float, weightless, working out what you need to do next. Whether you reach the hoop or not, you aim your leap for it. Thrust your body into a flight path carrying you in for a shot if no opponent blocks the way. Which old-timer said it first—You can switch a shot to a pass, boy. No way you switching pass to shot. Leave your feet better always be thinking shot first, boy. How can you hear the whole message in a fraction of the time required for speaking one word of it aloud. The whole thought blinking through your mind as quickly as the flash, materializing now, just as you anticipated it would, into one of your teammates who's sprinting in a lane parallel to the channel of air in which you're gliding down the court's middle. Two other bodies, arms flailing, attempt to shrink the space available for maneuvering. You've seen it happening before, seen the ways it can end. You don't have to choose an ending quite yet. You understand there's no rush. No time. All time. Just what's next and next till this finishes, next and next the only limit, the slow-motion tick and tick-tock of raindrops on a roof, punctuating your hang time till the play's over and in the book.

Your teammate airborne too now. Dish or keep. Keep or dish. The windmilling obstacle of two pairs of arms and legs porous as a prison's stone walls when the spirit cries, Freedom, freedom.

A small, perfectly round hole guarded by a ring of iron opens in the sky. You haven't even looked at it yet but know, given where you took off, where the hole should be, know where it will be when your teammate's hands you haven't seen yet either stretch up to receive the ball leaving your hands, catching the pass half a foot above the unseen target, him arriving just on time, on a dime to guide the ball down through the hoop. That's one dream of it happening. Maybe it will this time as you fly over the defenders or around them or blow through them. You don't know exactly how it will happen, just that it does. One more time. The play scores. Count it. You're still soaring as you strut in reverse, bouncing high off the balls of your feet, Jordan-style, backpedaling down the court to play "dee."

The game a string of beads, bright and colorful. You dance them to catch the light, coil them, let them spill through your fingers, mound in your cupped hands. You play the beads, observe how each tiny sphere's a work of art in itself. Time's an invisible cord holding them together, what you can't touch, can't see, time connects glittering bead to bead, forms them into something tangible, a necklace, a gift.

From my grandmother Freeda's house a short walk would take you to the basketball court behind Homewood school. Not much of a court. No more than two thirds the size of an average outdoor court. A cramped, unsafe space when ten large bodies are scuffling for running room inside its boundaries, a war zone separated from the street by a high, rusty Cyclone fence, twice as tall as the fence I took you to that runs along Finance now to keep people off the hillside below the busway and railroad tracks. This fence higher perhaps because it guarded the swimming pool adjacent to the court and also served to keep nonpayers a good distance away from Homewood field, where semipro baseball and football games were once contested on the oiled dirt surface beyond a second fence at the court's far end.

On a drab, dilapidated rectangle of asphalt straight up the street from 7415 Finance, my grandmother's house, it just so happened that in the early 1950s, when I was a kid, some of the best players in the world competed in some of the best basketball in the world. More than simply congregating and competing, the men were inventing day by day the playground game I'd learn and love. Not many people were aware then and not many more now of Homewood court's role in the history, the creation of hoop. Or hoop's relation to who we all are. I'd be lying if I said I knew it back in the fifties, but I do know I was driven, yearned every day for a chance to walk those few blocks, to step on the court and be part of a game even though at best my little walk-ons lasted five or ten minutes, yearned with fervor and an unswerving singleness of purpose, as if indeed I did understand there was nothing better anywhere else in the universe than the ball games on Homewood court.

Only recently have I become conscious of my habit of calling 7415 my *grandmother's house*. Both my grandparents, John and Freeda French, were alive during the first bad episodes when my father and mother couldn't bear to be under the same roof and our little family minus Daddy wound up—for days or weeks, then months—staying in 7415. My memories of the house on Finance across from the train tracks certainly include John French. His big easy chair in the corner of the living room full of him whether he sat in it or not. My regal view from his shoulders as I presided up there, touring Homewood, feet stirruped in his huge hands. Smell of Prince Albert tobacco and Limburger cheese in his flannel shirts. His gravel-voiced fussing at my grandmother when he couldn't find a bottle of straw-bottomed dago red he'd stashed somewhere out of sight and she'd restashed farther out of sight to confuse him into thinking maybe he'd emptied it or hid his wine from his own self when he'd stumbled in from gambling. Freed would come right back at him, lay his soul to rest. Don't you roll your eyes at me, Mr. John French. Don't want nothing to do with that nasty stuff. Don't drink it, don't like nothing about it, so don't come in here bothering me. If you big and bad enough to spend good money on that rotgut wine, you sure ought to be grown enough to keep track of it.

My grandfather an overwhelming presence from those days in Homewood. He keeps turning up in my fiction and here I am writing about him again. Then why the habit of saying *grandmother's house*. Perhaps it's simply because she outlived him by nearly thirty years, the years I was growing into manhood, or because I was raised in a household of women mourning lost husbands, lost fathers, lost brothers, absent men whose place I was being groomed, doomed to take. John French gone, how could 7415 be his house. But the women kept him alive in their hearts, their conversations. I overheard lots about him, and much of the recollecting intentionally directed at me, as lesson and example of the goodness and badness of a good man, proof of how much he'd loved and been loved. The women's stories painstakingly reconstructed his presence. They weren't willing or able to let go, savored their memories, cultivated the possibility that I might, for better or worse, turn out like him. The women depended on each other—the shared talk, rituals, history—to mend the rent in the fabric of their lives the passing of John French had made.

The women kept the memory of John French vital, vital for them in a fashion he couldn't be for me. Though they missed him, they didn't blame him for deserting them. No fault of his that God and a bad heart had cut him down. But for me his dying reneged on a solemn promise. He'd abandoned me. Like my father—and Daddy John was a father after mine defaulted once too many times—John French had left me alone to grapple with my sense of being other and different in the women's world of 7415. If he loved me, why would he leave me. Where did he go. No matter how hard the women tried to draw me in, include me, indulge me, I could only be *in* their world, not *of* it. Through the years, even now at this moment, calling 7415 my grandmother's house, am I suppressing the perplexing, hurtful, double loss of father and grandfather that occurred while I lived on Finance Street. Ceding the house to the women, am I cleansing it of ambiguity, removing the men whose loss haunts me. If they don't reside in the house, I don't have to miss them each time I call its name. I can stash memories of my father or John French in other places, hide and disguise them, forget them until I'm ready to reopen the door, reassemble the fragments I've scattered and buried. Until I'm ready to assume the responsibilities and burdens they've left for me. Until I'm ready to rethink the whole painful mess, if I ever feel strong enough to rethink it, and welcome my fathers back. Maybe then I'll rename the house on Finance. Wake, reunion, baptism.

If you walked down from the corner of Homewood and Hamilton to the intersection of North Lang and started up the steep grade to the court, the Carnegie Library would be at your back and behind it would rise the crenellated, gothic spires of Holy Rosary Church. The number 76 trolley once ran on Hamilton Avenue, its cobblestone-bedded tracks dividing the library from Homewood school. The school's brick walls, blackened by steel mill smoke like all Pittsburgh's older buildings, gradually cut off the sights and sounds of Hamilton as you climbed North Lang toward another set of tracks, invisible below the hill's crest, train tracks crossed by a green steel footbridge leading to Westinghouse Park, the same railroad tracks marking the shortest distance from 7415 to the court. On a hot summer day trekking up past Homewood Elementary School, you'd be grateful for the shade of its grimy walls, tempted by the splash, flash, and noise of the pool, then suddenly, because you couldn't see it till you reached it, the game jumps you, so close you could poke your fingers through the saggy chainlink fence and touch the players. Of course you wouldn't dare. Not unless you wanted to draw back a nub. You understood how serious it was out there, inside the cage where men were grunting, sweating, and banging into each other. Different rules on the court. Things happening at a different pace—quick, unforgiving, instant consequences you could neither foresee nor shrink from once you put yourself out there. Be like sticking your hand in the lions' den at Highland Park zoo. Finger, arm, whatever you stuck in there, a chance of losing it. If you think you want to dance with the lions, you best bring your whole load with you, bro. Do it right if you're going to do it. Play the game with all you have or leave it alone is what those dark, dripping wet bodies working, playing under the hot sun say to the passersby.

With the library and elementary school at the bottom of the hill, Westinghouse Park just across the bridge at the hill's top, the public swimming pool, ballfield, and basketball court strung in between, and Homewood Avenue's main strip of stores, banks, churches just two blocks away, the area I'm describing was Homewood's heart, and the hoop court for me the heart of that heart. Homewood's agora, its Carnival on weekends, where citizens converged to shop, stroll, picnic, play games, meet lovers, transact business.

Going to play on Homewood court meant you were making your game public. Wasn't about you and your little crew throwing the nearest thing to a decent ball you could scrounge up into some jerry-rigged peach basket nailed to a board on a telly pole on your street. Wasn't you launching shot after shot through the drooping lip of an eight-foot baby hoop behind the Catholic grade school. Taking your game to Homewood meant taking it Downtown, Downtown where most of the people you passed on the street looked vaguely familiar and even if you didn't exactly know their names and most likely they didn't exactly know yours, you'd probably heard each other's names and stories so in a way you knew each other, and passersby politely greeted one another, stranger or not, as was the custom. You knew the stories, and when you heard certain names, certain stories were attached.

Downtown a fun place for casual excursions but people also converged there when they needed to take care of important affairs. The heart of Homewood a marketplace among other things, where you discover the price of what you want. Where you brought your game to check out what it might be worth. What your game might make you worth. What name you could earn there and carry back home. Hear in the street. Where you could learn what a name cost.

Learning to Play

The body is the thread on which beads are strung.

SHE LOOKED *good enough to eat. And he wished he could start there. But first—half of him doubting, half of him absolutely certain, half of him stunned beyond words, half of him speaking in tongues, half of him scared, half of him willing to risk anything, half of him amazed his shaky whole could contain all these halves without exploding—he struggled to explain how bizarre it was to meet her here in this city where he'd loved her thirty years before, then lost her, not a glimpse until this moment thirty years later when she smiles at him, the exact smile on the exact face he'd loved before, appearing again in what must be a dream but here she is flesh and blood he could touch if she let him, can watch as her smile changes into something else he hopes is a sign she might be seriously considering the foolishness he can't help spouting, that she might be trying, giving him the benefit of the doubt, the eyes that had beamed the smile softening, turning quiet, thoughtful, averted downward, inward, attentive to him making an idiot of himself or perhaps if he could still read her, if he could recall how to decipher the code beneath the dazzle of her features—the simple, elegant arrangement and shape of nose, cheekbones, eyes, lips that took his breath away—maybe she had decided to listen and if he could cool it and let his story unravel so it suspended her disbelief as it was suspending his, word by word, sentence by sentence while he formed them, maybe she'd understand he wasn't crazy, not some nut laying down a corny, premeditated rap, but describing something impossible he couldn't quite believe yet either, a situation unreal as he spoke it and claimed to be witness, participant, and chronicler caught up in a scene that couldn't be happening because women don't drop off the edge of the earth and reappear with another name thirty years later, intact, unchanged, looking precisely as they looked when last seen, same age, same smile, same body, same power, yet that's the story he needed to continue telling, hoping she'd believe, hoping she'd entertain the possibility that she carried somewhere inside herself the spirit cargo of another person, memories of another soul, and that she might be, in some inexplicable fashion, both herself and the woman from the past he was seeing, the one he'd loved and lost, the one who'd inhabited this exact body, exact smile he'd found again in Philadelphia.*

He recalled one day, like Proust sniffing his little cakes and recovering a lost world, the smell of the room in which his grandmother lay dying. Summer. An open door he entered, drawn by the scent of baking bread, not one loaf but thousands, millions cloying the air you must breathe if you're going to breathe at all walking past the three-block-long brick walls of National Biscuit Company, *N-A-B-I-S-C-O/Nabisco is the name to know /For a breakfast you can't beat/Eat Nabisco Shredded Wheat.* On Penn Avenue, Pittsburgh, P-A, passing Nabisco on your way to Mellon Park to hoop. He steps back into the front room of the house on Finance Street, the house everyone called his grandmother's house, even though John French, his grandfather, paid the bills by hanging wallpaper till a stroke crippled him and then he sat enthroned in the big overstuffed chair, the big parts of him, arms and chest in flannel shirt or long johns top, legs sprawled so you could not enter or leave the room without stepping over them. You tiptoed around when John French, head flung back, mouth wide open calling hogs, filled the room at the front of the house we called the living room with racheting snores almost as loud as the trains across Finance up on the hill, you tiptoed past him, just as you tiptoed up the stairs into the thick, yeasty smell of a room hardly large enough to hold a brass bed, a low, mirror-topped bureau, and the folding chair you sat on each day that summer when your job was watching your grandmother die.

You are drawn by the smell of bread baking in an oven and it opens you, enters you, takes you back to being a boy in a world of smells you certainly noticed but did not try to name or classify much beyond nasty or nice, fresh or stale, good or bad. Then you must go into the tiny room, in spite of a smell you can't name worrying you as you enter quietly, quietly tiptoeing because she needs her sleep even though that's all she does it seems to you, sleep, sleep, sleep, resting and never rising from the bed in the little spare room in her house you or the other grandkids sometimes sleep in and one day her great-grandchildren, your sons and daughter, will watch TV there and call it, when they're visiting in Pittsburgh, the TV room, and never guess when you were their age you tipped in here to watch your grandmother, a woman gone too soon for her great-grands to recall, sleep the sleep of the dead.

A smell you did not think of then, forty or fifty years ago, as baking bread or anything else that comforting and clear. You thought stink. B.O. You thought the dirty-ditch odor of yourself after running around all day or two days and escaping a bath, lying, promising you did bathe though water never touched you, water and soap had no shot at the sweaty, gritty stink, the boogers of dirt you could rub from your skin when for a day or two or three you pigged out, storing up, rolling around in your own funk and enjoying it in a way, peeling back the foreskin of your penis and marveling at the cheese you'd grown there, its peculiar, not unpleasant scent surprising on your fingertips long after you picked it off, the odor clinging the way a fistful of lightning bugs ranked up your hands for hours after you stole their lights. You raise the covers a little while you're lying in bed and the smell funnels to your nose, unnamable except it carries your name, yourself, the leaky flesh house you live in, you and not you it says in waves of funk rising and breaking across your face when you slowly fan the covers.

A body stinking is not what you are allowed to think entering the room where your grandmother lies, not even if it's the stink of your own body not hers you're ashamed of and sneak and play with anyway. Freeda's trying to leave here. She's still chasing after John French, he had heard the grownups saying. Seems to me she caught ole John French long time ago. Uh-huh. Caught him good, somebody replied. Sure did love that paperhanging fool, one said. It happens all the time, another one said. You know, two people live together whole lotta years, one dies, the other surely don't want be left behind. But you do not think of either love or death, you think both in a word that is neither one, a word like somebody familiar passing you on the street and gone, gone before you can sort out who and recall their name, and then you unthink both death and love real quick, as quick as you unthink stink because it's your grandmother lying in the bed. You do not want to lose her. You do not want anybody to hear you disrespect her. There may be a thin line somewhere and the smallest lean or shove, the least little disloyalty someone listening might hear in your thoughts, could decide whether your grandmother stays or goes.

You don't know. Nobody seems to know. His grandfather was here one day and gone the next and nothing about him the last time he saw him snoring in the big chair said his grandfather knew he'd be gone the next day. His whooping-cough hacking coughs always terrible, no more or less the last day. Daddy John French smiled the last day as he usually smiled. Laughing out loud at something you could see and laugh about too or laughing more and more as he did since he stayed put all day in the chair at things tickling him invisible to everybody else. He had spoken a couple times to his grandson. Grabbed him once when he passed by, hugging him, pretending he was going to nuzzle him with his prickly whiskers. Plenty of chances to say something about leaving to his grandson. But he didn't. And probably didn't because he didn't know. Not his hands nor his rheumy, pouched, hound-dog eyes nor his big, bad Limburger-cheese stinky feet knew they would change after just one more night into something else as unnamable as the smell filling the hall when the boy stood at the threshold of the room where they'd laid his grandmother for her turn of dying.

I am lost now in the universe of wondering what thought I would have been thinking as I entered the little room at the top of the stairs in the house on Finance Street. The universe of a smell silently crackling with signals that might make sense of everything the particular smell was and wasn't, of everything period, if I knew how to decode what was entering me, stirring me. I waited for my nose to figure things out. To tell me good or bad, nasty or nice, stale or fresh. It didn't know. No one knew. Stepping into the room, I was more alone than at those times I sniffed myself under the covers. More naked than when I kicked out of my grimy underwear to get a better whiff. My nose poked out trying to do its dumb job. Like a hunting dog does. Points. Then you're on your own. You do or not do what you have to on your own, at your peril. You meet yourself coming back at you in the stink percolating off your body. Was I trying to make myself into someone else when I stayed dirty. Making a stranger. Two people where once there was one. Who did I expect to discover trapped with me, loving me in my unwashed flesh.

Lost is the word. Lost. Lost. Not any other words about how I might have felt, what I might have tried to think about the smell of my grandmother in a hot little room at the top of the front hall stairs the summer I was twelve and heartbroken over the death of my grandfather, the absence of my father, who'd deserted us and us with nowhere to go except back to Homewood, to my grandmother's house, her house we always called it for some reason, even before John French had left there. A reason as elusive as the smell. As the smell I had to step into sooner or later, easing into it gingerly, inch by inch, as I entered scalding hot bathwater when it finally caught up with me.

She seemed as small as a doll under the faded green sheet someone in spite of the heat had pulled up and tucked tight so nothing showed but the tip of my grandmother's head and one long braid, the great, floating fan of her hair twisted into a heavy, silver-threaded rope. Before she'd comb it in the morning, Freeda French would be busy in the kitchen, moving between stove and sink, and no one else would be up yet but the two of us and I was never exactly sure she knew I was there, with her humming and muttering to herself, busy fixing coffee and breakfast, lighting the oven burners to chase roaches from the stove, her long, fine hair glowing like an angel's wing when it caught sun through the little window over the kitchen sink. It crackled when she brushed it, hanging down to her butt after she unpinned it or unwound the kerchief binding it to comb out knots. I'd touched it and smelled it loose that way before I knew it was hair, before I knew she was my grandmother. Clumps of it gripped in my fist while I sucked the thumb of my other hand. My Aunt Geral has a photo of me holding on, half asleep in my grandmother's arms, a roly-poly baby with his handful of hair who maybe hasn't been half as happy since.

Once inside the room, inside the smell, something said to me, You will never forget this. You will not want to leave this room when it's time to go. You will look for it many times in the many places you will find yourself in after this. And what is *this*. Is the special state I'm recalling nothing more or less than the ease and peace of settling down to watch over her once I was inside what had seemed moments before a place I could never set foot in. For a minute I halfway sat on the card-table folding chair just inside the door at the bed's foot. More than a minute—three or four, I guess, time enough to feel the surprising ease of being in a place where I hadn't thought I wanted to be or needed to be, time enough to listen for her breathing, listening intently, then slightly, suddenly alarmed since I heard nothing, noticed no movement under the taut sheet. Was there room beneath that little wrinkle for a person. Sat long enough to think if my job is saving her, wouldn't it be dumb to spoil everything this first chance I get by sitting here doing nothing while she might be already going or gone.

If I'm remembering correctly, I must have been twelve. A skinny, gangly, all-arms-and-legs twelve but not particularly tall for my age so I can't account for the sensation I'm sure I experienced of looking down from a great height when I stood at the head of my grandmother's bed. Perhaps it was the job I understood I was taking on when I decided I would enter the room at the top of the stairs with its thickly present but strangely freeing unnamable smell, me slipping inside the eye of the storm threatening to carry her away and finding there, as people say you do, a silence and quiet at the center while the world tears itself apart around you. Peace of a clump of hair clasped or braided through your fingers. I was discovered. Claimed. Though I could not name nor claim it, whatever was happening to the body of my grandmother hidden beneath a sheet seemed also to be happening to me. Nothing about it more foreign, more apart than the smell, her flesh's invisible signature writing itself again and again till it ripped through the paper, her name alive, simmering in the close air I pulled in breath by breath, one careful, spaced breath at a time till I realized the smell was nothing to worry about, no problem as I looked down on the small, dying, faraway woman who was my grandmother but also a woman vast, close, and as unknowable as myself, as the stranger who'd lie in my bed with me at night, myself sneaking into bed without a bath, yearning for another body, desiring the excitement of someone's difference I tried to grow in the garden of my own ripe flesh.

This vision, a boy, myself, rising from a chair, edging sideways up the narrow passage between wall and bed, standing taller than he could have been to stare down at his grandmother's head, a long stare at what I didn't want to see, at death, love, at what happens to people if breath leaves them, at what's left behind if you love them and there is nothing you can do to rouse them, to summon breath back, just stare and wonder how such things happen one quiet moment to the next with no warning no music no screams only a fluttering as if your heart has dislodged and dropped into the whirling pit of your belly and beats too fast there, too fast to beat very long without exploding, and the thought of it in the wrong soupy place flopping like a fish out of water or in too much water so it's drowning, gasping faster and faster, that part of me out of control, queasy, nearly sick, but hides itself behind the long still quiet of staring down while I attempt to make sense, figure out exactly what is happening, is it too late or is she still here and is the mantle of smell enfolding me now, is it comfortable now, after I've moved closer, close enough to touch, to lean down and kiss if I dared, the sweat on the small, pale patch of cheek and forehead my grandmother's only skin not veiled by sheet or hair.

This vision pieces itself together as I think back and recall what it starts, what will happen next and next till now, my memory foreseeing the events of that summer, hot July and August weeks I will spend guarding her, sweat sticking my bare thighs to the vinyl seat of the little folding funeral-parlor chair, my desire and determination to be nowhere else, yet wild horses galloping in my chest, pulling me away to the basketball court in the park, to the moon, just go go go, flee far from here, as far and fast as I can fly away so what's haunting her, haunting 7415, won't catch me too. My plan to run stymied each day by the unbearable possibility that taking a single step away I might lose her. The vision of a boy, me, dancing on a pinhead of choices, choices he's afraid to make, choices chosen and not, even as he tries to dance instead of choosing, choices toppling like dominoes to bring me here, this vision the first part of a sentence I can't complete, a subject needing a verb, adjectives, adverbs, grammar, syntax, and whatever else is required to forge a sentence, make sense, move from one point in time, in thought, to another. This vision a head for which I can create no body. Just recall unnamable smells and sounds, the fugitive evidence of my hands touching here or there, events too insignificant for words, mattering infinitely more than words, fifty long years of my life telescoped into a sentence that might begin "This vision . . . ," a sentence bringing to bear, beginning to align events so I can feel them again, recognize the truth and mounting force patterning them, a sentence whose evolving rhythm and turns of phrase would unravel my story as it might be spoken aloud to another person, a sentence so pure the note of each word played correctly would unleash the whole composition like the scent rising from a single spring flower brings forth a season, the endless cycles and recycling of time compressed in a yellow flower I cannot name because I'm a city boy, it's very familiar, I've seen such tiny, teardrop-petaled flowers many times before, but it strikes me this once differently than it ever has so I bend down to sniff the bright splash, examine it closely, suck up its perfume.

This sentence I'm seeking wants to be what actually occurred between then and now, even though that wish dooms it to be elusive, daunting, and as fatal as the possibilities within any given moment. Moments can expand you or snuff you out, either/or and always a little of both hovering in time's marrow, in the narrow passage from chair to bed, from fear to hoping, remembering, trying to convince myself my grandmother has always been alive, part of my life, here where I am and why should I worry it could be any other way.

I didn't touch her the first day. Looked long and hard enough to see the sweaty roots of hair where they were pulled back from her temple to form a braid, to see her skin wasn't one color but many, paleness dotted and speckled with darker bits of various hues, see her jaw twitch as if the invisible part of her face pushed into the pillow was tasting something, chewing or fussing.

My aunt had said, Wait, honey. Lemme go upstairs and see if she's wake. I'll be quiet I promised and left Aunt Geraldine at the sink under the window where morning sunshine could turn my grandmother's long nightgown into a bright glass bowl, her dark shape slim as a fish swimming through it.

Though the clattering of dishes followed me up the hallway stairs, the house seemed empty. Only three weeks since John French had died, and barely a month ago my mother, my siblings, and I were living in this house, my grandmother's house truly now with John French gone. When he was alive, I had never given a second thought to the habit picked up from the grownups of calling 7415 Finance my grandmother's house. Like everybody else I continued to say grandmother's or Freed's house after my grandfather died. When did the words begin to sound wrong. Wasn't 7415 his house too. Where's John French. Where's John French. When did that question begin asking itself, when did it deepen the color of walking alone upstairs, deepen silence as silence was deepened by the noise of my Aunt Geral, suds to her armpits, wrestling a sinkful of dishes, pots, and pans.

The house larger with John French gone. No long, outstretched legs to maneuver around. Nobody shushing you so you don't break his nap. Nobody snatching your grinning face away from a room full of his singing and the smell of sweet wine. Vast new space loomed everywhere. Familiar rooms grew suspicious, unexplored extensions. Silence bigger too, layered with scary possibilities of sounds you definitely didn't want to hear. Took every ounce of nerve to negotiate this strange, new, unmapped territory of my grandmother's house. We continued to call it that and calling it Freed's house should have made more sense with John French absent, but somehow he had slipped back through an open window to claim his portion, shrinking the safe havens of the house with his invisible presence anywhere, everywhere you turned. *Where's John French.*

You could go the short distance from kitchen through the dining room, coast along the china cabinet with a cut-glass bowl on top, then turn left at the doorway just past the phone table, start up the hallway steps, and before you reached the second floor lose everyone you loved. Shed people one by one as you thought their faces, their voices. Each person you tried to make real beside you drifted off into an ocean of brown silence swallowing them, swallowing you as it swelled, stretching the rooms of the house, filling them even as it pushed back their walls. More space and less. You could keep thinking your tissue paper thoughts, always room for them. What you couldn't keep was your father, grandfather, mother, or siblings. As close as they seemed to be, they were not really attached to you. They drifted away. You could walk a few steps from someone and the silent emptiness surrounding you might last forever, leave nothing for you to hold on to, nowhere for you to return. Where did people go after you left them. Where did you go when they left you. No one in the dark staircase with you. No room. Only space for thoughts thinner than breath since you could think and think but barely breathe there. Where was everybody. Did anybody know. Where's John French. Where's John French. Would your grandmother stay alive in the room at the top of the stairs long enough for you to reach her. And if you gripped her bony hand, would she stay. *Stay.* And if you let go her hand.

My mother with the help of her sisters and one sister's boyfriend, Harry Bobo, the boxer, who hustled up a pickup truck for an afternoon, had moved us from 7415 to Shadyside just a few weeks before my grandfather's fatal, last stroke. School out till September and I begged my mother to allow me to stay at my grandmother's house for the summer. Mom wouldn't take a job with three little kids at home, so she didn't need me to babysit. More boys my age and color on one block of Finance Street than in all of Shadyside, the white neighborhood where my parents rented because people said the schools better. But no school in summer and in Homewood lots of kids to play with and a hillside with trains on top, what kind of dummy would choose Shadyside just because the houses nicer, streets cleaner than in Homewood. Even with my father not around, too many of us crammed in the second floor and attic of 702 Copeland Street, Shadyside, so why not. Please let me stay in Homewood.

Maybe, my mother said. Are you sure, she asked.

She knew her question would stop me in my tracks. Understood *maybe* was better than telling me yes or no. *Maybe* started me thinking about whatever I was asking and getting me to rethink meant a good chance I'd land in a different place with different feelings. *Maybe* meant I couldn't react. Couldn't pout or holler or stomp away until she exposed her hole card. Couldn't tell where she stood, except, except in the *maybe.* I saw her floating there, saw how well she knew me, how slickly she could play me, how she exposed my uncertainties, reminded me I was far from understanding my own will and desires. *Maybe* her strategy for dealing with me, and more, much more, because *maybe* could stump her too, reveal how much she was my mother, I was her son. At the core of both of us a nagging fear that whatever we thought we wanted, however carefully we chose, we'd always pick the wrong thing. So *maybe* when I asked if I could stay in Homewood for the summer.

I want to. Please, Mom.

Are you sure it's what you want. I'll miss you, baby. Your brothers and sister will miss you. You're getting grown enough to be a big help to me. My little man of the house now your father's gone. You know I don't want to hold you back from something you really want. Not much for you to do in Shadyside in the summer, is there. On the other hand be just you and Mama and Geral most the time if you stay at 7415. Sis in and out. Nobody expects your Uncle Otis back this summer.

Geral said it's a good idea. Said they wouldn't have to worry about someone to help Sis while Geral's at work. Happy to have me she said. Give her and Sis a break.

Spoke to them already. We know you'd be a big help. Proud of you wanting to help. I'm just thinking about you. Missing you. The kids missing you. Maybe you'd even miss us every once in a great while. And I'm thinking about you in the house all day by yourself. Are you ready to babysit your grandmother all day while Geraldine's at work. I'm afraid Freed won't be much company for a while.

Not all day. Just some. Weekdays. When anybody needs a break.

You think real hard about it. You know it'll be very different in Homewood without your grandfather around. You'll miss him. I can tell you miss him already. He's the one kept you busy. Took you everywhere when you were a baby. Never forget the fit Mama threw when Fred Clark stumbled home drunk and teasing her John French had you sitting up on the bar in the Bucket of Blood sipping Iron City.

That's when I was little, Mom. Daddy John's been sick a long time.

Just trying to talk this through with you, honey. Homewood might be a good idea. Don't like giving you up a whole summer, but it might help all around. Some of the summer anyway. Maybe.

Maybe almost stopping me before I get to the top of the steps. How long could I stand in the dark staircase before somebody comes looking for me. Would I disappear the way the people whose faces and voices I imagine disappear into silent emptiness. They aren't really gone, are they. Geraldine's noise in the kitchen. My grandmother's smell drawing me on, entering, enfolding me as I mount the stairs. No matter how alone and uneasy I feel—no matter the house is filled with rattling emptiness, with rooms holding nothing I want to see, with words I don't want to hear, questions I can't answer, layer upon layer of silence that just might begin to thaw, begin to crack and release all those unspeakable terrors I've worked so carefully to avoid by boxing them and stacking them in walls to the ceiling, as if after John French's death the sudden, threatening immensity of my grandmother's house could be partitioned, tamed, could be negotiated by slipping along skinny tunnels I've left in the stacked boxes—I must go up to the room where my grandmother lies.

She was alive. Sleeping. Sitting on the folding chair watching her, I must have been holding my own breath so hard I couldn't hear hers. Then yes. Closer, I hear a slow, rhythmic scratching for air, muffled by the pillow hiding her face. I'd arrived in time to do my job. Yes. There still is a job to perform. Part of her like the mice in 7415's walls scratching breath by breath for life and maybe I could help.

Why was the sheet stretched this tight across the bed. It seemed to pin her down, press her body into the mattress so she's barely visible under the faded green cotton. Who'd tucked her in like this, the sheet a wide rubber band fastening her in place. And did the covering have to be pulled up to her neck, to the heavy rope of braid Geral or Sis must have lifted and draped atop the sheet so at least it could breathe, stay cool. Should he loosen the sheet. Fold it back some. Was that part of his job. At night, in the darkness, did she awaken and swim under the covers like she glided through the bright glass bowl in the morning.

Would his grandmother be wearing under the covers one of those long nightgowns he remembered when it was just the two of them alive in the world, except for the roaches she cursed and flushed from their hiding places in the oven, tears in her eyes some mornings when the waves of insects won. Or were the covers pulled up because her shoulders were bare, her whole body bare and wet, and her sweaty skin might catch a draft and she'd cough and cough till she's gone like John French. Why was his grandmother—who could bake juicy blackberry cobblers so good he couldn't sleep some nights worrying if there'd be any leftovers for him in the morning or toss away his grandfather's half-full, straw-bottomed bottles of dago red and tell John French, You better gwan out of my face, man, drinking yourself foolish on that rotgut and coming round here blaming somebody cause you can't keep track of your own nasty business, or fuss at his mother and aunts as if they were little, silly kids ought to know better when they mess up and come crying on her shoulder, fussing till she tugs out the handkerchief she keeps pinned inside the front of her house-dress and wipes their eyes, then hers, then lets them unload their sad tales—why was she a little baby again herself needing somebody to dress and feed and wipe and wash her in this used-to-be-spare bedroom where he'd slept more than once with his brother when their parents were feuding and he couldn't beg his way into an aunt's bed.

There were reasons things happened, and reasons you should do things a certain way, reasons the grownups seemed to have figured out ages ago, and only now, lately, with people dying and falling out from strokes and a father leaving and households dismantled and moved, had anybody seen fit to say there were reasons things happened and tell him a few, explaining the reasons behind the reasons adults behaved in odd, hurtful ways with each other, ways he'd never expected they would. No one had told him there were well-understood truths and patterns and what you must learn to do is deal with those, conform to them whether you like them or not, forget acting according to your own lights if you want to be an adult, because what you want or how you feel doesn't matter, what matters is the experience of others, what other people have come to understand about the world and passed on, what gradually gets passed on to you because that's the way things are.

Why am I telling you this now, as if I'm an adult and there are certain things I've learned and done that you might take into account in order not to commit mistakes I made, as if there's a danger you would repeat my sins or could avoid them simply by hearing the dire consequences for me of mine, as if we're alike, as if I know enough about you to interest you in my story, more than interest, include you, address the story to you, you in a sense its main character propping up what would be a lonely, futile monologue without your ears listening, eyes watching, just words, words.

I want you here beside me, inside what I have to say, so you can see for yourself, judge for yourself what I might have been thinking in the room with my grandmother, in a household buckling like the steeple in the cute little hand-jive game my aunts chanted with me. *Here's the church/This is the steeple/ Down come the walls/Out come the people.* Tickling me as the roof caves in, finger-people like roaches scurrying up and down my chubby arms and legs, poking into creases of fat. I want to be that baby boy again tucked into somebody's warmth under the covers, the house quiet, everybody shrouded in sleep so deep the trains up on the hill across Finance punch through the night soundless, weightless. I'm the only one awake. I pretend to sleep but I must count the train cars, try to keep up with their headlong rush, register the quick, thrumping rhythm as each brace of wheels drops from a mile high onto the tracks, then is snatched up into the sky again before the car behind smashes into it. Huge iron cars falling like buckets of rain. Car after car of endless night freights striking the rails too fast to keep up with. I lie there worried, dreaming a blur of flying numbers, sheets of rain, a storm passing. If I stay on duty counting, no one's sleep will be disturbed, no flood, no fire, no giant squeezing fist will shake the house to pieces as long as I listen, on guard, sheltered by the warmth, the scent of my aunt's body, a pulse inside me matching the train's frantic pace, taming the fury of its passing.

Were you there too in the room at the top of the hallway stairs, your weight, your presence like the shine of distant stars, visible if human eyes could travel far enough, fast enough.

If I could, I would fold you into this story the way I stowed away in boxcars and let the trains carry me into the night, the way I curled against the soft bosoms of my aunts and closed my eyes after the last shudders of the last shuddering train I could bear to stay awake for echoed the last time in the thought of its hurrying retreat. There, spoon fashion in front or behind, nestled into the warm mountain of one aunt or another, draping them with a little kid's skimpy arms and legs, I'd finally drift off, my last conscious thought, and often also my first thought when I'd open my eyes in the morning, Is this sleep.

Believe it or not that first afternoon alone with my grand-mother in the stifling, airless room at the top of the hallway stairs, I asked myself, Who can I tell this story to. I guess I should have asked to whom. Does grammar matter now more or less than it did then. Who needs it, who doesn't to tell the truth. Point was, from the beginning I sensed something taking shape. This story I'm telling now. So yes. Maybe you were there at that first moment, the moment I cross the threshold, breathe the smell, sit myself down in it, ants in my pants so I can't stay put on the chair more than a couple minutes before I'm on my feet again, anxious to get it on, anxious to move closer. And if I ask myself, move closer to whom, *then you're in the room, I'm moving closer to the head of the bed, moving toward you, all the women you've been and will be, moving past you, closer to this moment alone. Back there at the beginning were you the one I needed to tell the story to, the one the story was aiming for when it commenced. You as present as my grandmother. As a dream merging you with her, her with you. You waiting for this to begin, to start its arc of reaching you now. Before I knew your name or you knew mine.*

I understand that what I'm saying is impossible. You are impossible given all my reasons, my desires that would split you and save you, ignoring bounds of time and place to have you when you are not around, missing you when I shouldn't even know you exist, jealous of lovers you took before I met you,

having you here, there, everywhere at once in places impossible
for you to be, sprinkling you like fistfuls of seeds over this land-
scape I'm imagining, seeds older than my hand, unborn in my
hand, the history of the land sleeping inside them, its future
waiting, a future we might have strolled through one day.

So much beginning that day I watched my grandmother
dying. But is my story possible without someone listening. An
impossible someone in many places at once watching and lis-
tening, listening and watching, entering my words the way I
enter the room and the smell of death. Are you here, weaving a
story with me, unweaving it also as we go since stories can't
change the fact we are separate, must return to ourselves at
night, to our different silences and dreamings.

When my Aunt Geraldine finishes at the sink and comes up the
stairs she finds me on the folding chair. Finds exactly what I
found upon entering the room—the tightly tucked sheet, my
grandmother just about buried under it, only the top of her
head showing and a tentacle of braid dead as rope, then it's a
giant caterpillar crawling on the sheet or a thick snake slithering out or a gray cat sneaking under to snuggle up and steal my
grandmother's milk.

Aunt Geral pats my shoulder. I see, though she stands behind me, the tender look she gives me before casting her eyes up
at the bed, a look, a stretch almost tearing her apart because
I'm a young boy, my whole life ahead of me, and the woman in
the bed, her mother, may have next to no time left and Aunt
Geral must take all of this in, hopelessly in love with both of us,
love's greed and blind hunger equally for what it can and can't
have, what it can and can't do for the beloved, love's confusion
seeing the boy's health and promise withered in the suddenly
old woman, this woman in a photo posing with her twin
cousins in cloche hats pulled down on their foreheads to the coy
arches painted above their eyes, cascades of fake pearls to their
waists, short, fringed, flapper dresses, patent leather shoes with

buttons and silver buckles, black cupid-bow mouths you know would be crimson if the photo in color, Aunt Geral sees all this and in a heartbeat must pull it together, absorb it, compose herself as her glance brackets me on the chair, my grandmother in the bed.

Is my grandmother really under the sheet, the frozen ripple of her scrunched up into a corner miles from the extra blanket folded lengthwise, neatly across the bed's foot. What was the soft weight on my shoulder. More alone now, absolutely sure I am alone now that my aunt has entered the room and touched me. Am I the last breath in a dead mouth that will never open again. How do I know anything. Why. Do I believe there's any chance my grandmother will get well. Do I believe I'll grow old, frail, and die.

As if she's worried about the same questions troubling me, Aunt Geral repeats my trip to the head of the bed and stands there, still as stone, staring down, studying her mother. Lighter even than her touch on my shoulder, her fingertip traces the thick braid. Then she smooths the crumpled pillow, shifting it slightly so my grandmother's face rests on a fresher spot. Often the first day I didn't understand exactly what my aunt was doing. A few more days and I'd learned to perform many of the little tasks we hoped might keep my grandmother as comfortable as she could be in the only place, the only way we could tend her. You lean over and cup the weight of her damp head in one hand, not lifting so much as trying to hold her in place while you slide the pillow, a halo of sweat cool, or was it hot, against the back of your hand, as your other hand digs into the pillow, presses it down, and tugs. Learning the bones of my grandmother's face, the hard kernels inside her jaw. Damp witchy strands to rearrange, the heat within the bun of hair, brittle parts of her, parts like the pillow sinking, giving way when my fingers dig, press for a hold.

What I have yet to learn, what's still to come in the story, I can't help sticking in here where it doesn't fit, really shouldn't go. Who doesn't jump ahead or fill in behind when they tell a story. No matter how carefully I try to keep things straight—dates and places and people's names—time just squats there in its rocking chair, grinning or frowning, blocking my path and hurrying me along, and I can punch, kick, tug, it ain't moving, ain't changing the expression on its face, terrible because it's not really an expression or a face, my words stick to it, trapped like other blows I strike trying to get past or through or over or under or around the glistening pitch-black trickster.

My aunt whispers, She's okay, baby. Mama's getting that rest she needs to get better. Let's leave her be. She don't even know we're here, whispers these words or words very similar, I'm certain of them, hear them now, as clearly as I feel her hand dropping to my shoulder, lightly, a pat, a touch briefer than the time death takes to swoop in and steal someone's breath. Quicker than the blink of an eye all my aunt's weight, all the burdens stooping her soft, round shoulders gather to bear down on me, heavy and smothering as the sheet pressing my grandmother into the bed. I know this in spite of the lightness of her touch. Know this large, grown woman's feet are not planted on solid ground, she's been sucked up, shivering like a kite in a draft, weightless an instant in a powerful wind of grief suspending her, driving her higher and higher till she remembers herself, remembers the room, the bed, the boy and old woman, and then she's plunging back to earth and knows the weight of her would squash me like a bug if she lets herself lean a fraction of a fraction of a second too long on her nephew in the chair.

Her touch speaks to me without words and what I say to her requires no words either. I look back over my shoulder, tilting my head to stare up at her face, waiting for her eyes to return from the dizzying fall and focus on me so she can see I've been listening to what she did and didn't say, that I understand the good sense of her words, we should leave my grandmother to her sleep, but then I drop my eyes and stare straight ahead at the bed where my grandmother's hiding so Aunt Geral also understands she would have to lift the chair with me on it and haul it out of the room to break my stare. Understands the weight of my need to sit a little longer, understands she better not risk lifting it, no more than she should risk her weight on my twelve-year-old boy's thin shoulder.

Climbing the pyramid, I keep my eyes fixed on the steps. Step after ancient step after step, I don't let my gaze stray from the next stone slab in front of me. Later I will learn the Great Pyramid at Chichén Itzá soars hundreds of steps from earth to the ruined temple on its flat top. Mounting them on all fours, I don't count the giant steps. Not with English numbers anyway, though I tallied the steps sure enough. Mayan architects had recorded on them a map for the soul's bumpy progress skyward, each stone step's vertical face inscribed with prayer and duties, a stage of the journey. I can't read this carved language of glyphs but feel its thrumming presence as I stare at one step after another, depending on them, begging them to give me strength and sure footing for the climb to the top. Fear of falling compels me to study the steps as the pious Mayans must have when they read the stones like rosary beads, reciting rules for proper living the gods had commanded humans to follow.

Why didn't I recall till I was sixty or seventy feet aboveground my gut-churning acrophobia. Yes, it's as active here in Mexico as at home. Yes, it's turning my legs to jelly. Yes. The fight was my fault. I ran away from you because I thought running would hurt you, bring you crying after me. I was wrong. Wrong to start the fight, wrong to run, wrong about you. Deserve this punishment. This exile. This lonely climb.

Why did I wait till now to look down and reaffirm my fear of heights, now stranded high enough from the ground to break my neck if I lose my footing. Desperate to steal back time we'd lost, I often had wished to be a fly on the wall watching your other lives, but I never meant a wall like this, a precarious stone ladder ascending forty-five degrees forever into the stratosphere, me hugging it, no sticky padded extra limbs, no wings, no net. My soul as earthbound as a worm. Why am I risking everything for a god's aerial view of the lost city of Chichén Itzá.

In Auden's poem about the flight of Icarus, the reader doesn't learn whether the doomed boy thought his brief, bird's-eye, panoramic view of earth was worth the dues he was about to pay, falling, drowning like Willie Boy in the deep, deep blue sea. Instead Auden inserts us in the head of somebody at a distance, a witness ignorant of the boy's story, of his arrogant father Daedalus chancing his son's life in a contraption jerry-rigged in his garage. The innocent bystander observes the scene and doesn't even know it's a boy splashing down, just sees a plummeting figure, white spray when it hits, the silent ocean parting, instantly zipping shut.

Clinging to the steps, I'm way too busy to write a poem, but I steal Auden's ploy, shift the weight of the drama from the mind of a poor black boy far from home, afraid he's about to lose his grip, his love, and pay dearly for a lifetime of bad choices. I pluck up the victim, turn down the volume of his thoughts, and let him imagine himself soaring soundlessly, observed through the eyes of a Japanese tourist, the only one who notices the leap or plunge, the only human being wondering whether the dark, flailing figure had been tossed or blown or slipped off the pyramid or decided free will to try the air. Whether the gods welcome or ignore the offering, whether the body flying through the air is male like his or one more drugged sacrificial virgin, heart ripped bleeding from her breast by the priests before they push her or she swan-dives into the bottomless green murk of the cenote. I deploy my Japanese witness so the frightened climber can stop shaking, see himself as somebody else might, somebody calm, safe, who's not falling, somebody aware of information the climber doesn't know. Someone who listened carefully to a small brown tour guide's rap, amazed by how much the fellow's face, carriage, skin tone, and *manner resembled the typical peasant fishermen at home. How the language the Mexican spoke, though incomprehensible till translated by a second guide into Japanese, sounded not altogether unfamiliar. As the tour progressed and he paid closer attention to the Mexican guide's tone of voice and mobile features, his gesticulating hands dramatizing his clearly proud responses to particularly gruesome Mayan customs and artifacts, the tourist learned that some speeches in the foreign tongue required little or no translation. He stopped trying to substitute Japanese words that would explicate the brown, gnarled, one-thumbed man's rapid-fire Spanish. Followed the indian eyes to a platform at the edge of a limestone pit. Though the site too old and eroded to ascertain if it's manmade or something the Mayans discovered already formed, waiting in this jungle clearing, the Japanese tourist doesn't need anyone's voiceover to see that the semicircle of boulders is a stage.*

Eons ago, the guidebook says, an enormous shelf of limestone, thrust to the surface by seismic convulsions at the earth's molten core, formed what is now known as the Yucatan peninsula. The Mayan warrior kings utilized this native limestone to construct their buildings and monuments, as grit to grind their corn. Limestone's porous, pitted texture also provided a perfect medium in an arid land for storing in deep natural pools and reservoirs the precious water needed for large-scale agriculture. Productive farms supplied the stable food supply empires require to expand and terrorize.

This particular oval pool at Chichén Itzá (cenote the italicized indian word for pool in the English text the tourist purchased and might have chosen even if a guidebook in Japanese available) sits at the center of a natural open-air amphitheater formed by steep rock walls and thick jungle. Inside the towering semicircle, an arc of ten-foot-tall, lichen-covered boulders frames a stone diving platform forty feet or so above the pool's bellyful of water, water turning from bright jade to ominous black as clouds cross the sun. Stumbling unexpectedly upon this site for the first time, who wouldn't believe it's a tunnel plunging straight to the underworld, a portal of green fluid distilled from rotting vegetation and crumbling rock, rainfall, silt, the decaying bodies of creatures who dwell in worlds above and below. Who wouldn't sense the danger, the opportunity this opening spawns. No one needs to explain the pool, no words in any language would prepare you. Standing at its threshold, you'll shudder. It attracts and repels. The oddly colored still water forty feet down inside the limestone walls reeks of life and death. It would slowly dissolve your skin, gently lick flesh from bone, patiently melt the white bones and sip them. You grasp truths for which there are no words. Understand how quick the passage, long the fall from one world to another, how thin the membrane separating them, thin as green water's skin, there and not there, always changing, never the same water twice, except here, this pool's thin skin a lens upon which things are doubled forever. The cenote a jungle-bedded, rock-cradled door words won't open, your words nor anybody else's. You got to go there to know there, the song says. In the clearing you will understand the Mexican's bloody Spanish, the stolen indian words. Acquire all other languages. Need none, the Japanese tourist assures the climber between one step and the next, between the holding on and letting go, between sky and sea.

Did I tell you the tourist's guidebook also confirms I'm on the right track, says the Mayans used to play b-ball here. In their fashion. A thousand years ago hordes of uniformed players competed in specially designed stone arenas here and in cities all over the empire, warring a hard nugget of rubber ball through a keyhole hoop fastened high on a limestone wall. They played ferociously because the game was about honoring their kings and gods, about ensuring the sun's passage from night to day, the soul's passage from life to death, about enacting the cycle of the seasons, about celebrating the flesh's glory, affirming its transience, about each contestant's slim chance for honor and glory, about the constant gamble of being alive, the

sudden cruel twists of fate, the thin line between victory and de-
feat. In short they played the game just like we do at home.
Their ball game an ancient ancestor of ours. Oh, and by the
way, entering today's Chichén Itzá on the tourist bus, where
you'd pass through city gates if there still were gates, an out-
door hoop court greets you. Surprise, surprise. I almost jumped
out my seat. It could be Westinghouse Park.

Meanwhile I'm still climbing, still inching along, still
sprawled on all fours. Hugging the stones, I look down again.
A challenge, a dare. I'm trying to expel fear of falling without
bringing up my lunch too. I'm gasping for breath. The air's too
thin. You know how my vanity, my worry about getting old,
keeps me jogging regularly, so it's not the hot, steep climb that
has me sucking wind. I'm dizzy. About to pass out. My skull's
pounding. A traffic jam of words clogs my head, words repeat-
ing themselves, fighting to get in, fighting to get out. Where am
I. Where am I. Do I really want to know. And where are you.
Can't risk twisting my whole body around, so I sneak a back-
ward peek through my straddled legs. Are you hiding in the
swarm of people behind me, below me, a carnival of all ages
colors sizes body types nationalities crawling up the broad
steps, intent on reaching the summit. If they can do it, why not
me, Bird-Jaguar Man, snout sniffing the pyramid's stony ribs,
reading the scent trails of other creatures who have passed this
way, inhaling the sour musk of fear rising from my own groin.

The name — Bird-Jaguar Man — jumped up and dubbed me
just like that. Said itself and I repeated it before I was aware of
what I was saying. Bird-Jaguar a name I probably picked up in
one of the fat library books you collected about ancient Mayan
civilization. Remember the books. The plans. The two of us fly-
ing here to research the roots of hoop for my book, your film.
The wonderful synthesis of both we intended to create. What
happened. Where are you. Bird-Jaguar a synthesis too. Sleek
haunched panther with a grinning face who wears a fanciful
winged creature perched precariously, ridiculously, atop its

head, a birdman wearing a feathered robe, snake and scepter clutched in its talons, resplendent in its own luxuriously plumed warrior's headdress with a world growing out of the feathers, panther birthing man birthing bird birthing birdman and somewhere in there Noah's whole crew propagating to infinity. The Mayan Life Tree's crown cracks the cenote's surface, shoots up to the sky, pierces a dark cloud. Sheets of rain flood the earth, feed the Tree's invisible underwater roots. A jailbreak when the Life Tree's crown returns to the heavens, when it skewers and unites earth, water, air so all living things, usually bound each in its own element, are free to play, to mingle, dance, mate. Strange couplings. Numbers and kinds never envisioned by humans or gods until the Life Tree like a giant fist thrusts up and casts the trembling dice—Bird-Jaguars, Rabbit-Turtles, a snake deity with wings and head of a hawk. Results as unnamable, unpredictable as the outcome of the ball game Mayan warriors stake their lives to contest on masonry courts erected at the centers of their cities. Not even the most powerful gods can divine the outcome when the Life Tree rattles dice in its fist. Like foolish mortals the gods wager their power, lands, their heads, and like us often lose. You never know till the contest ends whether victors or vanquished will be called upon to forfeit their lives in honor of the game.

A moment of weakness halting my climb, my escape. Am I fleeing from you, from myself, from too much love, no love. Did I run to be free. Run to hide. Am I stretching my heartstrings till they snap or will they boomerang me back to your side. I feel myself coming apart, my will failing, disintegrating, and then, surprise, surprise, the lost/found name mounts me, rides me to the top. Bird-Jaguar Man an unexpected boost just when I need it. I rise, beamed up at warp speed, propelled by the Life Tree's thrust. Bird-Jaguar Man one of countless figures inhabiting the Tree's vast spreading canopy, its teeming green hive a headdress the scribes and sculptors imitate when they carve portraits of nobles as gods on the stelae, on stone steps, on portals between worlds. When I reach the top of the steps, the pyramid's crown, the edge of the sky, eyes tearing, teeth chattering, buffeted by the wind's siren wail, will I remember how to fly.

I sat on the folding chair until Aunt Geraldine, downstairs again, hollered up and asked what I was doing. *Whatchoo doing up there, boy.* No way I could answer her. Didn't have an answer for myself, let alone another person. C'mon down. Fix you something to eat. She'd be rooting in the fridge as she spoke. No chance I'd say no to a meal. No chance I'd let whatever I was doing or thought I was doing come between me and a meal. Aunt Geraldine would assume that as she started pulling something good together in her mind from the odds and ends of other meals she's rummaging through in the icebox, as she called it. Nothing in 7415 ever thrown away, especially food. Waste not, want not. Sin to toss good food in the garbage, sin to toss out good anything—clothes, hangers, paper bags, rubber bands. Hard as it is to get your hands on a little piece of money. Or a piece of anything still halfway good somebody else don't want no more. Many a starving person in the world give their right arm for what's sitting there on your plate you fixing to leave behind. Don't youall ever forget to be grateful for what you got. Don't you dare forget who sends good food to fill your bellies every day. Bow your heads, youall. John, you bless the table this evening.

Cat got your tongue up there. Watchoo doing, boy. *Nothing,* I would holler back if I wasn't afraid of disturbing my grandmother's sleep. Instead I keep the word to myself, repeating it inside my head *nothing, nothing.* Then, break my stare, push up off the folding chair and scoot out the door, the unspoken sound of *nothing* echoing in my empty head till I see my aunt down in the kitchen, leaning into the open icebox checking out cans with gum-banded lids of wax paper, saucer-covered bowls, recycled margarine tubs, Mason jars, each preserving leftovers I always inspect first thing when I arrive at my grandmother's house, anticipating the permutations and combinations of these potential ingredients and how good they will taste whipped together by the women's magic hands.

When I think I'm beyond it, halfway down the hall stairs, the smell returns. Not me. Not my grandmother. Itself again. Something with a life of its own working its way back into my consciousness. It's spread thinner at the foot of the steps, the bulk of it seeming to have rushed up as I hurried down. I can almost pick out from the darkness hovering over the landing the shape of the thick cloud I'll have to pass through next time I climb to my grandmother's room.

She okay, baby.

Not awake yet. She turned over once and the one eye I could see not open. How's Freed sleep at night if she sleeps all day.

We almost lost your grandmother. She's still weak now. Very, very weak. Barely can sip those thimblefuls of broth we try to spoon in her. She had to fight her way back from the deep edge. And that's a mighty long way back, honey, and a mighty strain on a person's body. Thank God your grandmother's a fighter or we wouldn't have her with us today. She's still fighting to stay here.

She's quiet. Just sleeping very still and quiet. Didn't make a peep when she turned her head on the pillow.

Quiet fight sometimes the hardest fight. Takes all a person's strength. Can't be wasting one iota of energy on foolishness. Just quiet, quiet holding on. Not every fight about thumping your chest and hollering like Tarzan in the movies cause you stabbed some poor animal. Ain't Tarzan's jungle. Belongs to all God's creatures. Ain't no Tarzan's place to belly around killing things. Never did think much of them Tarzan movies. Always wanted the crocodile to win.

Aunt Geraldine, I heard in school there was a real Tarzan. Tarzan, lord of the jungle. Tarzan not his real name. He was an Englishman from a shipwreck supposed to live like Tarzan in the jungle till a boat came and carried him back home to England.

How long they say he lived in the jungle.

Long time. Years and years, till everybody forgot he's lost over in Africa.

Well, you can believe that lie if you want to. Me, I know no cracker wouldn't lasted a hot minute in a real jungle. You better stop believing everything those people tell you in that school. Believe half of what you see with your own eyes and almost nothing those people say. They lie through their teeth. I know. Didn't I go to that same sorry building my ownself every weekday God sent here. Doing time, locked down from first light till dark on those short winter days. Can to caint, like John French used to say, in that pitiful learn-nothing school. Went to school every day and every day they filled us full of lies. Barefaced lies.

Well, they're just teaching us now.

You listen to them and keep getting those high marks on your report card. We're all proud of you. Ignorant ole me the last one tell you not to listen and do your schoolwork. Just telling you be careful. Teacher's mouth no prayerbook. Never forgive those hunkies for lying about your great-great-grandmother, old black-as-coal Sybela Owens. She planted the first apple trees in Homewood. Everybody knows Sybela Owens run away from slavery with that white man Charley Bell. Came here and planted fruit trees. She and Charley Bell among the first who settled in Homewood. Ask any the old people round here and they'll tell you. Never forget the day teacher said to the class it was somebody else planted the first apple trees. Said some white woman. Some heifer trying to steal Sybela Owens's light, what it was. Shame how they do people. Take and take everything from us. Ain't bad enough we're poor. They try and take away things like your great-great-gran planting the first apple tree in Homewood. Give it to some ole rich white bitch and we're spozed to sing a song about her. La-di-da-dee. Sing the lie. Not me. Never did sing it. I knew who planted the first tree. Kept my mouth shut, head down on my little desktop while the others sang. Down there praying teacher and the rest of them choke on the lie.

Fixed you a meatloaf sandwich, baby. Know you must be hungry.

Can I eat it upstairs.

You sit right here. Don't want food upstairs attracting critters. Besides which you've been in that room a good long while this morning. You're a growing boy need your time outdoors. Don't worry about your grandmother. She's going to be all right. Tough old bird, ain't you, Mama. Believe me, honey, your Aunt Geraldine's not going to let anything bad happen to that ole gal. Sit right here at the table and eat your sandwich, drink your milk. Then you get on out here. Find some boys to play with.

Can I walk up to the park.

What did your mother tell you.

Said I could. Just ask you first. Said stay off the tracks.

I know you know better than to get close to the tracks, don't you. You're growing up to be a nice smart boy, and I know you know better. Walk to the park if you want to. Just keep your feet on Finance Street till you get to Homewood Avenue. And if you stay too long, remember you won't be going soon again. Better not make me trudge these sore dogs up there after you, boy.

Of the many ways to reach Westinghouse Park from my grandmother's house on Finance, the shortest and best was forbidden. I'd start slowly up Finance, on the sidewalk side exactly where I was supposed to stay all the way to Homewood Avenue, but after a block or so I'd hi-ho Silver across the street, gallop through high summer weeds to the hillside's top, the out-of-bounds path along the railroad tracks gleaming up there. A straight shot to the park then. Follow the tracks past the rotting old teapot-on-stilts water tower, cross over the narrow trestle above Homewood Avenue, a stretch next where you can look down on treetops, the patch of woods we called the Bum's Forest, then cut down from the tracks on a steep path through weeds and trees to a break in the fence that edges the ballfield and you'll see across the tarred dirt outfield the basketball court surrounded by its own web of fencing.

I didn't own a basketball. Hadn't played the game much. Each time I set out for the park I'd be hoping the whole way there to find somebody on the court, older players to watch so I could learn more game or kids my age and size I wouldn't need to be afraid of, who'd let me shoot around with them between the older boys' games till we could start one of our own, dreading the mean bigger kids who'd sometimes wreck our games and chase us away. Now I think of myself as a little shy ghost haunting the court, invisible at first to the others. I can laugh at my scaredy-cat ways and wonder why I felt like such an outsider that first summer I stayed in Homewood at my grandmother's house. Was it because, unlike Shadyside, everybody at the court brown. Or maybe it was just me, who I was and who I am, still shyly uneasy around strangers. All I knew for certain about the other brown boys who turned up at the court was that something drew them as it drew me. I didn't know their names, their families, the streets where they lived. Some were regulars, others came and went. None of the boys from my grandmother's street seemed much interested in basketball. Or maybe I never asked anyone to go with me to the park. Maybe getting away from everything about Finance Street the main point of going. Maybe I needed a place to be someone else. Somebody who could shoot, dribble, pass, and rebound, somebody good you'd want on your team. If I learned the game well, that's who I could be. Pick and choose what else people knew about me. Keep my secrets safe. Good if the other boys understood I broke rules to reach the court, scuffing along through the gravel bedding the rails, daredevil dashes over the trestle high above Homewood Avenue, hop-skipping from cross-tie to cross-tie, tightrope-walking a shiny rail. Not good for any of the players to know I'd spent the morning watching over a dying old lady. Pick and choose.

As summer progressed, my routine became more and more fixed. Mornings tending my grandmother, lunch, then about two in the afternoon the forbidden walk along the tracks to the park, hanging out a couple hours and back to 7415 around the time my Aunt Geral arrived home from work and Aunt Sis left to prepare dinner for her family. Long, mostly silent days, from the time Aunt Geral left to catch her morning trolley till she returned late afternoon, I might exchange only a handful of words, hello, goodbye, how you doing, how's Freed, with Aunt Sis coming in for duty as I'm finishing my lunch. The stroke had stolen my grandmother's voice. Weeks would pass before she recovered enough to begin emitting the peculiar noises that would be as close to normal speech as she'd manage the remainder of her days. At the basketball court I watched and played from a distance, no words necessary there either. Often the closest thing to conversation occurred on solitary walks back and forth along the tracks, my head hosting voices, the engineer warning me off the train's right of way, some grownup in the family reciting rules I was breaking, my arguments back for breaking them, me shushing and threatening with death a tattletale sibling I'd imagine catching me silhouetted against the Homewood sky as I raced to beat a train across the narrow trestle, the world shaking like dice in a black fist when the scream of twin diesels caught me, enclosed me as if God or death had decided to shut me up, shut up all my voices, remind us who's in charge.

I felt obliged to carry the morning quiet of the room at the top of the stairs with me all day. Breaking it seemed like betrayal not only of my grandmother but of all the women and what they strived to accomplish inside 7415's walls. I backed off from the loudness of the court—older guys bragging, playing the dozens, teasing, hollering nasty greetings and goodbyes. Laughing at each other's mess-ups. The quiet I carried with me from the room didn't fit in. I had to preserve a place within myself for silence, where I could steal away and be alone with it.

Quiet a defense and refuge, a refusal to connect with everything it wasn't, couldn't be. My grandmother peacefully asleep in a bed floating invisible thirty feet above the court's cracked asphalt, or maybe she's beneath the ground, her snores, hot breath, and baking-bread smell seeping up through a crack from the underworld where she lies enchanted. I remained constantly on duty, as vigilant at the court as in 7415, protecting the quiet, the rest my grandmother needed to get well. Nothing would startle her awake as long as I guarded the silence within myself. My time away from 7415 also and always preparation for returning, for conjuring the happiness of finding her safe. If I didn't let the quiet go, I could leave the house and not lose her. And that was an immense relief, a freeing, even if maintaining inner silence exacted dues I've never, then or now, learned how to stop paying.

The grownups were impressed by my dedication. How I could sit hours in the hot room with my grandmother. My Aunt Geral said, You don't have to stay up in there. Just keep checking in on her every so often. All Mama'll do is sleep whether you sitting there or not. You can go on about your business, honey, just so you remember to pop in regular and make sure everything's all right. Okay, baby. I said I liked to sit there. Liked the quiet. Was just fine sitting alone. Told her I read books and magazines to pass the time. Said there was nothing I'd rather be doing.

He's a good boy. Loves his grandmother. Everybody heard and repeated these sorts of nice things about me. When my mother and siblings visited 7415, they'd be greeted at the front door by news of how big a help I was. More responsibilities were allotted to me. I was left alone in the house with my grandmother for longer periods of time. As she gradually recovered from the stroke she could cooperate more, and many tasks I once couldn't perform solo became easier to manage, part of my watch. From early August on she'd sit up in bed a bit longer each day. Before Aunt Geral left for work she'd help my grandmother use the bedpan, *go potty* she'd say to her mother, using words and a tone I bet Freed had used with her and I could recall my mother using with me, *go potty.*

I'd run a basin full of hot water in the tiny bathroom down the hall and wait with it outside the door till Aunt Geral called me in to take the bedpan and empty it. Wait again outside the room with the freshly rinsed bedpan till the morning wash-up was completed and Aunt Geral would open the door, kiss me on my forehead, pat my shoulder, take the pan, and shove it under the bed. I'd remove the sudsy basin, dump it in the toilet where I'd dumped the bedpan. It would be okay then for me to go in and sit and watch while my aunt combed my grandmother's hair.

Wish I'd gotten Mama's good hair and not her bad teeth. God got it ass backwards. Mouth full of cavities just like her but when it comes to hair I look at Mama's and weep. Wonder what happened to poor me. Red and nappy and got the nerve to be falling out too. Be bald as John French soon. Mama'd be sitting on all this beautiful hair if she didn't keep the ends trimmed. Much trouble as it is with her the way she is now, we almost went ahead and cut it short. Then I said to Geral, no way. I could see Daddy frowning from the grave. I could see Mama crying first time she woke up enough to know her headful of glorious hair gone.

Aunt Sis started out talking to me while she combed but now she's whispering, mumbling into the cascade of hair spreading on a pillow propping up my grandmother against the headboard. Talking to one of the great wings of hair rippled like a washboard she lifts and combs, combs and lifts off my grandmother's pale neck. Freeda French's eyes closed, brow furrowed, as if she's intent on hearing what her youngest daughter murmurs. Papery, blue-veined eyelids shut tight except for fits of blinking, her eyes practicing unsuccessfully the trick of staying open, one or two blinks held a few seconds longer than the others, too long to be called a blink but no other word the boy knows for the wet, unfocused stare held two or three extra beats, his grandmother's eyelids clicking open and shut the way some curly-lashed baby doll's eyes do when you tilt its head.

It might be his favorite time of day. Watching the ritual of combing and brushing, braiding or unbraiding in the morning, afternoon, or at night, the hour doesn't matter, what makes it favorite is seeing the brown-and-silver tangles soften, shine, hearing crackles, the snapping knots, following the graceful weave of his aunt's arms, hands, fingers directing an orchestra, unleashing music asleep within the dreaming mass of hair. One morning while he watched he caught himself holding his breath. He didn't understand why. Felt vaguely ashamed that he didn't know why. Realized as soon as he became aware of the tightness in his chest, the coiled tension of his entire body, that he needed to figure out real quick why he was holding his breath. Needed to explain the heat in his middle to himself and everybody else penned up inside him waiting for an explanation. Though the face framed by a dark waterfall of hair was pale, old, sad, lined, and those overlong blinks exposed a drowned woman's spooky, unseeing gaze, he desired more, more, more of her. Prayed each stroke of the brush, pull of the comb would pass more life into the hair and the hair feed the face, the whole stubbornly unwaking body absorbing measure by measure the wish for life within every stroke and pull. Daughters nourishing their mother. The comb's teeth lifting a thick hank of hair toward the ceiling, the brush smoothing veils of it that drape her breasts, tiny, tiny increments of vitality passing through pampered strands of hair into injured, needy flesh that once at its peril had risked the daughters into being. They repair her, restore her. It's happening as he watches, life growing stronger by stages so minuscule, so fine, no stage is perceptible, just the flow, the gathering force and direction. Her eyes will open and remain open, her lips form words. He's counting on it, measuring unseeable progress. Any time he watches might be *the* time. Wasn't that why he was holding his breath. Watching.

Waiting for the charmed moment. Hoping as his mother's sisters groom his grandmother's hair that she will return, arms open, that calming smile, Let this be the time. Let it be the beginning of the beginning.

One reason I'm telling all this old stuff, the hard stuff and silly kid stuff too, is because it ain't over yet. Meeting you again after so many years of making do without you and finding you were my sister, brother, love, a lost limb recovered, I realized that nothing begins or ends as long as we have breath in our bodies, except, except perhaps our wishes and the power we relinquish when we stop wishing.

A light rain this morning before I awakened. Though it's stopped drizzling now, the air, the light still damp. Train whistle in the distance. Insect prattle. Crows high in the trees, barking. Funny, the train whistle takes me back of course to the house on Finance, maybe the tapestry of quiet returns me too, weaving itself around the noises figured upon it — crows cawing, crickets' static, shuddering train — absorbing them, stilling them, but last night's rain doesn't take me back. I can't recall rain the summer I babysat my grandmother and learned to play basketball. No rainy days, me sitting on the couch under the living room window sorry for myself because poor little Johnny did his duty all morning and now he can't go out and play. I've never heard anybody mention a drought that summer so my memory must be whiting out what it doesn't require to construct a representative day, a day with just enough hours to pack in the events I want to recall and no time for anything I wish to forget, a fictional day serving to give the summer a shape and meaning I haven't bothered to question until now, missing rain that may or may not have fallen nearly fifty years ago. There must have been rainy afternoons that summer. A boy grumpy, pouty, bored, pacing the rooms of the house, up and back, up and back like that pitiful ratel in its glass cage at the Highland Park zoo.

The version of that summer I constructed, tucked away, and believed I'd have no occasion to revisit, no necessity to climb the stairs and reenter the room, no need to worry myself for names of confusing things like the smell, mysterious today as it was then, that version, after I found you again, became inadequate. I believed I'd grown around that summer, the flesh of my life encasing it, locking it away like a harmless cyst. Not a mark on me. No bump, even. Then I became aware of a certain hardness under my skin I was afraid you might come upon as you caressed me. The surprise of its presence would disturb us both, you shocked and probably scared, me disappointed I hadn't prepared you nor prepared myself better. No calm story to relieve your mind. No adequate version of that summer to ease mine. The lump under my skin rising to my throat so I'd be as helpless as my grandmother after the stroke when she lost her power to speak and tried to make herself understood with grunts, whines, squeaks, squeals, twitches, racing eyes, wild nods, whirling hands, the noises of small, panicked animals replacing words.

Have I harbored some deep, dark secret. Do I own a face I cannot bear to behold, a mask beneath the other masks that would turn a lover's heart to stone. Nothing so melodramatic, I hope. Rather a reckoning. A slow threshing. Grain by grain I must dig and sift, lift and comb. Not to censor or reveal things I've wished away. Not to confess or beg forgiveness. To see. To name. To enter the room, then begin to find my way safely out.

Language attempts to divide and conquer. Its enemy darkness, the seamless mingling and shared identity of everything that exists, the overwhelming, intimidating, all-inclusive oneness and unfathomable chaos of being. Language would rend this dark fabric. Scatter it as stars splinter the night sky with light.

When I recall that summer of caring for my grandmother, a kind of peace follows from the long view. Memory shrinks and smooths those months. Those days feel long gone. I'm a different person now in the fullness of time. Then you appear again and the door opens. All time's always present. I can't fool myself. Not now. Not again. No more than I stopped missing you, yearning for you, those years time took you away, no more than I could turn my back and walk away from the room where my grandmother lay dying.

I never *touched* my grandmother. To touch without permission is trespass, sin. But touch is not the worst thing. If only because what's done is done, and in the fullness of time you can suffer to move beyond it. To touch is instinctive. To touch is a compelling, natural urge. Who can resist pinching a baby's freshness. Touching glass when it's so clean you can't really believe it's there, protecting what's behind it. Adam in the garden. Curiosity. Temptation. From one point of view, the need to touch is human weakness. Yes. But giving in to an irresistible urge, no premeditation, no malice intended, maybe it's beyond good and evil. Why should a person's world be turned topsyturvy, why should you pay an eternity, grieve ever after in heart and conscience, for one slip.

If I had touched my grandmother, maybe by now I could have forgiven myself. Touched her just once, the evidence left behind like a fingerprint in the perfect white swirl of icing crowning the layer cakes she baked on special days. If I'd done something stupid I couldn't conceal from myself or anybody else, I could have confessed, taken my medicine, moved on.

If I had touched her, wouldn't the word *touched* shed light on what I chose to forget about the summer, about myself. More light in some corners, less in others, of course. Part of the job of watching her made touch a necessity. Learning my grandmother's body so I could maneuver it in the bed, cover and uncover her according to the room's temperature, hold her head at the correct angle so chicken broth would dribble down her throat without choking her, every morning a round of tasks demanding my hands on her, adjusting nightgown, robe, bedclothes, drying her drool, sweat, and tears, times as her recovery progressed when she'd motion me to sit beside her on the bed and sandwich one of my hands in hers while she sat up and stared at the emptiness of the room, her hands wrapping mine, patting, *patty-cake, patty-cake, baker's man,* as if she weren't sure she believed the heat, the life in her own flesh, needed to be reminded by mine. As if she were trying to say Hello, I'm back. As if she were saying goodbye. As if she understood she was awakening from a nightmare in which she'd lost everything— her body, her voice, her stories, her man—a murdering dream that might stay real if she opened her eyes too quickly or let go the anchor of her grandson's flesh. As if she couldn't make up her mind, as if she were deciding inch by inch whether or not she wanted to bear the weight of returning. Each pat of my hand a petal plucked from one of the coveted roses in her front-yard garden: loves me, loves me not.

Touch instigating familiarity with a woman's body. Me learning too fast. Everything. Nothing. Like a blind man by touch. A twelve-year-old boy discovering that boundaries are as fluid as words. No names for what he sees, feels, hears, touches, smells. *Grandmother* a word, *woman* a word. Neither applicable, neither appropriate for the body in the bed. More heat than light shed by words. They divide without conquering darkness. Explain nothing. Words stun him, desert him, because suddenly they don't fit, don't work. A shock like the hot, hot damp of his grandmother's bony hands the first time, eyes bulging with fear, she seizes and presses his.

What was forbidden, unthinkable yesterday, okay today. Still, he's mostly clear about what he should do, what he's allowed to touch, what not. Why wouldn't he be. Everyone loves his grandmother Freed. They wouldn't let him near her if they thought he'd harm her. Would he have been trusted alone with her if the grownups couldn't depend on his good judgment, his love. He surely knew right from wrong. Then there are accidents, doors he does not open but they flop open anyway and the question's not whether to ignore them, not whether to leave them open or not, he knows they should be closed, but how quickly, by whom. Why. Then there are also blurry lines. When are eyes as guilty as fingertips. Or a nose guilty. Does a look touch the untouchable. Who can he ask. Who trust. What would his grandmother say if she could. Does she care if he looks. Is the room smaller than a needle's eye. Vaster than an ocean.

Was I *touched*, a little crazy, maybe a lot wicked, to use the failing body of my grandmother as a prop, to steal from her dying flesh images of the woman my awakening twelve-year-old's sexuality desired. *Touched* as in anointed or chosen by an angel or devil. *Touched* meaning moved to feel strongly by or about something or someone. *Touched* the laying on of hands. As I shuffle through various dictionary meanings, through subjective associations, repeating its sound in my head, imagining the letters of it arranged on a page, the word *touched* like all words grows less substantial, more arbitrary, finally a kind of joke, gibberish. Language doesn't separate, doesn't clear space or let in light. It's shallow tricknology. The emperor's clothes. Just when you need it most, language disintegrates, disappears. One word as good as another, as its opposite, when it comes down to holding back chaos. Words not points on a meticulously plotted graph. Words open black holes. Portals where living and dead traffic, where worlds intersect, dissolve, clash.

Like the word *court*. Atrocious puns, a finger of guilt lurking in the word *court* I don't discover until I begin to consider seriously what I thought before and what now about the summer of watching my grandmother and learning basketball. Playing on the ball court. Paying court to the phantom body of a seductive woman seeping like the smell from my grandmother, a ghost woman's body rising unnamable, confusing me, drawing me on, pushing me away, a presence in the room I courted like I courted you, impossibly, from a distance of years, of separate lives, separate pasts I tried to stitch together with words, the rituals of language.

Court rooms. Playing court. Court play. Court date. Here comes da judge. The primal drama of innocence or guilt. Trial by ordeal. The cracked asphalt basketball court in Westinghouse Park, Pittsburgh, Pennsylvania, the ancient masonry courts of the Middle American ball game. Gods on high sitting in judgment. Gods entombed below the asphalt paving. I courted her, attended her sickbed like a lover. *Courted* her, as in *shelved* her, set her aside when I escaped 7415. Let my concern for her dissolve into the hot, thin air of hoop games. Strange how a boy's bottomless adolescent yearning mimics the adult game of fleshless, bloodless, courtly romance.

Through a fence—and I can't push past this point to the next point where I wish this sentence to go until I say this fence around the ball court in Westinghouse Park recalls other fences, other cut-off, segmented views through interlocking strands of twisted steel, the fence at the bottom of the hill on Finance, for instance, other fences that haunt this view of a basketball court through the fence bordering it, so through the many fences enclosing it, barbed wire, razor wire, Cyclone wire, zoo wire, handcuffs, bars, six-pointed stars, the logs of barracoons, the stony ramparts of seacoast slave forts, the purring, invisible sweep of surveillance cameras, searchlight beams, quivering noses of bloodhounds, networks of rumor, innuendo, false witness, and flat-out, foul-mouthed rage, fear, and hate—I see a cramped, regimented space full of black boys and men, my destination day after day that summer I learned to play basketball. No days off for rain because no rain falls in my recollections. One hot perfect blue afternoon warming me as I walk along the tracks to the action. All my dying behind me. Free, free at last.

The sun perpetually shining on hoop. The thump-thumping of the ball drumming the asphalt always on time, in time, dancing moons, planets, and stars whose orbits, whose glide and shuffle and bump, figure the rhythm of the court. When I see there are bodies on the court I can't help picking up my feet and putting them down a little faster, half loping, half scuffing nonchalantly across the dusty outfield. Then hold back on the last fifteen steps or so, so they're slower than any since I started out from 7415. Why would I hurry, or rather why would I want any of the boys already on the court to think I think I need to hurry. I'm cool. Wasn't the game waiting for me. How could the fat part start without me. And if by some mistake it did start, who cares. Not me, certainly not me striding not a care in the world, all the time in the world, and I might stop to play or not, because I have other business to tend to just as important as hoop. As if it's my call, my world, my time, and nothing, no one, particularly the dusty-butt gang of brown boys on the court, can touch me.

No game without me is what I'd like the others to read in my last, slow, sugarfoot, ambling steps across the baseball field through the fence onto the asphalt. Trying on for size the regal walk of a court king. Years before I'd be a good enough player to mean what the walk is saying, maybe I'll never be that good but practice makes perfect and if I get this walk part down, this wish, aspiration, imitation, it might help me achieve the rest, achieve a game to match what the walk promises, and even if I never become a king, hey, the walk, the attitude, the confidence, poise, and dangerousness it broadcasts, ain't a bad thing to have mastered.

Here's how ball begins. There are no shadows on the court. No place to hide. Everybody alone, vertical. Each brown body composed of sticks and a stony burr head. Five or six kids not saying much, not looking directly at each other, milling around beneath the netless basket at the far end of a rectangular court. You'd think you are catching them afterward, after they have finished whatever they came here to do. You'd think maybe they'd been wilding in the Bum's Forest and perpetrated something pretty awful because now each one seems intent on ignoring the others, detaching himself, disassociating himself from the deed, from the group that executed it. Whatever crimes brought them together, whatever they've committed has lost its power to unite or direct them, because there is a random aimlessness in their movements, the postures they assume. They've forgotten their purpose or accomplished it and have no clue what comes next. Aimlessness, except no one wants to be too close to anybody else or too far away, as if they're sharing heat from an invisible potbellied stove. An aerial view, you'd see a disorganized cluster arranging and rearranging itself, changing shape but occupying more or less the same amount of space as it shifts position on the court. From above you'd also see close-cropped sweaty disks, still a bit too large in many cases for the boy's thin shoulders. Nobody's paying very much attention to anybody else till one player casually patting the ball separates from the others, draws somebody from the cluster with words or his eyes or signifying hand jive. *C'mon. I want you, boy.* Detached from the others, the dribbler tightens up the beat, hunches over the ball, shielding it with his body from the guy closest to him. The others align themselves between the goal and the two players thirty feet or so away, one on either side of the ball, dribbler patting it, defender swiping at it, trying to poke away the pill. Ball moves side to side, the boys at a distance move with it. A jumbled line dance, following the leader, left to right, right to left, a quick dip back, forward again as the dribbler stutter-steps, jooks, head-fakes a slash to the basket, feints again, upper body in one direction, the ball looped behind his back pushed out in the other. Three quick strides, then he pulls up as if he's slammed into a wall, spins away from the mock collision, back to the spot he just left only he's a yard closer to the hoop, to the other boys. Bodies more alert, alive now as they jostle for space, angles, snap talk at one another. Call-and-response chatter like the defender answering the stylized movements of the dribbler, mirroring him, keeping up, cutting off his path to the basket, funneling him to the minefield of other players whose eyes hawk the ball.

It's started. You don't need an invitation. None will be tendered. No whiteboy handshakes and introductions necessary. You slip into the group, careful at first not to step in anybody's way, a fluid blending in so you don't disrupt the tempo, the tone. Soon enough the pace will intensify. But raising the ante's not your role, not yet. No one's worried too much about scoring. If you try to score too much, too soon, everybody understands you're scared, trying to sneak your stuff in when it's easy because you know everybody else knows you won't be around, won't count at the finish. No one upset they've been scored on. You're welcome to join in if you can read the signs, understand your place, the place in the game you're entering. It's just getting started, plenty room, plenty time to get on board, and you glide, shuffle into an unoccupied area. You're invisible to the others it would seem till you've done this slipping-in bit for enough days, then somebody or another greets you *hey, man,* grins or frowns or checks you out with a stare that says, Here you come again nigger and I couldn't care less.

You take your spot, claim it. Wait for the game to pass through. Come to you. The rules are simple. Not rules so much as casual, flexible guidelines that make most sense of the circumstances. You only need half the court, one basket for this loosening-up action. Each person who gets possession of the ball keeps it as long as he scores. One on one on one. Every man for himself. First one to reach twenty-one points wins. When you make a hoop you earn two points and a chance for two free shots from the foul line, each worth a point. Drop in both free throws, you own the ball again, try to score a hoop against anybody, everybody who feels like stopping you. Miss a shot from the field or the foul line and the ball goes to whoever grabs the rebound. His chance to score. Gradually, as players rack up points, the court shrinks, goals are harder to score because every crowded inch is contested, everybody mugs the one closest to winning. The game sneaks up on us, then it gets so good nobody wants it to end.

I'm in too many places at once. On the court playing ball before I finish what I started—confessing, telling the story of a boy and his grandmother. Hoop a big part of it, obviously, but hoop also a way of breaking up the story, escaping then and ever since. It's taken thirty years to begin telling the story. Perhaps I needed thirty years to prepare for this moment, thirty years, not one second less, and I'm not going to rush now. There is no rush in the fullness of time and in the fullness of time is the only way stories play themselves out.

Sometimes I think about my life, and the things I think happen. I don't believe they happen because I think them, but I'm almost convinced we possess a faculty that knows what's going to occur, not just in a general sense but sometimes with the scary specificity of how, where, when, and what will shape us. The possibility of learning too much about the endgame, the certainty of uncontrollable change, of death, stops most people from cultivating such a faculty. Dreams, visions, déjà vu, premonitions, prophecy bypass the wall of fear and denial, remind us what we know. Maybe what I'm calling a *faculty* is nothing more or less than an unflinching view of our prospects in the world, a view informed by the knowledge that everything falls apart and dies. When stories embrace this view, perhaps they too speak the future.

After losing two fathers, I couldn't afford to love my dying grandmother too much. Or at least that's how it seemed to me then. It seemed important not to get too close, or rather, I needed to deny closeness, close down the room in my heart where she lived. Running to the court seemed one way out of the room. One way to prevent her from slipping away from me. With such confusion, such ambivalence rooted inside me, no wonder it continues to haunt my feelings, my understanding of love.

• • •

From the moment I found you again I couldn't help thinking ahead to the devastating thought of losing you. Losing love again. Thinking I'd do something stupid to spoil a second chance with you. And I did. Even though I tried to trump that future with other stories. The ones I told you. The ones I bugged you to tell me.

When we exchange stories, they're as much about tomorrow as about yesterday. Stories are wishes and predictions, dreams of a future. I wanted a story with a different ending from the end I expected. During our happiest times together, part of the happiness for me was how unbelievable. I couldn't keep my hands off you and each touch also a test. I kept reaching out to reassure myself, to get in a million, million touches as if they would make a damned bit of difference once you were gone. Couldn't help myself. I thought she's gone *with every touch. Missing you as I greeted you. Goodbye forever when we fell asleep in the same bed. Astounded in the morning, when you were still there turning toward me, the first soft bumping kiss, your lips always parted, moist, silently speaking* good morning, *and my unspoken reply—how could this be, how will it end.*

I needed to hear your stories, the secret wishes and prophecies they held. Eager to learn everything about you and also dreading each word. Your stories about yesterday and tomorrow. Words making real those parts of you I'd never share. Words separating us forever.

Interior. Night. A room candlelit, chiaroscuro. Neon pulse of the city blinks through an open window that frames the black bones of a fire escape. Two lovers sitting in bed. Naked from waist up and presumably naked from waist down under the sheet the woman has raised to partially cover her breasts. Been there, done that, right. Or you've seen the movie. One or both actors could be smoking, maybe the same cigarette slowly offered back and forth or no cigarette when cigarettes are out of fashion. Clearly they've been getting it on, either off-camera, just before we arrive, or their lovemaking's been staged for us in a stylized montage, bare body parts as close to private parts as the film's decency rating permits. Now it's pillow-talk time. The couple's tired, flushed, a dreamy, underwater languor in their motions, their voices, as they invent themselves for the benefit of each other and the camera. Talk a kind of meandering, casual straightening up of a room the morning after the blitzkrieg of a party has rolled through. Talk a way of asking, Where am I, what happened, who is this next to me, and who am I.

Hour of the wolf, when most people are born or die and the city's catnapping. I'm stone exhausted but feeling good, better than I've felt in a long, long time. You're back, I've found you again, and maybe we can call *time out,* stop the spinning world, step on or step off at our pleasure, end life as we've known it, start another life as easy as pie. A little more night chatter, more kisses, maybe a little bit more lovey-dovey, and *boom,* in the morning, Everything's going to be all right.

It begins innocently enough. New lovers swapping, on a sort of feel-good dare, erotic stories. I told you one about a grad student who successfully defended her thesis and wound up in my office after the defense, locking the door behind herself as she burst in. A huge hug and kiss, which didn't surprise me, we'd mock-flirted the two years I'd been her dissertation supervisor, but then, wow, she's suddenly atop my desk, her long peasant skirt hiked to her hips, no drawers, doing a slow, nasty bump and grind.

You like it. You like it. You know you do. It's all yours. You know you wanna lick it. You know you like it.

I did. She was a foxy young woman. Sylvia Manfredi. Big boobs, narrow hips. Small, dark, arrogant, and quick-witted, quick-tongued. Smart and smart-alecky. Put you in your place in a minute, she would, she would. A kiss-my-ass smirk for anybody who didn't approve of her gypsy earrings, see-through tops, miniskirts, foul mouth. Yes. She spoke truth. I liked the whole package and had let her know I did, stretching the limit, and maybe for some sticklers exceeding the limit, of proper student-faculty relationships.

From my point of view I'd been cool. Maybe even felt a little smug about how discreetly I'd behaved in a humongously temptatious situation. A little back-and-forth low-grade teasing, a little touch here and there, now and then, as far as it ever went.

What you're saying is you kept the door open. A married man and her professor, but you kept the door open.

Hey. This is my story. In my story my office door is shut. I'm minding my own boring business, stuffing stuff in my briefcase, and *bam,* she busts in, remember. Before I could say a word she's up on my desk, wild-eyed, wagging her bush in my face.

And you loved it, didn't you. Didn't yell, Get down from there this instant, Ms. Manfredi, did you.

Who's telling this story. As a matter of fact the next thing happens is I'm helping her off the desk.

And . . .

Well, you know. We get a bit tangled up negotiating her descent safely. She winds up sorta on my lap. I'm still in a state of shock. Not your typical day at the office. Still trying to catch my breath, which isn't easy with Ms. Manfredi's busy tongue crammed halfway down my throat.

Next thing I know she's slithered off me, to the floor, on her knees. Starts unzipping my what. What professorial pants would I have sported in those days. Jeans. Baggy tweeds. Chinos. Whatever. They're coming loose and coming down and she starts rooting around in there. Gonna have it her way.

Weird though. Instead of heating up, rising to the occasion, I'm bogged down by all this legalistic crap running through my head. Thinking, Okay, technically, Ms. Manfredi's no longer my student, so in theory anything goes. Or does it. Or is she. The committee unanimously approved her thesis and awarded it honors. Course credits passed—all A's. She's signed, sealed, and delivered. The cap, gown, and diploma rigmarole still to

come but that's only a formality. She's completed her degree re-
quirements. She's legit. Free, white, and over twenty-one. Kick
back and enjoy, son.

For some reason, I couldn't.

Couldn't. What do you mean, man, you couldn't. Isn't the
poor misguided thing down on her knees sucking her prof's
dick.

I'm going to tell this my way, in spite of your lewd interven-
tions, girl. Your turn's coming right up. You'll have your turn
but this is my turn. So listen.

I'm listening.

As I was saying, she *started* in on me. That's the way my
story goes. *Started,* but I pulled her up off the floor. Not now I
said. You're beautiful and desirable I said but this is not the
time or place. Hugged her. Tried to express how grateful I was.
Turned on I was. Didn't want to hurt her feelings.

Didn't want to close the door.

C'mon. Cut me some slack. I didn't want to make the young
woman feel bad. She's on my lap again. Still pretty pumped up.
Still coming on, You know you like it. Know you want it. My
present to you she said. Today's a special day she said.

I held her, squeezed her tightly because I didn't know what
else to do, what to say. If she'd started crying I think I would
have lost it. For once, maybe for the first time in my life, it was
me who couldn't handle. I mean she was way out there and I
couldn't catch up. I felt like Ms. Manfredi's teacher. Her uncle.
Felt old, lame. Used up. A cliché. Her hot tight little ass waved
in my face and me a salivating, toothless old dog. Shit. We
never got it on.

Is that the end.

The dance the best part. It was some dance. Not much else
to the story, I guess. Begins with a bang but then it peters out, if
you'll excuse the expression.

You men and your open doors.

You women and your open drawers. Or no drawers.

Right. Our choice of underwear or lack of it is why we wind up crazy on some man's desktop. Don't you see your Ms. Manfredi never had a chance.

I'd rather hear your story than listen to you rag on mine. *Next,* as we say on the playground. *Next.* Your turn to strut your stuff.

I don't think I have a story. Definitely not a strutting one.

Huh-uh. No chickening out. I showed you mine. C'mon. Tit for tat.

No story worth telling. Anything I can think of boring boring. It's depressing in a way. Wish I did have a bunch of wild tales to tell.

Bet you're just not trying. Bet you do.

I don't. And I am trying. Really trying to think of something you might find exciting, just can't.

Forget me. Point is I want to hear what excited you. A time, a place. Somebody or something that really turned you on.

I don't remember specifics. My mind doesn't work that way. Besides, for me things happen, then they're over. I forget about them. No reason to go back. No reason to remember. Every reason to forget.

Sounds like denial to me.

Maybe. Maybe it is. I think it's more about forgetting. Just plain forgetting. Okay, maybe I want to forget, but if something doesn't mean much when it happens, why hold on to it.

You know why.

No. You're not listening. I didn't say the past isn't important. I don't mean people shouldn't remember, either. Though sometimes I wonder if people ever do remember, because if they really remembered and really cared, why wouldn't they stop doing what they know hurts them and hurts other people.

Agreed. Folks bullshit themselves about memories like they bullshit themselves about everything else. Still I don't believe you or anybody else looks back and sees a blank screen.

I didn't say blank screen. Here's what I want to say. Listen, please. For various reasons I've let go lots of my past. As far as I'm concerned, it's gone, gone, gone. Maybe I didn't like who I was most of the time. Maybe part of me allowing things to happen, part never there. But much more to it than that.

Whoa. You're jumping way too serious. I just wanted a sexy story.

All right. All right already. I'll try. Here's one. A sort of funny one with a little surprise for you. Not as big a surprise as a bare-butt, hoochy-cootchy dance on your desk, but here's a story.

You deadpanned your telling, delivered a flat, cut-down version of events I've been rearranging, rewriting since.

You call over the little dog, whose name and breed are some of those specifics you have trouble recalling, *Fluffy,* maybe you say on another occasion, or big dog, maybe a great Dane you say when later I ask you to elaborate on the first, short, sweet telling, you call the dog over and say to the young man, your lover, on the chaise longue beside yours, whose shorts or swim trunks or towel or whatever he's wearing is pushed down past his penis, say Let him try, meaning let little Fluffy or Fido or Duffy the Dane, let man's best buddy have a go, ha-ha-ha, at your bare, aroused member, my friend, while I sit back paring my fingernails and wickedly watch. And that's it. Take one of your story, except for a few well-chosen words setting the scene I'll try to paraphrase.

Exterior. Day. Bright blue afternoon in a hedge-enclosed, manicured, English-style garden. Two lounge chairs and other assorted pieces of white wicker outdoor furniture arranged on a flagstone patio, and beyond the hedges, acres of lush green lawn stretching to a border of towering trees. Perhaps a small swimming pool at one end of the garden. You can't remember for sure, but you think there probably was a pool. You and your gentleman alone and private for a few hours during a visit to his parents' suburban castle, both stretched comfortably on lounge chairs, enjoying the sun, sipping cool drinks, perhaps gin and tonic with a slice of fresh lime split on the glass's lip, perhaps slightly restless, so you begin stirring things up, brewing the available ingredients into an amusing anecdote, pink man, brown woman, dog, you're sure of these particulars, these major players in your movie, and sure of the edenic pearl of garden, sure of sunlight, perhaps, yes, the glisten of a pool over your shoulder, maybe your skin, your hair still wet from a dip, maybe his whatever damp to your touch, your fingers digging below an elastic waistband and finding his elastic member, tugging down wet cloth to expose it—free at last, free at last—you softly stroke, consider the ramifications, the permutations, combinations, and amalgamations of race, gender, and species you might initiate, might generate, smiling to yourself, deciding not to have it the usual way but your way this time, whatever that way might turn out to be, a swelling firmness between the light pinch of thumb and forefinger you slide up and down the man's member, damp or not damp depending on whether or not whatever he's wearing is damp, whether there's a pool, a dip taken together, small ripples, gliding coolness, the surprisingly hot, always elusive, let's say Seattle sun ablaze on your bare shoulders when you climb out of the pool, sliding fingers of warmth, someone's sticky, sweaty, randy scent—man's, woman's, canine's, whatever—redolent in the warm air, and in your mischievous mood the possibilities are cute, kinky, smarmy, endless, so you smile your electric smile and delightedly call the dog over, say Let him (or her if it's a her), let Fluffy have a go at you, my sweet. Lots of frantic sniffing, licking, tail wagging, quivering in place till you're slightly alarmed, you never have quite trusted dogs, especially large, hairy ones, and shoo the poor excited beast away, tail drooping between its drooping, scraggly hindquarters.

And that little's much more than you give me in your bare-bones version of the story first time around. First time round both of us laughing, not so much at the story as at the incongruity of it coming from your mouth, shocking me, quieting me, the fox outfoxed, surprised into nervous laughter, then uncharacteristic silence.

That's it. You're finished, I asked after the burst of laughter, the silence. I sensed immediately there was more to the story than you were letting on. Thought maybe you'd appropriated someone else's tale, passed it off as yours. A story held at arm's length. Like those disembodied factoids on TV, delivered quickly, impenetrably. Voiceover, no live body underneath.

I started playing catch-up then. The panicky, know-you're-going-to-lose feeling of being down ten in the fourth quarter. Time running out. Who is this masked woman. Where'd she come from. Where's she leading me. I coaxed you to sing your siren song again and again. And again. Asked you to dance it. Wanted to play underwater with you in the dark pool of it, if pool there was. If the pool was filled and warm. If diving in headfirst wouldn't crack my skull.

Innocent enough. A garden. Pink Adam. Brown Eve. Fluffy's color unknown to date, perhaps irrelevant. Or did you say a little spotted black-and-white dog. Seems I heard that at some point. Did I also overhear the pink man chuckle slyly, No, not Fluffy, it's not that kind of story. Is the man, the third principal actor who too shall go nameless, isn't he the one who actually said, Let him try, let him or her have a go. Wasn't it the man in fact, looking across from his recliner to yours, at your black one-piece bathing suit draped to dry on a glass-topped white wicker end table, at your split-peach sweet Georgia brown bare bottom, your stripe of glisten within its furry garden, who hailed the dog and announced, It's her turn, let her have a go at you, my dear, or words to that effect, the excited mutt, tail whipping back and forth like a windshield wiper, nostrils quivering, sucking up the scent of bare, moist private parts, female, male, or both exposed, the family dog obviously taking notice, seized, engaged. Did the man pat her, scratch behind her ear to encourage her. Get down, little doggy. Get it on, Snoop doggy dog.

Who said what to whom when, where, why. I kept asking myself over and over even after you repeat unchanged your original tale. Why did I think my version true. Truer. What's my stake in a different story. What really happened in the garden. You admitted you aren't good at keeping details straight. Admitted you let yourself forget a lot.

How does the storyteller who doubts his own tale believe anyone else's.

Do I think new stories, different stories, will change the past. Free us of its burdens — our secrets, lies, failures. Free us to love freely, unhaunted by what we fear will happen again because it's happened before.

My long absence, my desertion of you in the enemy's camp, one of my secrets. Where was I. Where was I when you needed me, when we should have suffered together evils neither of us could prevent. Another secret: I feared the invisible wounds inflicted on your body. Would your stories map the scars — your skin scorched earth, crisscrossed like the frontiers of Europe where armies from east and west have clashed for centuries. Would your voice haunt the ravaged land, shame all armies, all invasions. Shame me. Would your stories be spring in the land or the land's lament or its freedom song.

One last secret, one you know too well already. I was drawn to your stories like a moth to flame. Scared I wouldn't survive if I listened, wouldn't survive if I didn't. Do I make up my stories so I can listen and not listen to yours.

In my version of your garden story, a smirking white man's always in charge. Caging me. Lording over you. Europe over Africa. Master over slave. That long, sad, bloody history recapitulated in a parable I fashion my way from your tale.

On the day in question, my story goes, you've been shamed, humiliated. You let the man, the frisky, licking dog steal your soul. For many years you suppress the incident, pretend to forget it, but the wound festers. In dreams the scene flashes back, the slobbery, saber-toothed jaws of the dog a yawning cave mouth sucking you into its foul black recesses. A certain kind of smile or tone of voice from a nice new man in your life and you'd want to beat him with stick, run screaming from the thought of his touch. You shrink into yourself over the years. You become a walled and gated city, a labyrinth of false doors, phony windows, dead-end corridors, a maze leading nowhere. You the sleeping beauty at its unreachable core, curled like a fetus in a stuffy, airless chamber at the top of a staircase with no bottom steps, waiting to be kissed awake. Over and over again in your sleep you replay the moment the man sics the dog on you. Ask yourself each time, What was I thinking. How could I have believed I loved him, believed he loved me.

I think you intended to tell me what actually happened in the garden. Purge the awful memory. You wanted to trust me, hoped, since I was brown like you, I might understand. You believed you were ready to share secrets you'd hidden even from yourself. Then you lost your nerve. The details, the specifics of the story, retained their power to incriminate and silence, fill you with self-doubt. You chose not to risk diminishing yourself in my eyes or your own. In my story you step back from the brink. You transpose the tale because that's the only way you can tell it.

I finish relating my version and you say, It's about race, isn't it. My choice of lovers hurts you.

When you told me I was your first black man, I wanted to cry. Yes. True. True.

I did cry, remember.

Of course I remember. And I remember the taste of the tears. Ever since that night I've been trying to figure out why I wanted to cry and didn't cry and why you did. But no, no, no. I don't want it to be about race. Race is some mad scientist's evil invention. I believe we're all colored folks down here on earth. I'd feel great if I could forgive and forget. But I can't. Not yet. Not while they're still chopping us down and trying to stomp life out of the pieces. Not while they're still stealing us from ourselves, separating us, using us, telling us we're strangers. They sold beautiful brown women like you, baby. Bought and sold you like livestock. Forced you to be their playthings, their mules. And it's never stopped. How can I afford to forgive or forget.

No. Not race. It's about color still determining who lives or dies. Who prospers. Big lies and little everyday lies. It's about not having real choices. Just little boxes—black or white—to check.

And you think my choices turned me into a sleeping princess in a funky room, huh. Like that room on 7415 Finance you've been telling me about. A mean metaphor, sir.

Okay. Yes. Maybe it starts there. Me learning about love in a room where my grandmother's dying. Me learning to fear love. I never touched my grandmother, but I did something just as bad. I imagined her to be someone else. A woman I desired. A woman she could never be. I wasn't loving her. I was denying her. Some days I wished my grandmother would die. Die so I could be free, free to love the woman I imagined, free to run to the court and play ball, whatever. And worse, I wanted her to die because I believed she heard everything I thought. Heard me desiring the woman she'd become in my thoughts. I couldn't deal with her knowing my secrets. I was scared she'd wake up one morning and tell everybody what a terrible boy I really was. So there I sat, day after day, on my little folding chair. Afraid she'd awaken, afraid she wouldn't. Knowing I'd lose her either way.

Let the room go. You can't change what happened.

I'm still there. Still trapped.

You pointed out in one of our pillow talks that my resistance to your garden story, my need to turn a silly incident into an allegory of racism and oppression, might be a sign I'm threatened more by the idea of a woman in charge than I am by the evil, imperial white man. You teased me. Said I couldn't handle a woman usurping male prerogatives, turning the tables, directing a porn flick her way, laughing through the whole bit. The almighty penis tossed like a bone to a puppy. Said I didn't approve of your story because no room in it for me to gallop in on my white (?) steed and rescue you from Massa's evil clutches.

You got it all wrong. Wrong, wrong, man, you said. Your story's interesting enough, things just didn't happen that way.

And I come back with, Yeah. But who really knows what happened. Doesn't the best story win.

Hmmm, you say. Turning this into a basketball game, aren't you, Mr. Hoopster. One on one. I score. You score. Who you think's gonna win.

Any chance to play with you is winning, I say. Just so the game never ends.

And maybe. Maybe it's as innocent and sappy and no-strings-attached as that. Part of me knows better. More at stake in the game or I wouldn't be so driven. Wouldn't play till I drop down exhausted. Wouldn't dream unsettling dreams of winning and losing. Wouldn't lie awake at night watching game films, the same scenes flickering over and over again, desperate to sort out what went wrong.

A poet said humankind cannot bear too much reality. Are the evil secrets of our past in this smiling land too much reality. I've glimpsed the spirit that shines forth through your flesh, so strong it can leave your flesh and quicken another body. And even though it clobbered me, reminded me how little of you I would ever know, how much still to learn, to lose, why wasn't that enough. What more did I need to know.

You shamed me into recognizing that I was behaving like the people I called our enemies, trying to steal your past, change you, rob you, fearing what turns me on most—your curiosity, independence, what's different and unpredictable, the erotic energy smoldering in your eyes, the way you bite your lower lip when you ride a wave of pleasure building in your body. Why

couldn't I accept all the creatures you'd been, the small panicked animals, animals squealing, squeaking, the roaring jag-
uars, the dolphins, eagles, speaking all at once through your
mouth.

Did I ask you to tell your stories so I could watch. Imagining
myself a fly on the wall. Invisible, powerless, watching. Could I
bear the sight of you in some white man's arms. A black man's.
Could I stand to lose you again. Could I watch or would I go
nuts. Testing. Could I trust you with my secrets. Was I a little
crazy, a little touched already, torturing myself unnecessarily as
you said, pestering you to tell me more than I was prepared to
hear.

Here's what I saw in my sleep one night. You're facing me
spraddle-legged in a soapy, steamy tub. You've scooted forward, your hips squeezed between my thighs, your ankles on
my shoulders. My fingers plug every orifice they can find under
the suds. Your pelvis thrusts forward *uh, uh, uh*. Your eyes are
closed, head thrown back, your shoulders resting on my feet
where they're propped on either side of the faucet at the tub's
far edge. Three of my fingers welded together like the multiple
barrels of a Gatling gun furiously pump. *Uh, uh, uhh*. Then you
let your ankles flop down off my shoulders. They splash like
boulders. The water goes crazy and when it's still again you sit
up, lean forward, dip your face into the soapsuds, gobble me
up. Fish nibbles of sensation as your lips pucker, slide up and
down. Bubbles burbling to the surface like someone's farting
underwater.

Your face masked in foam pops up, grinning.

Wow. Wow.

We're both laughing.

Looks like you have a faceful of you know what.

Thought I might look that way, you say, smiling as you wipe
your eyes, flip a Neptune beard of suds off your chinny-chin-
chin.

Wow, girl. You okay, girl.

I'm fine.

How'd you do that without swallowing half the tub.

Same as swimming. You blow out. Blow bubbles.

You figured that out just now.

Huh-uh.

This wasn't the first time.

Huh-uh.

You've done it before. Underwater before.

Yes.

Where.

Oh. I don't remember where.

In a pool. The ocean. A bathtub. C'mon. What do you mean you don't remember where.

No specific time and place.

You don't remember with whom then, either.

Huh-uh. No reason to. Maybe if I tried . . . Maybe not.

I find that very strange. I mean, you're supposed to be the shy one, the one who couldn't ever really cut loose. The inexperienced one with no stories and you can't remember doing this.

You're mixing up what I told you. I never said I hid in my room. You may have wanted to believe that, but I didn't say it. I hid sometimes, probably way too much, but not always. Afterward was the problem. Sooner or later a terrible emptiness and loneliness would hit me. I'd feel guilty, depressed, mad at myself because I'd done something I knew I shouldn't have. Afraid I'd be punished sooner or later.

Well.

Well . . . I'm still afraid.

Disappointment and distress cloud your eyes and your features begin to blur. You are leaning away, pushing back. The bathwater chills instantly to absolute zero. My parts shrink. No smiles, no laughter echoing off the tiles. I'm shivering, alone. A riff of anxious questions builds, works its way into the gray dreamscape. Where are you. Where are you. An empty room, empty house. A deserted city. Someone knocking door to door, never any answer. I call your name again. Holler it. Will scream it next. Then I realize you won't hear a word no matter how loudly I shout. You've slipped into another dream. It wasn't me in the tub with you. I'm the wrong color. On the wrong side of the door. I've been outside the whole time, watching, wishing, believing I was the lucky guy having a ball until other stories bleed in, encounters I badger you to share, other times, other lovers, other places, as if you could take me there with you, as if *there* is anywhere I need to go. *Stop doing this. Why do you torture yourself.* I have no answer for you. Can't help myself. *No more. No more dredging up stuff I halfway remember at best. None of it matters now. Why are we wasting time on it.* I drive you away with questions that wake me in the middle of the night. In the middle of other dreams.

A cracked door. Another dream. My grandmother blank-eyed, suds to her chin, sitting in a clawfoot tub that barely fits in the tiny room, the great fan of hair pasted like a helmet to her skull, she sits, then begins to totter up, splashing, dripping, I'm sure she's going to fall but Aunt Geral steadies her, she leans on Aunt Geral's arm, my grandmother a gaunt winter tree planted in the water, leafless, wind-scarred, more a rootless toppling than a lean that Geraldine catches, guides as I hover in the darkness outside the bathroom squinting through the cracked door that isn't really cracked but ill-fitting, the wood warped, shrunken, so there's always a sliver of light escaping where the door's pulled away from its frame, my window into the bright sanctuary the door's supposed to conceal and I know I shouldn't look, I try to blind myself, stare past my grandmother's helpless nakedness, ignore the parts I know I shouldn't see, shouldn't look at, none of my business, parts mercifully veiled by foamy suds, but I'm desperate to see all there is to see aside from what I shouldn't, everything that compels me, that I ache to discover, that might save her, that freezes me crouching silent in the dark hall so I can't turn away.

Games end. Do stories. Do dreams. They must. When. How.

Do they. I drag back along the tracks to 7415. Sneak down the hillside to Finance Street a block before home. My grandmother's still at the top of the stairs dying. No pockets in my short pants to hide my filthy hands. I bound up the steps two at a time to clean up for dinner. Yes. As always I peek in at her. Remember the smell of bread baking, bread turned slightly sour the way old meat turns.

She's lying on her back with her glazed eyes wide open staring at nothing. I move to the head of the bed, frightened, wondering where she might be, what she might be seeing or thinking, because she's not in the room, the mirrors of her eyes hold the room on their surface, I see myself floating there as I lean down, but she's gone, long gone in the space behind those marble eyes. A hot, hot day but for some reason the door's been shut and wherever she's escaped, my grandmother needs no clothes. She's kicked off the sheets, almost worked herself free of her twisted nightgown. Was it her sleep sweat or myself fresh and funky from the court I smelled with each breath as I hovered over her way too long, waiting for her to come back, wishing her gone forever. Where are you. Please hurry back. Please don't stir. Her eyes still wide open as I stopped again at the door, unable to unlock my gaze from the naked woman sprawled on the bed until I close the door between us and run, run down the steps for supper, stumbling and almost breaking my neck in the dark stairwell.

The images converge, bathtub, bed, pool, this room, that room, yearning, loving, loss, the possible and impossible converge and confuse and shame me still. It all came back recently, me peeking across my bare chest at a rippling cascade, a glorious blanket of hair, black hair threaded with silver, gray, and white draping the back of the woman working on my legs. Lying flat on my back, all I could see was hair, and it brought back my grandmother's hair, its color, its enormous wild spread and energy, as Miranda, my friend as well as a skilled, professional body worker, leaned over the far end of the massage table, facing away from me, lamenting over her shoulder the wretched state of my basketball beat-up toes, busy mothering them while she fusses at me, cooing *poor babies,* pampering my abused dogs, dogging me because I refuse to follow the exercise regime she prescribed to save them from becoming blocks of wood at the end of my legs. For a moment behind the screen of hair I had imagined Miranda wearing only her skin. She is a very smart, good-looking woman with magical hands so nothing unnatural about fantasizing inappropriately, thinking about what wasn't going to happen. Miranda my friend in a different sense and I knew better than to cross certain lines so a little tingle of embarrassment stung me for spying on her while she concentrated on doing her job. But that hair. I couldn't help visualizing the instant she'd turn and expose her body, naked as mine under the sheet. There, in front of me again, I saw the even more disturbing allure of my grandmother's long, rippling hair, plunging me back, tying up my insides, me twisted, coiled again, and I didn't like it, fought it and quickly won the battle against the tightening, the thick rush of fuzz to my brain, blood to my groin as I imagined Miranda's bare back, her bare breasts when she'd give up on my hopeless toes and turn, smiling, her slim arms outflung, fingers fluttering, gesturing, reminding me how difficult I make the job of keeping my aging hoopster's body halfway cleared of aches and functioning semismoothly more or less. Miranda in her baggy sweatsuit, as innocent as Eve of my daydream, sighs and I sigh, watch her graceful movements, the simple perfection of a woman's body executing the dance of its particular array and unity of parts, its possession of weight, balance, function, how it can dispense to a man's attentive gaze the overwhelming knowledge of difference and how much that difference can matter, can express.

Not the worst thing in the world, getting turned on for a moment by a woman who's off-limits, but it brought back the confusion of other moments, shamed me the way just recently I'd been shamed shaving one morning, seeing and remembering you on another morning, your brown face beside my lathered cheeks in the mirror and thinking how we'd both disappear from its unspeaking surface without a trace and being very sad because you seemed too beautiful ever to disappear and besides I needed you too much so I told myself you were a stable fixture there beside me, you'd never go away, and of course the next thought, yes, I *could* lose her, I certainly *will* lose her, *did* lose, and devastation set in that quickly as I glanced at myself in an empty mirror. I can't tell you how upset I felt, and how helpless and stupid, and then as I said when I started this confession a wave of shame washed over me. I understood finally, without doubt or equivocation, that what I mourned was not the fleeting image of us twinned in the mirror, not the immediate flesh-and-blood absence of you, nor the long-lost lover from my distant past I'd talked myself into believing you incarnated. No. But what I was experiencing did hurtle me into the past. Way back. Too far back to be about you or another you in a body perhaps your spirit once inhabited. I was mourning time all right but a time excluding you—the thirty-odd years of a marriage that had failed. Missing the woman I had loved and failed and thereby also failed myself, our children. Those many years lost. Mourning them.

Not lost exactly, but gone, gone. Consumed. For better or worse. Richer or poorer. In sickness and in health. I'd been with her through those marriage years. They belonged to us still, only to her and to me, and maybe in a way to the family we loved and who loved us. Anyway I understood staring in the mirror that one meaning of those years would not happen. And that's what I was missing, had been mourning all along. The meaning of shared talk, shared recollection and reconstruction, keeping that time, those thirty years alive the way Africans used to keep alive their ancestors, their history, themselves cycling in Great

Time. We, she and I together, would not talk these shared years down through the rest of our time on earth. I'd let go of my partner, my mate, the only soul who could sustain with me the conversation keeping alive those years of our marriage, maintaining them, passing them on. By betraying her, leaving her, I had betrayed that possibility. Meaning in that sense the time we'd spent together wouldn't survive. Meaning a kind of death.

That's what flashed in the mirror in your eyes and wasn't you but invested in you during an impossible time, a hard, hard time of great unease and fear. I invested in you, transferred to you, incredibly, illegitimately, the memories, the power, of another woman, my talking partner, who, in another dream, if I had been a different kind of dreamer, could have saved my life.

Still confused, still too scared and troubled to engage forthrightly those incriminating, humbling thirty years, that collapsing history, I had let the force of the emotions connected with what I was losing become attached to the present tense hot surging of our passion. Laid unrealistic burdens on you, on myself. Like the burden of a boy's newborn desire I'd placed mistakenly on my grandmother as she lay dying. Only a matter of time before the weight crushed us. Before you slipped from the edge of the mirror where you'd been gazing at our faces. Before you too disappeared. One love missed, merging, replaced by another, becoming the other in mixed-up, daunting exchanges. More for less, less for more gained each time. My grandmother preparing me for all the women to follow, preparing me for confusion, for loss, for shame, for love, for hope, for the painful separating of what's possible from what's impossible, what's allowed from what's not allowed, exchanges, transitions haunting me because I've never understood, never exactly figured out, how to love without the guilty shadow of transgression, without fear, without the specter of death, without acknowledging how mercilessly desire breaks all rules, forges its own rules.

I must learn to tell myself old stories I really don't want to hear. Face my heart's truth in them, in the words I'm telling now, this attempt to sort through the past, prepare for what's next.

Rebound. In hoop language the word means grabbing the basketball when it ricochets off hoop or backboard. Means you've won possession of the ball. Means you're gripping it in your hands, in control, with a chance to do something with it — pass, dribble, score. *Rebound* in the language of love means almost the opposite. Like the ball recoiling from impact with the backboard, you bounce mindlessly, automatically, into a new pair of hands. Attempt to restore too quickly, seamlessly, what's been lost. A predictable, clichéd reaction I was far too enthralled, too proud to admit. Huh-uh. Called my head-over-heels passion everything but *rebound.*

One of the nicest things my college coach Jack McCloskey ever said to me was something like John, you're the best rebounder for a guy your size I've ever seen — college, pro, whatever. Years later after Jack had general-managed at least two NBA teams, one to a world championship, and become a master talent scout, horsetrader, franchise builder, I looked him up in Minneapolis, where the Stanford University Cardinals, my daughter's team, were competing in the NCAA women's Final Four tournament. Somehow that old compliment my coach had paid me came up. Jack smiled, ran his thick hand through graying ripples of what used to be thick crew-cut black hair, cocked his head to one side and said, Well . . . you know, I've been in this basketball business for a lotta years, John, and I can still say you were a great rebounder, damned good, but the best . . . I don't know now about the best.

Hey coach, I'm still rebounding. And still pretty good at it, too. Thought I was too smart, but I elevated with the rest of the pack, snatched at the ball, believed I snagged it. Squeezed like you taught us. Squeezed it dry. Didn't notice till too late my hands were empty. Game had passed me by. I didn't believe I was subject to the cliché, but I rebounded like a champ, coach. Maybe nobody ever did it better after all.

Where were you, Jack, when I needed you. Needed your cold, flinty, Irish-eyed stare. Keeping me in line. Calling it like you see it on the court.

One story never ending before another begins. Is it always the same story. Everything always at stake. Maybe not so innocent then, the story swapping that began as sort of a game between us. Perhaps it always was my game, not yours. My attempt to shape, control the past, the plot. You played along because you believed you had nothing to hide, played along until it stopped being fun. Until you realized I always wanted more. More. You show me yours, I'll show you mine. Tit for tat till somebody blinks. Or somebody goes blind. Goes mad.

My past scared you and yours frightened me. I frightened myself when I found I was falling too fast, too hopelessly in love with a woman I hardly knew. Knew not at all, in truth, beyond the possibility of another life we'd spent together, a history propelling me backward and forward in time when I met you in Philadelphia, the myth I conjured to give you a habitation and name in the past, the future. To fashion my story I needed to learn everything about you in a minute, and when your answers to my questions didn't match the person I was dreaming up, I'd back away. Hide. Trust nothing. Not love. Not myself. Not you. The scared little boy again trapped in an unforgiving room, watching, not understanding what he sees, what he feels. Fearing what comes next. Next. Did I want you to say the past is real or say it's not real. Whose voice did I expect to hear when you spoke. Whose secrets.

The metaphor of a verbal ball game breaks down. Too simple, too transparent to carry the weight of what motivated me to question you. My questions not about getting to know you better, no more than a desire to learn to play basketball explains why I wanted to stay in Homewood that summer my grandmother was dying, no more than fear of losing her explains my vigil in the hot, stuffy room.

Our stories one story, yours inseparable from mine. Was that my impossible wish, my dream. The story of a boy guilty of love, guilty of loving his grandmother, guilty of desiring her, leaving her, running to the ball court to save himself, become himself, that story call and response to what you tell me about the years we were lost to each other. Were you also frightened away from love. Running. Coming back. Both of us telling and retelling and untelling, trading riffs, losing our places, fracturing the music like that morning in bed we sang the old gospel songs together. Stories nested in other stories, unfolding and enfolded longer than we've been alive—brother and sister, brown man, brown woman, lovers since the primal darkness, the green forest, the burning village, the terror, the coffle, the petri dish in which we writhed to satisfy the curiosity of a pale, monocled ghost who amused itself by turning up the flame beneath us, the two of us lying spoon fashion, naked, chained in barracoons, in slave ships, in brothel beds with white snakes slithering up our legs, then together again spoon fashion in tiny cabins, in tenements, in songs and dances, in the marriage bed, in the grave, inseparable always, no matter how distant, always spoon fashion, matching what's different and the same.

In a novel called *Damascus Gate* I read about a cult dedicated to seeking Tikkun, the pure light of God's perfection that, once-upon-a-time, according to the cult's priests, dwelled right here on earth where we dwell. Through a severe regimen of mental and physical exercises, these mystics believed they could earn glimpses of the world as it was before God's exit. I wondered if moments of ecstatic vision experiencing God's perfect presence compensated for the devastating reality day after day of his perfect absence.

Will storytelling always feel like Isis gathering remnants of her missing son/brother/father/husband Osiris, each recovered fragment a cause for celebration, for hope that someday the broken body will be restored, renewed, lovers united, but also each fragment bearing memories of ancient crimes, ancient pain and loss.

We were seekers of sorts too. Homewood boys and men running to the court to find our missing fathers. Playing the game of basketball our way of telling stories, listening to stories, piecing a father together from them. Practicing bittersweet survival whether we find fathers or not.

Recalling your stories, telling mine, I'm practicing survival again. Remembering what's lost. Remembering my stories can't save you. Remembering the fullness of time no story encloses. Remembering that the miracle of return is only a story, only a dream.

Who Invented the Jump Shot (A Fable)

The native American rubber-ball game played on a masonry court has intrigued scholars of ancient history since the Spaniards redefined the societal underpinnings of the New World.

— *The Mesoamerican Ballgame,* Vernon L. Scarborough and David R. Wilcox, eds.

THE SEMINAR ROOM was packed. Packed as in crowded, packed as in a packed jury or Supreme Court, packed as in a fresh-meat inmate getting his shit packed by booty bandits. In other words the matter being investigated, "Who Invented the Jump Shot," has (a) drawn an overflow crowd of academics, (b) the fix is in, (c) I'm about to be cornholed without giving permission.

The title of the session let the cat out the bag. It broadcast two faulty assumptions—that at some particular moment in time the jump shot appeared, new and as fully formed as Athena popping from the head of Zeus, and that a single individual deserved credit for originating the jump shot. "Who Invented the Jump Shot" would be a pissing contest. And guess who will win. Not my perpetually outnumbered, outvoted, outgunned side. Huh-uh. No way. My colleagues of the Euro persuasion will claim one of their own, a white college kid on such and such a night, in such and such an obscure arena, proved by such and such musty, dusty documents, launched the first jump shot. Then they'll turn the session into a coming-out party for the scholar who invents the inventor. Same ole, same ole aggression, arrogance, and conspicuous consumption. By the end of two hours they'll own the jump shot, unimpeachable experts on its birth, development, and death. Rewriting history, planting their flag on a chunk of territory because nobody's around to holler *Stop thief*.

And here I sit, a co-conspirator in my blue plastic contour chair, transported, lodged, fed free of charge, waiting for an answer to a question nobody with good sense would ask in the first place. Even though I've fired up more jumpers than all the members of the Association for the Study of Popular Culture combined, do you think anybody on the planning committee bothered to solicit my opinion on the origins of the jump shot. With their lock-step sense of time, their solipsism, and their bonehead priorities, no wonder these suckers can't dance.

I prefer anonymity since I'm trashing my colleagues and biting the hand of the profession that feeds us—feeds us luxuriously on rare occasions such as the buffet luncheon preceding this seminar, hosted in the penthouse suite by our corporate sponsors, long tables draped in glistening linen, groaning under mounds of bloody roast beef, crab, shrimp, smoked salmon, etc., etc., that we swarmed around and stripped of everything but chopped veggies and dip in five minutes—so call me Ishmael. I like the sound of the name, the preparatory juicing of my lower gum, the stiffened tongue pressing against the roots of my bottom teeth to *Isssh* before the dying fall of *My-ell*. A name sensuous to pronounce and also right on because it recalls faraway lands, ancient times, outcasts wandering in the desert, looking for a home. Ishmael continues to collect his university salary, but he's defected. Lost faith in teaching, research, the enfranchisement and vending of knowledge. Though his heart remains out there, pumping good wishes to the good of heart, Ish doesn't sign humanitarian petitions anymore. Please don't talk about him when he's gone.

Let's quietly exit from this crowded hall in a mega–conference center in Minneapolis and seek the origins of the jump shot elsewhere, in the darkness where Ishmael's lost tribe wanders still.

Imagine the cramped interior of an automobile, a make and model extant in 1927 since that's the year in which we're touching down, backward in time on a snowy January night inside a medium-sized, let's say, Studebaker sedan humping down a highway, a car packed with the bodies of five large negro basketball players and a smallish driver whose hairy white knuckles grip the steering wheel.

Chug. Chug. The hot engine strains through a colder-than-cold night, emits an occasional arrhythmic flutter, *fluup*, warning the man hunched over the wheel that his Studebaker is severely overloaded, a *fluup* like the irregular heart murmurs of certain tragic athletes, usually long, lean people, often Americans of African descent, who will appear half a century later in the headlines after they suddenly expire, young and healthy, in the prime of life, then disappear, unlucky victims of a disease just as teasingly present and undetectable and fatal in their bodies as whatever it is under the Studebaker's hood worrying the driver. Who, listening for *fluup*s, loses track of time. Miles become minutes and minutes hours and hours melt into the space between one chug and the next, an infinity of time or a split second as the engine cycles. The driver listens so intently he's not sure in the overheated, drowsy space whether he actually hears a *fluup* or imagines it. Simulates a wet *fluup* with his lips. Does he miss the sound. Does he really want to hear it again if it's the sound of doom. He sees the whole carful of them marooned, stuck together like popsicles till spring thaws this wilderness between Chicago and Hinckley, Illinois.

Maybe he listens to distract himself from the claustrophobia, the scotophobia he can't help experiencing when he's alone, the only white man somewhere in the middle of nowhere with these colored guys he gets on with so well most of the time. C'mon. He rides, eats, drinks with them. Will sleep in the same room with one tonight to save money. In the same bed, for Chrissake, if there's only one bed and they fit. He'll be run out of godforsaken little midwestern towns with them after thumping the locals too soundly, nearly get lynched when Foster grins back at a white woman's lingering grin. So don't question my motives. Who are you to throw the first stone, anyway. Who gave you a striped shirt and whistle. He listens to stay awake, stay alive. For their benefit as much as his own. Stuffed like sardines in the tin can car; nobody would survive a wreck. Everybody out here tonight driving way too fast. As if they can outrun the weather, outrun accidents, gas pedal pressed to the metal, feeding the heart's last open artery.

So when the motor *fluup*s you listen. Or try to listen through the daze of driving. Windshield iced over except for a semiclear half-moon swatch maybe ten inches by four, the size more or less of his bunkmate Cooper's long, skinny paw. Like looking at the world through one of those slotted deep-sea-diver helmets. Squinting's giving the driver a headache and he still can't see shit. The thought of colliding with some bootlegger's giant rattling truck shivers through his body. He stomps harder on the gas. Do the others believe he sees where he's going. Do they care. Is anybody paying attention. He spies on his players in the rearview mirror above the dash. Too many stocking-capped, stingy-brimmed, big heads in the way. Blind as he is peering through the stubborn snow grit studding the glass, he might as well swivel around, strike up a conversation with anybody awake in the back seat.

Why am I first thing inside the driver's head. A carful of bloods and look whose brains I pick to pick. Is my own gray matter hopelessly whitewashed. Isn't the whole point of this fieldwork to escape what people like him think of me. The steamboat hauling us to Memphis glides steady in a broad stretch of river. Massa promised us we could come up on deck later and play. Is that why we serenade him, mind his business even now, in the hold where he can't see or hear us.

> *Hi de good boat, Neely*
> *She row bery fast, Miss Neely*
> *Ain't no boat like a Miss Neely*
> *Ho yoi Miss Neely*

In my defense I'll say it's too easy to feel what the players trapped in the car in the snowstorm feel. Simple to slip inside one of them. Not all of them, mind you, each player different from the others as each is different from the driver, but I know how athletes' bodies absorb them, save them, a house of refuge as you consider with truly deep, appalled curiosity your own body parts and wonder, really wonder how they accomplish the deeds, do the damage, your body always you and not you, it lives separately no matter how close to others, lives in your hands, shoulders, or your cramped buttocks or an arm squeezed numb under somebody else. Crammed in the Studebaker you patrol and explore and practice within the precincts of your body, fit and don't fit, cause when you get right down to it, ain't nowhere else to go. Rooted in their bodies, players kick back for the long haul to Hinckley. The ground we pass over may be unfamiliar and the body can be broken, unravel, smoke up the chimney, but players enjoy the temporary sense of belonging, of substance and weight, as they hunker down, anticipate action.

A kind of semi-hibernation during this long ride, eating yourself, nourishing your muscle with muscle, fat with fat, consuming yourself to survive. You must be ready, whatever's left, whatever still belongs to you, ready to explode when the cargo door bangs open. Saving yourself. Body a comfort and chain. Huge white flakes fall outside and you crouch inside your body's den while dreams of winning or losing, of being a star drift through like clouds changing your weatherscape, tossing and turning you as in sleep. Doesn't matter what rages outside the window. If it ain't one thing, it's another, my brothers. Let it snow, let it snow, let it snow.

I am them. One of us. In our ancient, thatched village of round mounds aboveground covering our hidden entrances. Circled like covered wagons at night to protect ourselves from these great howling plains, howling savages. *Howling. Savages.* Where did those words come from. Who invented them. Treacherously, the conqueror's narrative insinuates itself. Certain words attract us, their sound, their weight. It's easy to stray. Say the words as if you believe them. Lost again. Found again. *Savages. Howling.* Once you learn to speak a language, does it speak for you. Who comes out of your mouth. As I pleaded above, the mystery, the temptation of being other than I am disciplines me. Playing the role of a character I would not choose in most circumstances to be renders me hyperalert. Pumps me up and maybe I'm most myself.

In other words—if you believe nothing else, please, please believe I am always struggling for other words, my own words even if they seem to spiral out of a mind, a mouth like the driver's, my words are words I've earned, words if they fail me, I'm bound to fall on like a sword—in other words, I already understand what it's like to be one of the dark passengers. Been there. Done that. Swapped stories. Shared rides. What I haven't done and never will be is him, a small, scared, pale, hairy mammal surrounded by giant carnivores asleep just inches away in the dark and any move I make, the slightest twitch or shiver, the tremors, stutters, and *fluups* it's my nature to produce, might awaken them.

Though he wears a uniform under his business suit just in case the refs foul one of us out and he's forced to play, you know, the way some men sport bra and panties under their clothes, the driver's not an athlete. He's all business. A wannabe wheeler-dealer but so far no big deal. So far every time he's signed on the dotted line, the dots, the deal peel off the page, skitter away. Now he's got a better idea. White people pay good money to see negroes do what white people can't or won't or shouldn't do but always wanted to do as soon as they see negroes doing it. Big money in the pot at the end of that rainbow. Old-time minstrel shows and medicine shows, and now black-faced hoofers and crooners and tooters starring in clubs downtown. Why not basketball. Step right up ladies and gents. Watch Jimbo Crow fly. Up, up, and away with the greatest of ease. Barnstorming masters of thin air, of flim and flam and biff-bam-thank-you-mammy jamming.

The Globies' first tour had commenced in daylight, the dregs of it anyway you get at 3:30 P.M. on overcast gray days in a gray metropolis. Slocumbe Rucker, the last pickup, fusses as he squeezes his pivot man's bulk into the back seat, and we're off. Soon the first highway bug, *splat,* invents the windshield. The driver's happy. Whistles chorus after herky-jerky chorus, mangling a Satchmo jump. He believes in daylight. Believes in the two-lane, rod-straight road, his sturdy machine. He believes he'll put miles between us and Chicago before dark. Believes he'll deliver his cargo to Hinckley on time. Mercifully, whistling stops as giant white flakes surround us. Shit, he grunts, then hollers, No sweat, boys. Cooper twists round from the front seat, rolls his lemur eyes at me, *Right,* and I roll my eyes back at him, *Right.*

It's later. Imagine someone in the car at least as wired as the driver, someone who, after night's fallen blackly and falling snow piles against fences bordering the highway in ghostly drifts taller than the Studebaker's roof, watches the driver and tries to piece together from his movements and noises a picture of what the man at the wheel is thinking. Rooted there, maybe it's me, fresh from the conference in Minneapolis, attempting to paint this picture of the driver's invisible thoughts. Or perhaps I'm still sitting in my blue chair inventing this car chase. You can't tell by looking at my face what's on my mind. Who besides the person making it up ever sees the world each of us dreams inside our head, the play world supposed to function in certain crucial situations as a reasonably reliable facsimile of the world outside our heads. Is each inner world different. Are we all pursuing the same world, a reality somewhere, somehow, once and for all the same for everyone, even though no one can go there or know there. Who knows. Stories pretend to know. Stories always true and not. Real and unreal. Outside and inside. Stories swirling like the snowstorm pounding the Studebaker. Meaning what.

Doesn't meaning always sit like Hinckley somewhere in the darkness beyond the steamy peephole, meaning already sorted, tagged, logged, an accident waiting to happen.

It's the night of 27 January 1927 and we're on the road from Chicago to Hinckley, Illinois, population 3,600, no colored to speak of, a town as white as Ivory Snow except on one bedraggled, dead-end street a dozen or so shanties inhabited by negro hewers of wood, toters of water, bootblacks, janitors, whores, laundresses, waiters, maids, future presidential candidates, unemployed professional athletes.

One Hinckley negro in particular anxiously awaits the Globetrotters' arrival. A boy named Rastas whose own arrival in town is legendary. They say his mama, a hoboing prostitute, so the story goes, landed in Hinckley just before her son, landed butt first, hard enough to break every picked bone in her body when the flatcar she was standing on, last car of a mile-long freight, zigged when she thought it would zag and whipped her off her feet, tossing her ass over elbows high in the air. Miraculously, the same natural-born talent that transforms negro athletes into skywalkers and speed burners enabled this lady to regain her composure while airborne and drop like an expertly flipped flapjack flat on her back. In spite of splitting her skull wide open and spilling brains like rotten cantaloupe all over the concrete platform of Hinckley station, the maneuver preserved the baby inside her. Little Rastas, snug as a bug in a rug, sustained only minor injuries: a slight limp, a sleepy IQ. Imagine the fruity mess if she'd belly-flopped.

Poor Rastas didn't talk much and didn't exactly walk or think straight either, but the townsfolk took pity on the orphaned survivor. Maybe they believed the good luck of his sunny-side up landing might rub off, because they passed him house to house until he was nine years old, old enough to earn his keep in the world, old enough to stop playing doctor in back yards with the town's daughters. Grown-up Rastas a familiar sight in Hinckley, chopping, hauling, sweeping. A hired boy you weren't required to pay except with a few scraps from the table. Rastas grateful for any kind of employment and pretty reliable too if you don't mind him plodding along at his lazy pace. Honey dipping, exhumations, porn flicks, wet nurse— Rastas could do it all. If somebody had invented fast-food joints in those days, Rastas might have aspired to assistant-assistant-manage one. Rastas, Hinckley's pet. Loved and worked like a dog by everyone. No respect, no pussy, and nothing but the scarecrow rags on his back he could really call his own, but Rastas only thirty-six. There's still time. Time Rastas didn't begin to count down until the Tuesday he saw on a pole outside the barbershop a flyer announcing the Harlem Globetrotters' visit.

Of course Rastas couldn't read. But he understood what everybody else in town understood. The poster meant colored people. Niggers. Maybe the word *Harlem,* printed in big letters across the top of the poster, exuded some distinctive ethnic scent, or maybe if you put your ear close to the word you'd hear faint echoes of syncopated jazz, the baffled foot-tapping of Darktown strutters like ocean sound in seashells. Absent these subtler clues, the cartoon colored boys cavorting on the flyer worth a thousand words. Folks get the point. And if other illiterates (the majority) in Hinckley understood immediately who was coming to town, why not Rastas. He's Hinckley if anybody's Hinckley. What else was he if he wasn't.

So let's say our boy Rastas sniffed opportunity knocking, and decided, with an alacrity that would have surprised and shocked the townsfolk, to get the hell out of Dodge.

Given Poe's rules for composing a short story, have we meandered too far from the Studebaker's steamy interior, a site suspiciously like the inside of whatever car it was John Cinicola drove back in the days when he chauffeured us, the Shadyside Boys Club under-twelve hoop team, to games around the city of Pittsburgh, digressed too far from the *fluup*s which, recalling now those cramped rides in Mr. Cinicola's car, might not have been warnings of a bad engine or bad heart after all but muted farts, as discreet as possible in close quarters, almost involuntary, yet unavoidable, scrunched up as our intestines needed to be in the overpacked car. Last suppers of beans and wieners from moms who could conjure filet from neck bones didn't help. On the other hand, subsisting on the same low-rent diet homogenized as much as possible, given each individual's peculiar body chemistry, the sneaky, unseeable bubbles of gas nobody could keep from expelling, grit your teeth, squeeze your sphincter as you might. Mize well ask us to stop breathing and snoring. Smells from our bodies rising and percolating, a foul miasma that might have knocked you off your feet if you were too close to the Studebaker's door when it opened at the Hinckley Armory, but no big deal if you'd been along for the ride. The looming thunderhead of bad air above our heads like gloom or history or civilization and we couldn't disown it, couldn't deny our complicity, without disowning ourselves.

Yes, stone funky inside the car and one game the driver played to keep himself alert was every now and then taking a hit of this raunchy air, a deep junky snort, then a blast of icy air when he rolled his window a quick down-and-up inch. Overloading his senses, gorging to purge, purging to gorge, that eternal channel-surfing to overcome the insufficiency of human enjoyments. The old black magic fiddling that keeps us going. Till we stop.

In other words not much happening in the single-car wagon train, its pale canvas cover flapping like a berserk sail, our ship yawing, slapped and bruised by waves that crest the bow in blinding surges of spray, wind roar, foamy fingers of water scampering like mice into the vessel's every nook and cranny. Splish-splash. A monotonous sameness in the sea's monumental assault, and even though our hearts pump madly, though our throats tighten and bowels loosen, after a while it's same ole, same ole whipping till the storm gets tired whipping. Thus we're really not missing much if we flash forward to Hinckley.

Rastas gazes raptly at the crudely drawn figures on the flyer. He's the ugly duckling in the story first time it sees swans. Falls in love with the long, dark men, their big feet, big hands, big lips, big eyes, shiny white smiles, broad spade noses just like his. Falls in love with himself. Frowns recalling the first time his eyes strayed into a mirror and it revealed how different from other Hinckley folks he looked. Until the mirror sneaked up, *Boo,* he'd never considered he might be the beast dwelling in the fearful depths of other people's stares, the beast he'd encountered himself from time to time, daring him to look into its blazing eyes, eyes that could steal his soul, eat his flesh. The world full of devils. They assume many shapes. A hairy-fingered fat man coming at you with a knife. Soft-limbed, blue-eyed things wearing tiny dresses who'd turn your joint to fiery stone, then skip away giggling at your agony. He'd learned not to look. Taught himself to ignore his incriminating image when it floated across fragments of glass or the surface of still puddles, even in his thoughts sometimes, tempting him to drown and disappear in glowing beast eyes that might be his. Hiding from himself no cure. Each and every Hinckley day eyes penetrated his disguise. Eyes chewing and swallowing and spitting him out wet and mangled. Beast eyes no matter how artfully the bearer shapeshifted, fooled you with fleshy wrappings make your mouth water.

One day at closing time Barber Jones had said, You look like a wild man from Borneo, boy. All you need's a bone through your nose you ready for the circus. Put down the broom and get your tail over here to the mirror. Ima show you a wild cannibal.

See yourself, boy. Look hard. Filthy naps dragging down past your shoulders. People getting scared of you. Who you think you is. Don King or somebody. Damned wool stinks worse'n a skunk. Ima do you a favor, boy.

Barber Jones yakkety-yakking as he yaks daily about the general state of the world, the state of Hinckley and his dick first thing in the morning or last thing at night when just the two of them in the shop. Yakkety-yak, only now the subject is Rastas, not the usual nonstop monologue about rich folks in charge who were seriously fucking up, not running the world, or Hinckley, or his love life, the way Barber Jones would run things if just once he held the power in his hands, him in charge instead of those blockheads who one day will come crawling on their knees begging him to straighten things out, yakking and stropping on the razor strop a Bowie knife he'd brought special from home for this special occasion, an occasion Rastas very quickly decided he wanted no part of, but since he'd been a good boy his whole life, he waited, heart thumping like a tom-tom, beside the counter-to-ceiling mirror while fat-mouth Jones keened his blade.

A scene from Herman Melville's *Benito Cereno* might well have flashed through Rastas's mind if he'd been literate. But neither the African slave Babo cutting Captain Delano's hair nor the ironic counterpoint of that scene, blackface and white-face reversed, playing here in the mirror of Jones Barbershop, tweaks Rastas's consciousness of who he is and what's happening to him. Mr. Melville's prescient yarn doesn't creep into the head of Barber Jones either, even though Rastas pronounces Barber as *baba*, a sound so close to *Babo* it's a dead giveaway. Skinning knife in hand, Baba Jones is too busy stalking his prey, improvising Yankee Doodle–like on the fly how in the hell he's going to scalp this coon and keep his hands clean. He snatches a towel from the soiled pile on the floor. He'll wrap the bush, raise it in his fist, chop through the thick, knotty locks like chopping cotton.

Look at yourself in the mirror, boy. This the way you want to go round looking. Course it ain't. And stop your shakin. Ain't gon hurt you. You be thanking me once I'm done. Hell, boy, won't even charge you for a trim.

Lawd, lawd, am I truly dat nappy-haired ting in de mere. Am dis my bery own self, the ugly ole pestering debil what don't look lak nobody else in Hinckley sides me. Is me, Rastas confesses, confronting the living proof. His picture reversed right to left, left to right in the glass. Caged in the mirror like a prisoner in a cell is what he thinks, though not precisely in those words, nor the word *panopticon,* clunkily Melvillean and appropriate if Rastas's vocabulary had been somewhat more extensive. No words necessary to shatter the peace in Rastas's heart, to upset the détente of years of not looking, years of imagining himself more or less like other folks, just a slightly deformed, darker duck than the other ducks floating on this pond he'd learned to call Hinckley.

Boom. A shotgun blasts, as cold as the icy jolt when the driver cracks the Studebaker's window, as cold and maybe as welcome too, since if you don't wake up, Rastas, sleep can kill you. *Boom.* Every scared Hinckley duck quacks and flutters and scolds as it rises from the pond and leaves you behind, very much alone, watching them form neat, V-shaped squadrons overhead, squawking, honking, off to bomb the shit out of some Third World somebody, so high in the blue empyrean, so far gone and distant so quickly, you should have known long ago, should have figured it would happen like this one day. You all alone. Your big tarbaby feet moored in miring clay. You ain't them and they ain't you. Birds of a different feather. They coo and gobble-gobble and chirp and peep and you might mistake them for geese flying way up in the sky, but you sure ain't never heard them caw-caw, boy. No. They ain't blackbirds. Not ravens, crows, grackles, jackdaws neither. Huh-uh. You the cawing night bird and the shotgun ain't gon miss next time. Your cover's busted, boy. Here come Baba Jones.

You sure don wanna go around looking just so, do you boy.

Well, Rastas ain't all kinds of fool. He zip-coons outta there, faster than a speeding bullet. Maybe he didn't rise and fly, but he didn't Jim Crow neither. No turning dis way and wheeling dat way and jiggling up and down in place. Next time the Baba seen him, bright and early a couple mornings later, Rastas had shaved his skull clean as a whistle. Gold chains draping his neck like Isaac Hayes. How Rastas accomplished such a transformation is another story but we got enough stories by the tailfeathers, twisted up in our white towel—count em—so let's switch back to the moment, earlier in storytime, later in Hinckley time, months after Rastas clipped his own wings rather than play Samson to Jones's Delilah.

Rastas still stands hoodooed by the Harlem Globetrotters flyer, welcomed and undone. Rastas who's been nowhere. Doesn't even know the name his mother intended for him. Didn't even recognize his own face in the mirror till just yesterday, Hinckley time. Is the flyer a truer mirror than the one in the barbershop, the mirror Rastas assiduously keeps at his back these days as he sweeps, dusts, mops. He studies the grinning black men, their white lollipop lips, white circles around their eyes, his gaze full of longing, nostalgia, more than a small twinge of envy and regret. He doesn't know the Globetrotters ain't been nowhere neither, their name unearned, ironic at this point in time. They haven't been invented quite yet. *Globetrotters* the owner/driver's wishful thinking, his vision of international marketing, prodigious piles of currency, all colors, sizes, shapes promiscuously stacking up. Not Globetrotters yet because this is the maiden voyage, first trot, first road game, this trek from Chicago to Hinckley. But they're on their way, almost here, if you believe the signs tacked and glued all over town, a rain, a blizzard, a storm of signs. If Rastas wasn't afraid the flimsy paper would come apart in his hands, he'd pull the flyer off the pole, sneak it into the barbershop, hold it up next to his face so he could grin into the mirror with his lost brothers. Six Globetrotters all in a row. Because yes, in spite of signs of the beast, the players are like him. Different and alike. Alike and different. The circle unbroken. Yes. Yes. Yes. And *whoopee* they're coming to town.

As befits a fallen world, however, no good news travels without bad. The night of the game Rastas not allowed in the Armory. Hinckley a northern town so no Jim Crow laws turned

Rastas away. Who needed a law to regulate the only negro in town. Sorry, Rastas, just white folks tonight.

I neglected to mention that the little burnt-cork, burnt-matchstick tip of the particular dead-end street noted earlier as I speculated on Hinckley's racial composition had been razed, spontaneously urban-removed, and the negro inhabitants of that portion of the street, those who survived the pogrom, had disappeared into the night, the same kind of killingly cold night roughing up the Studebaker. That detail, the sudden exodus of all the town's negroes, should have been noted earlier in story-time because it had registered many years before, Hinckley time, imprinted indelibly in the town's memory. Now you see it, now you don't, but always present. A permanent marker separating before and after. Hinckley a white man's town from that night on. A billboard at the edge of town said NIGGER, DON'T LET THE SUN SET ON YOUR BLACK ASS.

And just to emphasize how white a town, the night of the house-razing party everybody wore sheets bleached white as snow, and for a giggle, under the sheets, blacked their faces. A joke too good to share with the niggers, who'd see only white robes and white hoods with white eyes in the eyeholes. We blacked up blacker than the blackest one of them. Yes we did. Blacker than a cold, black night, blacker than black. Hauled the coloreds outdoors in their drawers and nightgowns, pickaninnies naked as the day they born. You got five minutes to pack a sack and git. Five minutes we's turnin these shacks and everythin in em to ash. Ash and cinders. Like what we'd smeared on our faces they couldn't see under our hoods. A double ha-ha. White blacks burning out niggers so scared they lost their color. Ashy white. Ashy black. Poor coons don't know there's a party going on.

They hobbled off cawing and moaning, singing melancholy songs they stole from us when we used to cork up and pretend to be them. A flock of blackbirds without wings. *Shoo. Shoo.* Time to strike the match. Catch you stealing one scarecrow peek back at those raggedy shacks, scorch you white as a pillar of salt.

So Rastas the only negro left in town, and with that fact established just in time we're in a better position to imagine how he would react seeing himself duplicated on the flyer. Can't you identify with his excitement, expectation, anxiety. His hunger. And then, just a few hours later, the absolutely deflating, prostrating sense of loss and unfairness when he's told there's no room in the inn.

The gillies transporting the Globies into town sported billowing canvas covers, noisy as wind-whipped sails, and their wooden sides, steep as clipper ships, were splashed with colorful, irresistible ads for merchandise nobody in Hinckley had ever dreamed of, let alone seen. A cornucopia of high-tech goods and services from the future, Hinckley time, though widely available in leading metropolitan centers for decades. Some stuff packed in the deep holds of the wagons extremely ancient. Not stale or frail or old-fashioned or used or useless, though there was plenty, plenty of that rummage sale trash too in the capacious holds, trinkets and baubles Hinckley hicks would see as new and gotta-have-it. No, the oldest, deepest cargo consisted of things forgotten. *Forgotten?* Yes, forgotten. Upon which subject I would expand if I could, but forgotten means forgotten, doesn't it. Means lost. A category, none of whose contents are available to list or describe because if you could, the items wouldn't be forgotten. Forgotten things are really, really gone. Even if you remember them. Like a *Free Marcus* button you tucked in a drawer and lived the rest of your life not knowing it lay there, folded in a bloodstained headkerchief, until one afternoon as you're preparing to move the last mile into senior citizens' public housing, the Le Roy Irvis Homes to be precise, and you must divest yourself finally of ninety-nine and nine-tenths percent of the junk you've accumulated over the years because the cubicle 610 you're assigned in the highrise isn't much larger than a coffin, certainly not a king-sized coffin like pharaohs erected so they could take everything with them—chariots, boats, VCRs, slaves, wives—so you must extricate yourself from what feels like layers of your own tender skin for a while as you appraise and toss, appraise and toss layers of who you've been and are, flaying yourself patiently, painfully, one precious forgotten thing after another, toss, toss, toss. Forgotten till you come across it in the gritty bottom of a drawer and realize you've not been living the kind of life you could have lived if you hadn't forgotten. And now, remembering, it's too late.

The wagons carried tons of alternative pasts. Roads not taken, costumes, body parts, promises, ghosts. The Hinckley hicks line up for miles at these canvas-topped depots crackling whitely in the prairie wind. Poor folks who can't afford to purchase anything mob the landing anyway. So much to be exchanged, so many bright hopes in the bellies of the schooners, they might still be docked there doing brisk business a hundred years from now storytime, my time, your time, the globetrotters in their gaudy, revealing uniforms delivering stuff to the sea of waving hands, grappling, grasping hands, but hands not too busy to clap, volleys of clapping interspersed with collective sighs of relief, ohing and ahing, hands brought together, then sighs so deep and windy they scythe across the Great Plains and bow mile after endless mile of wheat, corn, barley, fields of grain rippling and purring as if they'd been caressed when a tall globie dangles aloft some item everybody recognized, a forgotten thing all would claim if they could afford it, a priceless pearl the dark ball player tosses gratis into the grateful, huddling mass of Hinckleyites, just doing it to do it, and the gift would perform tricks, loop-de-looping, sparkling, gliding airborne long enough to evoke spasms of love and guilt and awe and desire and regret, then disappear like a snowflake grown too large and baroque, its own weight and ambition and daring and vanity ripping it apart before it reaches the earth. A forgotten thing twisting in the air, becoming a wet spot on a finger reaching for it. A tear inching down a cheek. An embarrassing pinpoint of moisture at the crotch of somebody's drawers.

Wheee. Forgotten things. Floating through the air with the greatest of ease. Hang-gliding. Flip-flopping.

Clippety-clop. Clippety-clop. The horse-drawn caravan clomps up and down Hinckley's skimpy grid of streets. U-turns at the abandoned, dead-end former black quarter where the foundations of a multiuse, multistory, multinational parking garage and amusement center already yawn, gouged deeper into the earth than the stainless-steel-and-glass edifice will rise in the sky.

Is that going to be the mall of America, one of the Globie kids asks, peeking out from behind a wagon's starched canvas flap. A little Hinckley girl answers the little boy: I dunno.

And then she's bright and chirrupy as Jiminy Cricket after the gillies saunter down the block, the last horse's round, perfect rump swaying side to side like Miss Maya's doggerel. The girl feels delicious about herself because she managed to be polite to the small brown face poking out of the white sheet just as her mother said she must, but also really, basically, ignored it, didn't get the brown face mixed up with Hinckley faces her mother said it wouldn't and couldn't ever be. Always act like a lady, honey. But be careful. Very careful. They are not like us. Warmed now by the boy's soft voice, the long lashes like curly curtains or question marks, his cute size, the dreamy roll of the horse's big, split butt, she's chattering to herself in a new language, made up on the spot, as if she's been tossed a forgotten thing and it doesn't melt.

Daddy said after the bulldozers a big road's coming and we'll be the centerpiece of the universe, the envy of our neighbors, and said I can have anything I want, twenty-four seven, brother, just imagine, anything I want, any toy or exotic taste or evil thought. Wow. Gumby-o. Opp-poop-a-doop.

After the dust cloud churned by the giant tires of the convoy settles, the little girl discovers chocolate drops wrapped in silver

foil the chocolate soldiers had tossed her. In the noise and confusion of the rumbling vehicles, before she'd answered the boy,
she'd thought the candies were stones. Or bullets. Aimed at her
by the dark strangers in canvas-roofed trucks her mother had
warned her to flee from, hide from. Realizing they are lovely
dark chocolate morsels, immaculate inside their shiny skins, she
feels terrible for thinking ugly thoughts about the GIs, wants to
run to the convoy and holler *Danke, Danke* even though her
mother had told her they're illiterate, don't speak our language.
As she scoops up the surprises and stuffs them in her apron
pocket, she imagines her chubby legs churning in pursuit of the
dusty column. Maybe she could catch it. The convoy had taken
hours to pass her, so it must be moving slowly. But war has
begun to erode her innocence. She's learned the treacherous distance between appearance and reality. Even after crash diets
and aerobic classes her pale, short legs would never reach the
retreating wagons, so she settles for lip-synching, *Danke,
Danke,* where she sits. Little Miss Muffet on a tuffet, eating not
curds and whey, whatever curds and whey might be, but Her-
shey's chocolate kisses, although from a distance, through the
eye of a casual observer, the difference would have been negligi-
ble. A starved urchin cramming food into her mouth with both
hands, as if she'd forgotten how good food could be and
wanted to make up for all the lost meals at once. Licking, sucking, crunching, chewing. The melting, gooey drops smear her
cheeks, hands, dimpled knees—chocolate stain spreading as
the magic candy spawns, multiplies inside her apron pocket, a
dozen new sweet pieces popping into being for every one she
consumes. Eating, eating till the poor child's about to bust, till
the sweet chocolate coating her outside and that chocolate
welling up inside transform her into a glistening, sticky tarbaby
her own mother would have warned her not to touch. Instead
of busting wide open like a cantaloupe dropped from one of the
twin towers of the imminent amusement center, she tilts on her
round bottom, rolls over into the dust.

(*Dust?* What happened to the snowstorm?

The snow? Oh In expectation of the mega–convention center, Hinckley's been domed for years.)

Believe it or not, it's Rastas who discovers the girl. Night now. Since being refused entrance to the Globetrotters show, he's been wandering disconsolate through the dark streets of Hinckley, when suddenly, as fate would have it, he stumbles into her. Literally. Ouch.

Less painful than disquieting, this abrupt contact with something soft and squishy underfoot freezes Rastas in his tracks. Instinctively his leg retracts. He shakes it, scuffs the bottom of his shoe on the ground; something Velcroishly tacky clings. He remembers the parade earlier in the day. Horses large as elephants. Sniffs the night air cautiously. Hopes he's wrong. Must be. He smells sugar and spice, everything nice, overlaid with the cloyingly sweet reek of chocolate. Another time and place he might have reared back, kicked the obstacle in his path, but tonight he's weak, depleted, the mean exclusion of him from the Globetrotters extravaganza the final straw. Besides, what kind of person would kick a dog already down, and dog or cat's what he believes he'll see as he peers into the shadows webbing his feet.

Rastas gulps. His heart *fluup*s as he kneels to be certain. The chocolate can't hide a cherub's face, the Gerber baby plump limbs and roly-poly torso. Somebody's daughter lying out here in the gutter. Hoodooed. Stricken. Poor babygirl. The frail— make up your mind—chest rises and falls faintly, motion almost imperceptible in the bad light since they never paved or installed streetlamps on this street when negroes lived here and now the cunning city managers are waiting for the Dutch-German-Swiss conglomerate to install a megawatt, multicolor, mesmerizing blaze of glory luring crowds to the Omniplex.

Rastas sees enough in the darkness at his feet to nearly break his already overtaxed heart on this night of nights, a night he expected his new life to begin, riding off in the Studebaker with the Globies, laughing, rapping, picking salty slivers of the town they just sacked out their teeth, exhausted but hungry by nightfall for another town. Yet on this penultimate night before the dawning of the first day of his new life, Rastas displays patience and self-denial worthy of Harriet's old Tom. Accepts the sudden turn of fate delaying his flight from Hinckley. Takes time out to rescue a damsel in distress.

One more job, just one more, and I'm through, outta here. Riding with the Globies or trotting on my own two feet. I'm gittin. Giddyup. Yeah. You tell folks it was Rastas sung dis song and now Rastas long gone.

Determined to do the right thing, he stoops and raises the girl's cold heart-shaped face, one large hand under her neck so her head droops backward and her mouth flops open, the other hand flat against her tiny bosom. Figures he'll blow breath into her mouth, then guide it, pump her rib cage like you would a bellows till her lungs catch fire again. In other words Rastas is inventing CPR, cardiopulmonary resuscitation, a lifesaving technique that will catch on big in America one day in the bright future when there are no rules about who can do it to whom, but that night in Hinckley, well, you can imagine what happened when a crowd of citizens hopped-up and confused by the Globetrotters' shenanigans at the Armory came upon Rastas in the shadows crouched over a bloody, unconscious little white girl, puckering up his liver lips to deliver a kiss.

To be fair, not everyone participated in the mayhem you're imagining. They say only the portion of the crowd returning home to the slum bordering the former colored quarter. In other words the poor and fragrant did the dirty work. The ones who'd contracted colored diseases generations back when they lived where no self-respecting white person would. This unruly element, soon themselves to be evicted when Consolidated Enterprises clears more parking space for the pleasure center, these people who, experts say, constituted by far the largest portion of the mob that had burned and chased all the negroes out of town, these embarrassing undesirables who disrupt city council meetings fussing about the huge, nasty, wet hole at the end of their block and the constant braying, hooting, clanking of pre-historic iron beasts digging the hole, these unemployables who, under their garlic breath, curse the foreign CEOs and would lynch them too if they could get away with it, they're the ones about to perpetrate the horror I'm asking you to imagine. And imagine you must, because I refuse to regale you with gory, unedifying details.

Not everyone's to blame. Still, who wouldn't be upset by an evening of loud, half-naked, large black men fast breaking and fancy dribbling, clowning and stuffing and jamming and preen-ing for women and kids who screamed their silly heads off. Enough to put any man's nerves on edge, especially since you had to shell out hard-earned cash to watch yourself take a beat-ing. Then, to top it all off, you're home, bone-tired, trying to fall asleep, and here comes your old lady bouncing into bed, squirmy, flush-faced, grinning from ear to ear, like she's just bungy-dived naked from one of those goddamned twin towers.

The wipers flop back and forth, bump over scabs of ice. The view isn't improving. The Studebaker's in a long, long black tunnel. Its headlights illuminate slants of snow that seem to converge just beyond the spot where a hood ornament would sit, if Studebakers, like Mercedes Benzes, were adorned with bowsprits in 1927. Bright white lines of force, every kamikazi-ing snowflake in the universe, sucked into this vortex, this van-ishing point the headlights define, a hole in the snow we chug-chug behind, deeper into the tunnel that charts our course, an ever-receding horizon drawing us on, drawing us on, a ship to Zion, the song says.

Our driver's appalled by the raw deal Rastas received. I'd never participate in something so mobbishly brutal, he swears. I would not assume appearance is reality. I would not assume truth lodges in the eye of the more numerous beholders. After all, my people also a minority. We've suffered unjustly too. And will again. I fear it in my bones. In this hot, *fluup*ing car. Soon after the Great Depression that will occur just a few years from now, just a few miles down this very road we're traveling, some clever, evil motherfucker will say, Sew stars on their sleeves. It'll work like color. We'll be able to tell who's who. Keep them apart. Mongrels. Gypsies. Globetrotters. Constantly coming and going. Sneaking in and out of our cities. Peddling dangerous wares. Parasites. Criminals. Devils. Through the slit in his iron mask he watches gallows being erected by the roadside, flyers nailed and taped all over town. Wonders if it's wise to warn them we're coming.

So *who* invented the jump shot. Don't despair. All the panelists have taken their seats at the table facing the audience. The emcee taps a microphone and a hush fills the cavernous hall. We're about to be told.

The Village

The bead artist continually changes perspectives while working on the design. The direction of strands shifts throughout the work, breaking up the surface to create the impression of segmentation, division, and separation that are so characteristic of composition in much Yoruba art.

—Rowland Abiodun, "Beads"

IT'S THE FIRST SUMMER of a new century, a new millennium, and I find myself with a friend in New York City on a hot July evening, strolling through the Village to a movie. Forty minutes to kill after we purchased tickets for Bruno Dumont's *Humanité* and I suggest we walk back to a basketball court we'd passed a few blocks from the theater. I thought it might be fun and useful to try to explain to my friend, who is a woman and French, what we'd see on the court, especially since I'd been hard at work for about two years attempting to explain to myself the power of playground basketball, its hold on me, on African-American men, the entire culture.

I could have said to my friend, Catherine, You whisper the secret of who you are, who you want to be, into the ear of the game, and once it knows your secrets, it plays them back to you and you must dance to them, the sense, nonsense, and music nothing less than revealed and revealing truth—your song of self the game makes real. Like the ancient Mayan ball game enacted to ensure through sympathetic magic the rhythm of the cosmos, the sun rising and setting, the wheel of the seasons, the cycle of birth and death. For a moment on the court you can play at that level of seriousness. Those are the stakes of the playground game.

I could have expanded these thoughts, broken them down further for her, for myself. Said, The game's a way of perceiving the world. It ritualizes what's significant in men's lives. The playground game is molded to express perceptions, ideas, feelings men have discovered about themselves, and it tests their beliefs about what's important, establishes a sense of identity. Once these attitudes are folded into the game, the game bristles with their force, the power of hard-won, self-identifying, self-preserving notions men have of themselves and their world.

A counterreality is dramatized. Playing hoop, African-American men act out a symbolic version of who they are, who they want to be. This is what will be manifested on the court just up the block, what's verified, the shadows proving substance.

In the cage abutting intimately the busy sidewalk, a few yards from nonstop honking traffic, inches from the chattering pedestrians, a zone is preserved. Not unlike the prisons, jails, detention centers, detox centers, asylums, hallway houses, ghetto blocks of public housing plunked down in the midst of cities. Everybody knows such preserves clutter the urban landscape and everybody knows you don't have to pay attention to them unless you choose to raise your eyes from whatever business you have in the street and peep through the Cyclone fencing, the spools of concertina wire, the steel bars, brick walls, across an expressway or a filthy moat. At the corner of 6th Avenue and Houston in the Village, caged men working out their fate, on display if anyone cares to spectate, invisible if you don't care to look.

I could have said a lot, but as we walk along the crowded street, I become aware of a silence inside myself I'm reluctant to break. Almost like I'm holding my breath, almost like I want to sneak up on the game. Months, maybe a year since I'd stood and seriously checked out a playground game. If I stayed away, wouldn't it help me forget. First step in the cure. Cold turkey, total withdrawal. No more hoop. Out of sight, out of mind.

At one end of the small court you could ease through a narrow gate in the twenty-foot-tall fence of twisted wire separating the hot and heavy action from civilians, step into the hoop

scene, mingle with the hardcore chorus of watchers, with players waiting on the sidelines for a turn to run. A game had just
fired up as we arrived. Three, I heard somebody shout, backpedaling, three fingers on his outstretched arm pumping at the
sky after he dropped a jumper from the top of the key.

Catherine lagged slightly behind when I crossed from the
sidewalk into the playing area beyond the fence. She must have
understood without being told how it was one thing to observe
the players through the fence, another to enter their domain.
I gesture she should join me, coax her with my eyes, *C'mon,
girl, over here, girl,* to the wide margin, neither sidewalk nor
playing surface, along one side of the court where I've planted
myself.

Thinking all the things I could say and don't, I begin to understand the filling, waiting silence inside me. It is a wound.
The wound of what's been lost and missing. Lots of it's about
giving up playing the game. But there's more, much more. Once
this side of the fence, the brawling traffic sounds and constant
babble of passing pedestrians a barely audible background to
the silence welling up inside me. The sounds of that outside
world shrinking, dispersing, absorbed by the bouncing ball, the
big, squeaky sneakers rushing up and back, up and down, leaving, landing on the asphalt playing surface. The game generates
its own soundtrack, a music and mood my guts, from blocks
away, had begun to quiet themselves to receive, discipline themselves to meet and be taken in, refreshed, energized, spoken to
by name, my heartbeat echoing a pounded dribble, a hush, a
holler in the space I prepare inside myself, space liberated,
space granted to this game or it would not just enlarge me, it
would bust me wide open. Here, close to the action, a sea
change. Not exactly relieved and not exactly stymied either.
Words I'm ready to speak now won't tell the whole story. They
don't need to. One kind of silence simply replaces another, the
other kind of silence words never quite defeat. I imagine a tam-
bourine in a cartoon morphing into the music it shakes out of

itself and dances to. A wind stirring the cage, blowing the fence away, the howling, screeching, siren-scraped street away, the whole neighborhood gone. I blink away the image I haven't been able to escape till now, watching the game, the image that assaulted me first thing in the morning while I looked for weather on TV, a swarm of cops descending upon a wounded suspect, burying him under a rippling blue blanket of angry, stinging wasps, blue men and women, blue blacks and blue whites punching, kicking, stomping some invisible, allegedly black somebody named Jones into the grime of a Philly street.

My head's full again of everything I could or should be saying about the game to a smart, curious woman who's spent most of her life in another country. See. Although all the fellows on the court now are various shades of brown, a sprinkling of white guys roam the sidelines, organizing a team or a spot on a team to challenge the winners of the present match. I could say it, but I'm glad a mixed crowd of players allows Catherine to see for herself that playground hoop is not about race. Not about gender either, though no women for Catherine to see today. If we had more time before the movie, maybe we could discuss how the court both reflects and challenges attitudes about gender and race. When I was coming up, women never played on the serious courts. Now in small numbers they do. Recently I'd played in heavy-duty matches with women on both teams so no doubt things are changing. A women's pro league suggests the propriety and glory of women doing their own thing. It also reinforces the fantasy of separate but equal, a fantasy because in the present ideological climate, league or no league, political equality remains a fantasy. A lot to talk about, but in the meantime Catherine has ocular proof playground hoop not based on the race of those who participate, anyway. Race does figure strongly in the thinking of those who would profit from defining and controlling the picture of playground hoop in the media. As long as racialized thinking prevails, as long as it distorts how we view American society, cultural activity at the margins will respond accordingly, appear to express itself in a racialized paradigm of division and confrontation. *In your face.* Appear to be about *us* exclusively. Us instead of them. Ours versus theirs. At a deeper level, however, playground hoop transcends race and gender because it's about creating pleasure, working the body to please the body, about free spaces, breaks in the continuum of socially prescribed rules and roles, freedom that can be attained by play, by a game not without rules but with flexible rules, spontaneous, improvised according to circumstances, rules based on a longstanding, practical consensus about what's important— rules whose only reason for being is to enhance play, radically democratic rules that are a means not an end, not a jail cell but a mutually agreed upon set of restraints, an imaginary labyrinth testing how ingeniously, elegantly players can actually work their way out.

As much as basketball might be hyped as a rosy consummation of multicultural, multiracial, melting-pot togetherness in ads featuring NBA stars, in NBA promos fronting ecstatic white faces who *love that game,* in the self-serving pontificating of sportswriters and sportscasters, in the platitudes of banquet speakers, in the selling of the NCAA tournament's March Madness as frenzied proof of the American dream, a red-white-and-blue lottery in which anybody with a ticket, big dog or underdog, has a chance to be number one, basketball also functions to embody racist fantasies, to prove and perpetuate "essential" differences between blacks and whites, to justify the idea of white supremacy and rationalize an unfair balance of power, maintained by violence, lies, and terror, between blacks and whites.

It's no coincidence that pro hoop's explosive rise to popularity coincided with the emergence of a Great White Hope in the person of Larry Bird and his old-school Boston Celtics to do battle with Magic Johnson's Los Angeles Lakers, West Coast wise-guy kings of shake-and-bake. Never mind that Magic's grin and Bird's tight-lipped Yankee stoicism were both masks disguising many identical features. Never mind that both were products of endless hard work, ruthless determination, love of the game, supreme court intelligence and vision, the willpower to jujitsu certain not very extraordinary physical endowments into strengths. Never mind that both men constantly learned from each other, appropriating the other's skills and tricks, flattering each other by sincere imitation.

What played in the media was the masks. Showtime versus lunch-pail ethic. Pleasure versus duty. Helter-skelter versus planning. Athletic ability versus intelligence. Nature versus nurture. Ego versus teamwork. Grin versus scowl. Familiar plotlines, stereotypical characters, commentary featuring coarse humor and homespun, cracker-barrel asides, often turning on thinly disguised gender or racial jokes, have been staples of American popular entertainment, preserving intact its origins in blackface minstrelsy.

Rather than treating Bird and Magic as fixed, different kinds —Bird as bedrock symbol of mainstream values and Magic as the wild hair, the nigger in the woodpile, whose act is entertaining but needs some major cleaning up before it's acceptable in the mainstream (although we'll grab the cash his mainstreamed battle with Bird produces)—the media could have examined how Magic and Bird created each other, how they are inseparable, an amalgamation, how together they achieved something more, probably better than either could have managed alone. Unfortunately, such a treatment doesn't sell sneakers or cars or beer. Purity of blood and kind, the fixed, predictable qualities of racial types, the rhetoric attaching warning labels to mixing, to miscegenation—that stuff sells. Good vs. Evil, Black vs. White, a battle royal with only one winner left standing at the end. No prisoners, no compromise sells. And even if the Celtics lose a particular championship series, they win. They started out as the good guys, so they'll never be anything else. You saw the games. You listened to the story. Remember. Blood. Essentialism. Race. Wait till next year. Basketball has been exploited to illustrate a sorry tale again and again. To sell itself and the soap selling it, the soap it sells.

Like blackface minstrelsy as it developed in the volatile working-class theaters of early nineteenth-century New York City, basketball mounts competing attitudes about race onstage, where they are contested, publicly shaped, and reshaped. What's instructive, even exhilarating about such a contestation is how stubbornly uncontrollable the outcome remains, one bare-bones side jooking, rope-a-doping to counter the overwhelming resources the other side employs to rig the game.

In the early 1800s, African-descended oystermen who fished the waters off Long Island would bring their catch to the wharf at Catherine Street on the East River, a busy marketplace then, a site of thriving cultural as well as commercial exchange, an area where coincidentally I'd found myself in the course of a recent morning walk along the waterfront.

Reading books by Eric Lott (*Love and Theft*) and Thomas Lhamon (*Raising Cain*), I'd been fascinated by the history of Catherine Street wharf, by the authors' speculations and theories about blackface minstrelsy's origins in the urban Northeast. The story goes something like this. After selling their oysters, some African boatmen (immigrants, though their passage to the New World coerced, not chosen) earned a second payday by dancing for money. Observers at the time reported being amazed by these exhibitions, especially when the dancers confined their routines — jumps, spins, skips, hops, songs, somersaults, rhythmic clapping and tapping, imitations of animals, birds, and gods — to the compass of a narrow board or plank. These displays of explosive athleticism and elegant control, spellbindingly executed within a severely constricted space the dancers disciplined themselves to honor, delighted the multinational, multiethnic crowds drawn to Catherine Street market. Through imitations by blackface white entertainers, versions of these popular performances found their way into Lower East Side theaters, then gradually spread beyond New York City as corked-up minstrels troubadoured across the country, seeding with African influence the burlesque song, dance, skit reviews which were creating America's first indigenous, truly national popular entertainment.

Proprietors of theaters on the Lower East Side and Bowery had discovered that their primary clientele—recently arrived, male, European, immigrant laborers—would plunk down hard-earned cash to watch other whites in blackface prancing, dancing, mangling English (the language, incidentally, many in the audience hadn't mastered yet) in comic skits ridiculing black difference. Though one obvious purpose of staging black buffoonery would have been to elevate the self-esteem of poor, beleaguered, immigrant laborers by scapegoating an even more lowly black underclass, there also must have been something else at stake, something alluring, entrancing, about the white imitations of black folks. Why couldn't theatergoers seem to get enough of these shows featuring corked-up, synthetic versions of African song and dance. Why did the crowds keep returning. What did they really see. What did they eventually attempt to plunder and master.

Satire, ridicule, and financial gain may have been the impetus of white professionals who purloined African speech habits and habits of movement in order to earn a living. However, to be effective mimics, these entertainers were required to observe their subjects minutely (as a lover's gaze longs to memorize the details of the beloved's body?), thus undergoing a kind of forced immersion in blackness, whether or not they admired or understood what they were simulating. White minstrels became agents of cultural dissemination, not only passing on external, material signs of blackness—color, clothing, dialect, a bouncy, Jim Crow, wheel-about-and-jump-about-and-do-just-so walk —but also conveying to their greenhorn audience styles of deportment, encoding (among other messages) silent resistance, defiance, and independence. Styles of self-representation and self-presentation honed in a hostile world, styles designed surreptitiously to alter imbalances of power. From a displaced African's perspective (whether a newly arrived slave in the nineteenth century or B-boys today in the Bronx), the world is never finished, never just the oppressive here-and-now of subordination; it's also *elsewhere*. A primal burden of Americanized African culture, from dancing oyster vendors to hip-hop, has been to invent the techniques and sustain the will to address this *elsewhere*, call it forth. Consciously or unconsciously, minstrel performers picked up the African habit of simultaneously addressing multiple audiences, multiple levels of reality, including the transcendent, imminent *elsewhere* where the minds of captive bodies freely play.

Despite itself, blackface minstrelsy conveyed lessons from an underworld, taught by underdogs, black others, very definitely other and very definitely black (didn't the message of greasepaint or cork or soot double blackness even while denying it), lessons as black as they seemed, also mirroring in a curiously affecting fashion what it means to be white, poor, and underclass, subject to a version of reality dictated by white people, a ruling elite imagining itself above you. European immigrants, like the youthful legions of white middle-class hip-hop fans across the globe today, could see mirrored in a glass darkly what it might mean to escape elsewhere and turn a harsh, unwelcoming, burdensome world topsy-turvy.

Unfortunately, during these same decades preceding the Civil War, when impressive, evocative displays of African competence and the transformative power of African culture, whether acknowledged as African or not, were working their way into the consciousness of the nation, an increasingly virulent, totalizing variety of apartheid was also becoming institutionalized in America. Many of today's unresolved tensions and contradictions that follow from the inadequacy of official racial categorizations to account for what we see, hear, and feel, the frustrating failures of theories of racial difference and racial accommodation to dislodge the evidence of our hearts and minds, in short, the seething, destructive stalemate, a.k.a. the "race problem," has its source here. America's neurotic ambivalence toward African-rooted cultural practices continues: commodified versions of hip-hop style aggressively exploit a lucrative worldwide market, while at home "black" kids are demonized, marginalized, and victimized by the stunted versions of themselves that hip-hopped commercials imprint.

Playground hoop, like Homewood stories and music, is also rooted here, in the vital remnants of African-derived folk culture and in the dynamics of struggling for survival in a hostile land. Here also at the interface of play and pay. Were the planks upon which African oystermen danced miniature ancestors of the hoop court. Were the disaffected young immigrant males who formed a Bowery streetcorner culture precursors of today's white chocolate point guards, vanilla ice rappers, wiggers, and hip-hop wannabes. Playground hoop carries forward the folk tradition of direct, immediate participation, of doing rather than observing. Carries it forward to an inevitable clash with the mainstream.

Folk arts are practical, functional, arise from the activities of everyday life. They are communal, choral, help you do what you must do to get along, help you join with others around you to enliven, enhance, make sacred what's routine, transform the ordinary into the extraordinary. Folk culture produces art without necessarily stipulating art as a separate, privileged province. Until yesterday European notions of art imported to America valorized product and permanence, encouraged the veneration and preservation of what's been done before, especially, almost exclusively, what was achieved "back home," the monuments of the Old World. Museums are the temples (tombs) of European arts, displaying the portability, the alleged independence of context, the assumedly intrinsic power as object that high art enjoys. Folk arts such as playground hoop are about the doing, one-time and one-more-time play in a saturated present tense, live performances immaterial and transient, enduring over time only if faithfully repeated. Time the thread stringing the beads. Great Time separating yet also connecting the individual and communal experience, the particular and general, high and low, the past, present, and future. Every Sunday morning the services in Homewood African Methodist Episcopal Zion Church, like ball games the same day in Westinghouse Park, initiate various levels of active participation. The preacher and choir may be the primary players, but sermon, song, prayer draw out all worshippers, rely on the entire congregation's fervor, everybody's immediate, communal response *going there, knowing there* to seek the spirit, feel the spirit, raise the spirit.

Though playground hoop offers 'buked and scorned participants an outlet for energies stifled by the mainstream, players don't thank the mainstream for providing this opportunity. Rather, playground hoop repudiates the "mainstream." Insists on separate accommodations, separate destinies. Pleasure unhinged from conventional incentives of duty, utility, responsibility. Playground hoop is a witness to the bankruptcy of America's promise of democratic equality. As popular as basketball is among Americans of African descent, we also understand basketball (and sport in general) as just one more glaring example of missed opportunities for whites to make good on the promise of equality, a promise that's been blighted over and over again by the double standard of racial prejudice. Playground hoop is partially a response to the mainstream's long, determined habit of stipulating blackness as inferiority, as a category for discarding people, letting people crash and burn, keeping them outsiders. And if that's what race means out there in the mainstream, and it surely does appear to mean all that from the point of view of an insider, here within the cage where playground ball is contested, then fuck it. Forget it. Let's start here. Keep it here. In the house. Do our thing. Enjoy the shit out of it. God *blesses* the child who got his own.

The culture of playground hoop begins at the point of experiencing, imagining zero positive connection to the mainstream, then builds, borrowing, bogarting what it needs from the common, already thoroughly creolized social environment. The process does not evolve into some essentialist "black" thing, but through amalgamation, crosscultural fertilization, bricolage, hybridity, collage, etc. builds toward self-sufficiency. Turning its back on the officially sanctioned routes of integration and assimilation, those problematic fates the mainstream grudgingly would bestow, playground hoop advocates apostasy, independence. Not the false bravado of gangster rap's simulated toughness nor Dennis Rodman's clownish tweaking of the hoop establishment, but the belligerent, radical, resolute, badass independence of Miles Davis that Quincy Troupe evokes in his memoir of the man and his music. Not leaning, not waiting. Few if any of the guys on the Village court are busting their butts because they expect someday to be rewarded with an NBA contract.

Playground hoop, like the Creole of Martinique, for instance, is a self-sufficient language. Speakers of Creole don't practice their vernacular in order to become better speakers of the island's official French dialect. Creole speakers aren't aspiring to "whiteness." Creole isn't a stopgap variety of language on its way to being some other language. Everyday speakers of Creole, as well as authors such as Martinique's Patrick Chamoiseau, winner of the Prix Goncourt, who incorporate the alternative reality of unwritable Creole orality into fiction and essays, are keeping vital a language aspiring toward goals all languages seek—expressiveness, communication, full-service functionality to name the mysteries inside and outside of us. Isolation and rejection by the mainstream may be necessary conditions for Creolized cultural production, but isolation and rejection are not sufficient to explain Creole's survival. Nor its proliferating, wondrous creativity. Nor its resilience, confidence, self-sufficiency.

Core folk culture not only generates rituals for ameliorating and surviving the daily grind, it also contains instructions for destroying the oppressor, those who turn the daily grind into a deadly struggle. Two sides of the same coin: *Fight the power.* Like any attractive folk cultural production, playground hoop is subversive because it crosses borders between margin and mainstream, and these crossings can destabilize, erode borders, eventually even abolish the distinction between mainstream and margin.

Though potentially subversive elements are the first thing culled, emasculated, cropped when mainstream (mass) culture adopts or integrates folk cultural products (Uncle Tom's welcome, not that wild buck, what's-his-name nephew), the mainstream is seldom sure what's most threatening, and when sure, confused about how to treat the threat, the love/hate ambivalence the threat often teases out. During slavery days Africans were deprived of drums because drums could communicate information African to African and leave non-Africans out of the loop. Yet drumlike percussive effects like hand-clapping or foot-stomping, as well as their structural analogues of driving, repeated beats and propulsive rhythms, have been main attractions of the African-descended music demanded and avidly consumed ever since by non-Africans, and these ingredients preserve the role of drums, continue to carry culturally specific, culturally coded messages. Appropriation of folk culture poses a paradox: how do you take over something appealing, use it, display it as your own, and simultaneously render its presence, its origins invisible. If medium and message are one, how can a medium be employed without signaling its messages.

Because its identity and integrity, its very life depends on the power to define its borders, maintain them, regulate traffic across them, the mainstream jealously guards these prerogatives. Yet the mainstream also desires controlled, sanitized access to its vital margins. De facto apartheid, economic segregation, a politicized climate that generates fear and suspicion minimize actual, everyday contact between majority and minority populations. Relations between margin and mainstream (between self and other, among layers of the self) resemble more and more, like sex with condoms, a species of virtual reality. Technologically generated and enhanced to approximate the real thing, intercourse between margins and majority is channeled into profit-driven media representations, simulations, "spectacles" in Baudrillard's sense, staged primarily by the entertainment industry. Through performing this function the entertainment industry has become, arguably, the contemporary world's most powerful, perhaps its only, industry, gradually usurping and incorporating all other businesses as it achieves a monopoly over the consuming public's "free" time and space. Colonizing all available time and space (including dream time, play time, thought space, pleasure space, as well as billboards, cereal boxes, airwaves, etc.), relentlessly penetrating, reconfiguring time and space in both private and public spheres (for instance, who owns now the quiet space around you that cell phones routinely claim and violate), the entertainment industry expands its domain.

The entertainment industry has become the archetypal riskless capitalist enterprise. A self-perpetuating system, the sow, as James Joyce said of Ireland, that feeds on its own piglets. Instead of playing, we're seduced into paying. Like the descendants of African slaves still motivated to work hard every day and accept the status quo because they've been brainwashed into believing they're on the path to "freedom." Virtual, vicarious pleasures displace good old-fashioned face-to-face encounters. No room, no time for immediate, sensuous participation and intimate immersion. Our disembodied surrogates go on vacation while we remain always-on-duty, clones of our jobs. Video games, beepers, porn on the Internet, chat rooms, portable phones, e-mail—these fabled electronic extensions of ourselves, and the humbler reassurances of received religions and ideologies, in fact incarcerate us, cyberize us, transform us to locked-down fans, voyeurs, travelers on a guided package tour that teases and beguiles us by whisking us through exotic highlights of our own bodies and lives, keeping us too busy to do much more than wonder occasionally—slightly stunned, slightly resentful and jealous—what it might be like to live here and now in this strange land of ourselves.

What once seemed intimate, private, unalienable property is curiously estranged, occupied, signposted ominously like medieval maps of terra incognito—*Dragons be there*. Our passions, enfolded within time and space that is chopped up, trademarked, cluttered, regulated, are casualties of this dispossession. Recirculated into the social economy under the sign of pleasure, commodified so we must purchase what we used to believe was a birthright, time and space unsettle us. Instead of welcoming unstructured possibility and surprise, we recoil from what appears to be a threatening, chaotic vista, simultaneously a void and brimming with our fears, yearning, hungers. The entertainment industry consolidates its power, its Prospero-like grip, by charming away this anxious dreamscape and substituting another—predictable, measured, named, disposable.

You taught me language/And my profit on it/Is, I know how to curse.

The game James Naismith invented in a Springfield, Massachusetts, YMCA Training School gym in 1891 was intended to serve as an indoor substitute for rigorous, competitive outdoor sports impractical during New England winters. Naismith's game, with its emphasis on hearty physical exercise as a means of promoting and inculcating good, clean, muscular Christian virtues, caught on immediately, spread widely and rapidly across the nation. For better or worse, the burgeoning appeal of his creation attracted not only folks who wanted to play basketball but many more who wished to watch. By 1896 a professional league had formed.

From the 1920s on, two related but distinct tracks marked basketball's development. One track documents the game's potential for maximum participation, how its unique blend of fun and demanding physicality has hooked players of all ages and levels of ability, how the game itself mutates, assuming a variety of forms to serve the needs and desires of different constituencies. The other track's about distilling from the great masses of participants a chosen few, players certified to be the very best, to perform *for pay* as entertainers. Though the first track is ritualistically celebrated in public discourse as confirmation of America's democratic ideals, it's the second track that dominates the public's imagination. Basketball has become a highly visible, successful commercial enterprise. A tightly structured corporate network controls the game's production, access, distribution, and image. Official sanctioning bureaucracies have emerged, consolidating monopolistic control of a standardized version of hoop. "Organized" ball has evolved a separate, segregated identity and destiny, removing it light-years from its origins in a YMCA gym. What once was conceived as open space for individual participation and pleasure has been "privatized." Pay displaces play, participation means watching. Basketball has been branded in two senses: stamped with a brand name and branded as the skin of cattle and slaves is burned to display who owns them.

When you're paid to play a game, a different game results, many different games dependent on the kind of payment, its scale, who's paying the players, who buys tickets to watch them play, who writes the contracts, who controls the venues for play, who sets the stakes. Playing for pay leads to the NBA, to barnstorming black professional teams like the Harlem Globetrotters, to cutthroat winner-take-all gambling matches and tournaments on ghetto courts, to fixed college games, to millionaire players, to the hypocrisy of so-called amateur college or scholastic players whose labor generates millions of dollars for corporate sponsors and advertisers.

Obviously professional basketball, school ball, amateur leagues, pickup ball, playground hoop are deeply intertwined and always have been. Just as *black* hoop and *white* hoop have always been mixed. Even while apartheid remained the league's official policy and no black bodies appeared in NBA games, the more wide-open styles—horizontally accelerated, vertically elevated, rapid passes, cuts, and ball movement—developed by African Americans in their pro leagues, college teams, club and YMCA squads, church leagues on segregated playgrounds and in segregated gyms exerted profound influence on white pros. Occasionally black teams challenged and defeated white pros in tourneys and exhibition matches. Furthermore, just as the popularity of blaxploitation films of the seventies—*Shaft* et al.— revived Hollywood with a sorely needed infusion of new cash and new urban audiences, during the NBA's cash-strapped, no-blacks-allowed, fledgling days, team owners, to pump up gate receipts, begged the crowd-pleasing, seat-filling Harlem Globetrotters and New York Renaissance to play exhibition games before otherwise poorly attended league matches.

Documenting basketball's history, especially its segregated existence, the often ironic, secret, surprising, shameful, illuminating relationship between African-American and mainstream hoop, is a necessary, crucial endeavor, a job that sorely needs doing, but it's not the story I'm going to tell here, now. Suffice to say one way playground hoop distinguishes itself from other varieties of basketball is by carrying forward the emphasis on democratic, inclusive, grass-roots participation, on play for its own sake. For pleasure. Play without pay. Except, except as Mr. Naismith divined, play in the form of rigorous, demanding team competition teaches and preaches, instills many virtues as you work hard at it. Yet the game remains, like virtue itself, its own best reward.

Has it taken me this long to figure out again that the deepest, simplest subject of this hoop book is pleasure, the freeing, outlaw pleasure of play in a society, a world that's on your case to shape up, line up, shut up from the moment you emerge squalling, shivering, culture-shocked from the most comfortable playground, pleasure dome you'll ever inhabit: Mom. From that stunned exit when the body's nearly perfect fit with its environment ends, we're plunged into an unceasing tug of war. Voices yell at us to become social beings, to internalize the rationalizations, appreciate the compensations of delayed gratification. Tell us to ignore the body's discomforts, its inconveniences. Say, don't whine about alienation. No big deal that the body becomes a stranger to itself, that it forgets what once made it happy.

Then the tug of other, oppositional voices—mine, here, for instance, proclaiming that pleasure is knowledge and knowledge pleasure, and don't you ever let anybody tell you different. Don't allow anyone to steal your body or rent, buy, disembody, tame, virtualize, shrink, organize, defang it. Don't let anyone stand between you and your body or stand in for your body by disciplining the kind and quality of experience it should seek. Even if you can't go home again to the wondrous place elsewhere from whence you arrived, that site of pleasure and contentment doesn't exactly disappear forever, either. In this tug of war contesting who owns you, playground hoop's fun confirms at least two simple facts: you have choices only when you seize them; there's time to play only when you play.

Meanwhile, back on the corner of 6th Avenue and Houston, as he intends, given the show he puts on with every inflection of his body, every riff of trash talk, every emotion he pantomimes, laying it on thick with broad, exaggerated strokes like actors in silent films so nobody misses the point, one short, extremely quick guard rivets Catherine's attention. A satiny blue do-rag wraps his head, and the man's endowed with the arm-length-to-body-height ratio of an orangutan. Exploiting his gifts of speed and reach, he can beam more of himself faster to wherever he and the other players want to go, so he dominates the game. On defense he seldom bothers to guard anyone in particular, just shadows the ball and often steals sloppy passes, converting his thefts to easy, breakaway lay-ups. On offense if the ball's not in his hands he flies to where it is and demands it. His signature move a low, slashing burst toward the basket almost slamming into the chest of the man guarding him, freezing the defender, forcing him backward onto his heels, then the do-rag guy straightens from his low-slung crouch to sample a stand-still Chubby Checker twist, both long arms extended behind him as if he's whipping an invisible towel side to side, furiously drying his back and butt, except what he's really doing is patting the basketball low and fast, tiny detonations on the asphalt, the ball almost as invisible as the towel, as the six-inch yoyo string controlling the ball, pat-pat-pat, as it skips between his legs, behind his back, cross over and under, right, left, in, out, up, back, pat-pat-pat how many times a second while his shoulders feint, rocking one way, head the other, hips another, the syncopated, staccato drumming of the ball a baseline for the separate rhythms of his body, the fake moves, real moves blurring, the ball's thump stitching the whole multimetered performance together as he poises, gathers himself, revving up momentum for a final thrust to the rack, down and dirty again, past the bewildered defender still frozen in his tracks.

His drive to the hoop part serious business, part mesmerizing razzle-dazzle like the flying rags of shoeshine boys, the airborne hand jive of three-card monte hustlers over their little handkerchief-covered, folding tables on the tracks of Harlem and Times Square. Now you see it, now you don't. Guess where. C'mon. Try your luck, baby. Yeah. Shiny and pretty, ain't it, babe. Now show me some money, honey. Huh-uh. No-no. Too late. Guess again, sweets. Sucker. The drive also determined, fearless, powered by a body seasoned for years by the specific demands and stresses of the playground game, ropy muscled shoulders, arms, and torso bump opponents out of his path, protect his stuttering, skittering dribble dashes into a crowd, stumpy legs, their power evident even camouflaged in baggy sweatpants precariously drooped to the crack of his ass, steel-thighed to launch him, buy him hang time, up, under, around, and over maneuvering time, so he glides past the hoop and flips the ball back over his shoulder or brakes in midair and arcs it high over a taller player's hand to kiss soft off the perforated metal backboard into the iron rim, its wisp of chain skirt.

I'm impressed too, in a fashion. Say so to amen Catherine's excitement. Then I find myself needing to qualify. Complain. Yes, an extraordinary display. The little fella can do it. Uh-huh. He possesses the kind of refined skills and rare natural gifts and flair for expressing them that's showcased by NBA ads to sell its product. So what. What's most of that flim-flam have to do with the game. You could say that the NBA, with its hunger for fans, its hunger for a few cash cow Hollywood-style icons, for circuslike spectacle, its preening self-congratulation, its micromanagement of every aspect of the game, its up-close-and-personal moments of corny sentiment, its accountant's steely eye for squeezing every penny out of every hustling enterprise stamped with the league's logo — you could argue it all fosters a pay-trumps-play, cartoon version of basketball ultimately destructive for players and the game.

Is the guy with the flashy do-rag crowning his skull exhibiting *showmanship* (profiling, styling his play to enhance and personalize the action, make it more fun, more challenging, more impressive, while not interfering with, maybe even forwarding, the purpose of the game: to provide an opportunity for ten people to work hard, work well at winning, consciously respectful of the game's traditions) or showboating (calling attention to himself as if the game's only about him, about accumulating his individual style points, damn the score, the game, everybody else on the court now, yesterday, or whenever).

What seems to count in this Village game we're watching is each solo, not the dynamics, not the dramatic synchronicity of five players on a team interacting. The action freezes each time the ball winds up in a different person's hands. Everybody else stands and looks. Waits. Players become spectators like us. Each player when it's his turn performs a little fancy-stepping, fancy-dribbling soliloquy, attempting to beat his defender and penetrate for a lay-up or liberate enough space to rise and fling up a jumper. The rhythm of the game herky-jerky, stop-and-go, predictable, boring doggerel about nothing important. Superficial in-and-out, stop-and-go. No deep, sweet, abiding, exploding, many-places-at-once, layered, lyric flow.

Maybe I just don't like the do-rag man. His cocky expression, his smirks and putdowns, the attitudes he expresses with florid body language. His playing to the grandstand. Or maybe it's as visceral as not approving of the guy's physique. Or could I be jealous. Of Catherine's attention. Of the fact he's out there and I'm not. Am I letting him distract me for no good reason at all, anything better than falling again into those places haunted by so much loss, so much pain and love.

Whatever's rubbing me the wrong way nasties up my voice and when I hear myself whining, judging, I'm bothered, a little ashamed. Realize I'm acting like an old man the action has passed by, fussing with the poor guy, fussing at the game. Am I mad simply because playground hoop has changed. Different now from what it was before, when it was *my* game. Is that what's annoying me. Is that why I'm worried about the balloony, nearly ankle-length shorts. Cornrowed hair. The ritualized extremes of self-congratulation, the ceremonial duels of dismissive, demeaning, confrontational trash talk.

Have I forgotten how it works. This game's rawness, the roughness, what's unfamiliar, what goes against the grain may, of course, be exactly those areas where a new generation of players are pushing the boundaries. Claiming ownership of unnamed, unexplored territory. The no-man's-land of innovation and/or loss old-timers and youngbloods will always contest in heated discussions on and off the court, because the game changes. Must change as it's always changed. Or die. Playground hoop birthing itself again and again in the flexing margins, turf no one owns.

I back off from my critique of the game we're seeing on a cramped Village court, stop my badmouthing of the guy wearing a silk bandanna to cover his hair. What is this man's playing telling me about his life. My life. What might he be saying that I don't want to hear. What truth about him. About myself. The game. Our tangled lives in these daunting, unhinged, uneasy, challenging days and times. I try to see what's going on with fresh eyes. Catherine's, for instance. So for the little time left I shut up and watch and listen. Remember.

A long-legged stringbean, six-foot-seven, very dark, one of the best quarter-milers in the state, Cook, who also played basketball for Fifth Avenue, Pittsburgh's blackest high school, located in the just about 100 percent black Hill district, wore the best stuff to the outdoor courts. In the middle fifties on the playground *best* didn't mean earlier versions of today's expensive, miracle fabric, logo-splashed athletic gear. Cook wore pants and shirts from the Claypoole Shoppe, the exclusive menswear boutique of Kaufmann's, an upscale downtown department store. If you passed him on the street, you'd think Cook on his way to party not to hoop. And in a way you'd be right. The playground then as now about party and display. Display as in Carnival, good time, let-it-all-hang-out showtime. And party as in Carnival. Carnival as it's been practiced from the sixteenth century on, all over this "New World" hemisphere anywhere significant populations of African-descended immigrants have settled. Carnival signifying masking, pageants, costumes, processions, parades, music, dance, news, gossip, satire, parody, mockery, syncretizing of sacred and profane, coronations of kings and queens, fancy dress, fancy stepping, elaborate balls, turnabout or reversal or suspension of normal social roles and rules, the sometimes forbidden, sometimes hesitant, sometimes riotously abandoned participation of all social classes and "races," a break or temporary nullification and unplugging of the linear, quotidian clock to acknowledge other ways of figuring time, keeping time, deferring to time, to the cycle of seasons, to Great Time, play time, where many worlds, many orders of beings mingle, converge — ancestors, spirits, immortals, the living and dead—the mythic time of origins, gods and goddesses, storytime.

You could call going to hoop at the playground going to Carnival since so many salient attributes of Carnival are mirrored in playground hoop, a number of which I've briefly identified and described, but plenty of others still await closeup, detailed, scrupulously analytic, and imaginative study by scholars dedicated to continuing the task I've only just begun in this book: to demonstrate how sport is art and, like any other African-American art form, expresses and preserves, if you teach yourself how to look, the deep structure, both physical (material) and metaphysical (immaterial), of a culture.

We won't even begin here to delve into the headgear, warmup suits, beads, rings, glasses, chains, shoes, mean rides, fine ladies, the retinue of homeys young brothers adorn themselves with in a Carnival spirit of extravagant, sumptuous, elegant, fecund, over-the-top possibility and presence. Just take one item, for instance, for a brief minute—basketball shorts. Of course basketball shorts would be longs in Cook's case since he hooped in slacks. And long is high fashion again today. The myriad bright colors and kinds of shorts reflect Carnival's plenitude, its festive air. Taken a step further, shorts are costumes, in some cases part of a complete body mask. NBA lookalikes in full-drag masquerade parade their official, authentic team regalia bearing their favorite star's number, the whole kit exact in every detail. Then there are carefully coordinated or mix-and-matched tops and bottoms, a team jersey and ragged cutoffs, or nostalgic, old school, shorty shorts (like Utah's John Stockton's) proclaiming, All you guys out here in those damned bloomers look like fools, but I'm serious, or swim trunks, or Bermuda shorts, long sweats, baggy hip-hop jeans (Hey, I'm so bad I can do this shit in my street clothes), etc., a vast array not simply of fashion statements but of assertions of possibility—of possible personae, possible values and affiliations that bottoms topped or topless can express.

How shorts are worn just as significant, as rooted in the practices of Carnival, as which shorts you pick to display and display you. Carnival nothing if not erotic politics, a site for celebrating and contesting the body's overarching, primal power to attract attention and desire. Body's on display, yes, but also an embodied discourse about who owns bodies, who controls them. Shorts reveal and cover skin. The color of bared skin itself unveils the secret erotic history of *liaisons,* of crossing-over, time out of mind, between Africans and Europeans. A rainbow of naked skin resplendent during Carnival and on the court tells a different story from the official narratives of difference, of separate destinies, apartheid, segregation, of legal, moral, aesthetic, and *natural* barriers between the so-called races.

The issue of how much skin is shown could be embedded in the context of fashion but also adumbrates, resonates, in the sphere of body politics. Did basketball players at some point simply become physically uncomfortable competing in skimpier and skimpier, tight-in-the-torso, crotch-hugging scholastic, college, and pro uniforms (weren't these snug little outfits vaguely contemporaneous with hot pants and miniskirts). Did styles begin to change, fuller, longer, blousier, purely for comfort's sake or perhaps also because players (like women) decided they wished more say about how much or how little they wore in public and decided to wrest control from whoever dictated overexposure, whoever's gaze they were obliged to entertain. Who other than skin's possessor should mandate the skin–material ratio, determine how much is displayed, to whom, when, where, and how.

A new day dawned of more and more cover, more fabric in each pair of hoop shorts, then lo and behold, players started wearing their long shorts lower and lower on their hips. Peek-a-boo. I see you beholding me. And yes, I'm still in here, my fine bod, my skin. Long shorts slung so low the cracks of players' asses peek out, or their underwear, the colorful boxers from an earlier stage, when basketball shorts were shorter and boxers stuck out like a slip below a dress, symbolically extending a player's shorts, shorts laughing at shorts, decorating them, compromising them, also covering up more leg, preparation for the next stage when hoop shorts lengthened past the knee and their bottom edge began to approach the ankle.

So up and down, the *you see me I see you we see each other seeing each other* polymorphous playfulness of bodies at Carnival. Exposure both enticement and a sign of pride of ownership. Separation and desire. Control of the body's power. Self-possession. Sharing. Daring. Seduction. Uncovering here while covering there, the sliding scale, up and down, now-you-see-it-now-you-don't play of a feather fan, a flounced dress, hoop shorts on streamlined, hoop-playing legs.

And if you care to go further, what about the relationship of XXX outsize—huge contemporary hoop shorts or the zoot suit's extravagant enveloping—to a body inside that's symbolically shrunken, perhaps even infantilized by too-big garments, a kid lost, buried inside, who needs a parent to dress him or her in something other than ragmuffin, Orphan Annie, Big Sis, Big Bro's cast-off, castaway clothes. A message of dependency, of missing TLC, of lost and needful. Are we still searching for a Big Daddy, dressing to attract him, mimic him, *be* him in our large duds. Costumes of court and Carnival present layered meanings, dramatize mixed messages. Are court and Carnival joyful reversions to childlike innocence, spontaneity. Are they mini-rebellions, practice for dismantling the status quo. Or do they defuse rebellion. Are they radical cries for independence or conservative nostalgia. Matched hoop tops and bottoms signify uniform and uniform brings to mind the idea of teams and teams are cooperative groups, little clubs, bands, miniature societies signifying working together, unity, competition, and that leads to the gorgeously luxuriant matched costumes of the *tribes* and *nations* so crucial to organizing Carnival, keeping alive its roots in ancient African ritual.

But now, as promised, let's leave the masks of playground

demeanor, the minidramas performed by storytellers on the sidelines, the ancestor worship of former great players, their evocation and return in the bodies of new stars, the bartering of goods and services, the stylized kinesics, the dancing, the music of boom boxes and bongos, the courting, etc., etc., for other observer/participants to explore.

Forty years ago, for my age set, wearing expensive articles of street clothing on the court was calculated transgression. Something we understood we weren't supposed to be able to get away with, but we could, so we did. Maybe none of us would have explained it as such—as transgression—but I believe we knew exactly what we were doing, knew why Cook arrived to play in clothes none of us could afford. Of course Cook couldn't afford them either except by way of the five-finger discount extended to him by highly organized gangs of boosters operating out of the Hill district who systematically pillaged the best stores downtown. If you knew the right people, you could custom-order your shit from the boosters—give them your measurements, specify style, color, material of the desired garment. Not all of us on the playground equally connected with the boosters and not everybody dressed like Cook but we all got off on his example. What he practiced we copied to the degree our wardrobes, wallets, and ingenuity allowed. Cook spoke to us. For us. Not only did he snatch what he wanted from the best white stores downtown—the clothing we weren't supposed to be able to afford, clothes white people displayed in spaces semirestricted, saturated with signs of race and class exclusivity, clothes tended by white clerks and floorwalkers, paid to exhibit nasty, prejudiced attitudes, clothes from stores whose intimidating prices and foreign decor were calculated to make us feel uncomfortable if we dared enter them, uh-huh—well, Charley grabbed the best shit from those exclusive temples, then wore it to Homewood or the Hill, our spaces, where we watched him run up and down the court, publicly, disdainfully destroying it. Insult added to the original injury inflicted on folks who clearly didn't like us any more than we liked them, people whose everyday casual mistreatment of us we could every now and then, symbolically mostly, get away with returning in spades. Payback. In your face. Carnival.

Why that long, tall Sally fool out there tearing up good clothes. You youngbloods crazy, boy. Right on. Exactly. No. Cook certainly didn't behave normally, but in his canny, silent assassin fashion he also fucked with the norms. We knew it and loved it. Imitated him when and as best we could, him and others like him with their hands deep in the cookie jar. Copied the idea behind the act, anyway, so we could exclaim without saying a word, Here's what we really think of your shit, nice and expensive as it is, good as we look in it, as much as it suits us better than it suits you, you know you don't look half as good as me in this button-down collar bleeding madras plaid shirt and these ivy-league tiny-belt-in-the-back khakis I'm about to play in, sweat in, stain, rip, throw away cause it don't mean a thing, ain't nothing to me, got more and better at home, uh-huh, uh-huh. Nothing but a party out here. And I'm dressed for it, ain't I. Sharp as a tack. Looking good. Go on with your bad self, Mr. Cook.

Split high in the crotch so his upper body like a lean lollipop on long sticks, Cook ate up the quarter mile with high-kneed strides, and by the homestretch turn those knobby knees just about hitting his chest as he galloped out of the pack of other runners into the last thirty yards or so of the race. Everybody in the stands whooping and carrying on, and he'd start imitating his ownself, chop, chop, chop, knees almost to his chin now, a drum major's bobbing, high-kicking strut across the finish line.

To resist being ripped off and redirected, to escape being kidnapped and whitewashed by the mainstream, playground hoop like all cultural practices at the margins engages in a constant struggle to reinvent itself, pump out new vibrations, new media and messages of yea-saying, saying loudly, clearly, *Yes.* We're here, still here, and we're human, we're beautiful. Look at us. Through the steel bars, the wire, the walls. Look if you dare. If you're able to keep up with our flashing feet, flashing hands. We're looking at ourselves and we like lots of what we see. And see the rest too. The cages. The frightening rest. The hurting rest.

The enormous fecundity of core folk culture a testament to its will to survive, its determination to generate its own terms for survival, to speak in tongues articulating, protecting these hard-earned terms. *Next. Who got next.*

Not today, good brother. Not today on this Village court. But I'll be back.

Naming the Playground

How shall I see thee through my tears.

ONE DAY we might rebuild and rename the basketball court behind Homewood school. Name it in honor of Maurice Stokes or Ed Fleming or Chuck Cooper perhaps, all three great players who grew up in Homewood and went on to distinguish themselves and the game, in college and as professionals at the highest levels of competition. It would be a fine day, a long overdue day of proper glory and tribute and legacy embodied in those names and the naming, and such a transforming of the park would be appropriate, but also inadequate because it leaves out too much. I'd be happy and proud to see that fine day come, but also wistful because I'm pretty sure in the discussions of what the court should be called no one would have suggested L.D.'s name. On the naming day would anyone miss him, Eldon Lawson, or his court handle L.D., yet the court belongs to him too. A stage for King Lawson's rise and fall. Because yes, for a day he was king. And if you don't believe me, you could have asked L.D. and received the whole story from the king's lips, but it's too late now, the king is dead. So I'll ask my brother Rob instead. My brother pushed a legless, shrinking L.D. into the prison yard on his wheelchair throne and listened like the rest of the crowd L.D. always drew. A tough crowd not believing much of what L.D. proclaimed, but damn, if the big, stuttering, cripple-ass, candy-sucking dude couldn't tell some lies.

The court belonged to L.D. and hundreds, thousands of

other anonymous players who, according to most people's standards, didn't do shit with their lives. Played, got too beat up or too old to play, maybe hung around on the sidelines awhile, talking that trash, sipping wine, a toke on the occasional circulating spliff or sitting quiet off by themselves the way some do, almost invisible, staring at the game sometimes, sometimes at nothing anyone else can see, just hanging, or show up at the court a couple times over the years for hugs, grins, skin, *How you doin, home, You lookin good, bro,* till they pop in and no one pops up, no one remembers, the regulars hanging, others sometimey, some away a year or a long, long time nobody needs to ask where because you see in a face it was a bad place, bad time, and who needs to hear about it, someone you'd forgotten gets mentioned or nobody mentions anymore one you often recall, till each player disappears, back into the limbo from whence he'd come. And wasn't that the court's story too. Its many stories, many names. What it might be called the day we get around to choosing a better name.

A well-told story recites something's name. Every word of the story part of the name, a necessary part of a unique, complicated something unsayable in any fashion except the story's exact words, their sound, sequence, sense, suggestiveness. A good story does not simply label or reduce something complex, it expands, spins out possibilities, presents new information, poses more questions than answers with every word it contains. A story expresses the unique name of something, doesn't try to explain something.

The words of a story perform a ritual of song and dance to summon a spirit, give substance and body to something that until the act of composition hovers nameless, unnamable, something vital and present even though it inhabits an immaterial dimension, a something unfolding that seizes the writer's attention and compels the writing, the saying, the suffering, the praising of its name.

Stories place you in the presence of something perhaps experienced before, but since not named, in a sense unrecognized, though mysteriously tangible like the painful throbbing an amputated limb leaves behind in the space it once occupied.

When an accomplished storyteller ends his narrative (the very best never end, coil like the sacred python, twisting back upon itself, mouth swallowing tail, tail birthing mouth), you've felt what a calling forth, a saying of a particular name summons, felt what happens to a summoner, felt what it's like for the characters in the story to hear and learn the unexpected presence of something impossible to experience except as it has been delivered, enacted word by word. Something as plain as day so once you see it you say, touched as people are by déjà vu, Of course, it's been there all along, once you hear its name.

A story is something's name recited, but a story isn't a name. No more than you are your name. Stories are a summoning. A seeking. Just as we can innocently invoke the whole history of a word by uttering it, another person, whether he's well acquainted with you or not, saying your name to your lover can call you forth, bring to bear an entire, unsayable, one-of-a-kind history-in-progress that's embedded, layered, in your name. Word by word, compressing time, opening time, a story identifies something total, never more than partially understood by the one hearing, the one telling.

It also seems to be true that certain people's names carry the force of a story. Recite stories. It's difficult to hear or say the names without being aware of specific facts, in a familiar pattern. Certain people's names are their stories. Mandela. Sojourner. Martin. When we repeat the name we're bearing witness to an indelible, inevitable parable residing in the public domain. Some names leak glory, but often names also leak tears, especially when the names are drawn from the history of African peoples in the New World. *Malcolm.* Tears and more tears till the ground beneath our feet is as wet and slippery as those cobbled alleys behind slaughterhouses in colonial Philadelphia.

How shall I see thee through my tears is a question asked by Ismene, the second daughter of Oedipus, when she finds her father and sister, Antigone, at the gates of Colonus, the city where the old, blind king is seeking sanctuary but once more has found himself rejected, a question sung by Jevetta Steele in a musical version of the ancient Greek legend. *The Gospel at Colonus* is one of the few live shows I've seen on Broadway. In 1988 I was collaborating with Frank Pearson on a screenplay of *Brothers and Keepers,* a book I'd written about my relationship with my youngest brother, Robby, who's serving a life sentence in a Pittsburgh prison, and Frank, a financial backer of the Oedipus production, treated Judy, my wife, and me to dinner and a premier performance of the show.

The show stunned me, shook me up. One number, "A Voice Foretold," renders Oedipus's prayer for sanctuary, and I've listened to a recording of it many times since for the pure pleasure of the music as the voices of Clarence Fountain and the Five Blind Boys of Alabama wring every ounce of harmony, rhythm, emotion from the song, and listened just as often when I needed to be reminded of the possibility, if not the promise, that trouble, even the kind no one sees the end of, don't last always. Maybe the fact my imprisoned brother was so much on my mind set me up to be overwhelmed by master gospel singers, by the uncompromising lyrics of Greek tragedy, the homeless, beaten-down old king wandering the land like a ghost, seeking a place to rest in peace, a place to shelter him from the demons of his past pursuing him, the terrible story of his name. By that time my brother had been incarcerated nearly fifteen years, and attempting to retell his story on the screen would be one more effort to secure sanctuary for him. Ideally, if Frank Pearson and I told Robby's story right and anybody bothered to listen, they'd understand enough was enough. Robby had repented, suffered for his crime. He'd been there, an accomplice in a botched scam, but he hadn't killed anyone. Nothing useful would be gained by more punishment. More revenge would not restore the victim to life. Clearly my brother posed no threat to society. He'd paid and learned. Learned and paid. He could be a force for good. Yearned for an opportunity to continue outside the walls work he discovered he could do well inside: talk to young men like he'd once been, young guys a corrupt social order was breeding in frighteningly increasing numbers, outcast, desperate, dangerous to themselves and others. It was time, way past time to set Robby free, lay to rest the furies dogging him, settle the spirit of the young man murdered in a holdup fifteen years, before, quiet the unflagging demand for more blood, more vengeance plaguing the victim's family, plaguing the legal system's dispensing of justice.

But it was not only Robby's face bleeding through the mask of the Greek king's ravaged features. First, unbelievably, unaccountably, unless our family too had been cursed like the dying old king's, there was my youngest son, also in prison, condemned at sixteen to a life sentence for murder. And then, all across the nation, drug wars, turf wars, and the plain, gruesome stupidity of having nothing better to do were driving young African-American men to kill each other, destroy themselves. I mourned them all, mourned our seeming powerlessness as a people when the despairing king lamented *Oedipus is not the strength he once was.* And when he invoked the *sweet children of original darkness,* I understood he was addressing those fearsome, pitiless deities who arrange men's fate, but wasn't he also calling out our name, because who were we—me, my sisters and brothers—if not refugees from the primal darkness of Africa's womb, her sweet original children orphaned in a strange land, stolen, lost, strayed, no place to run, no rock to hide our face, no sanctuary.

I brought such thoughts to *The Gospel at Colonus,* and looking back, no doubt for some tastes, maybe even mine, the emotions, the parallels, the rhetoric appear strained, untidy, but I feel no need to apologize or rationalize or temper my reactions to the play. If I stop today, this very moment, hesitate at the gates of any great city in this nation, pause like the fallen king paused outside the gates of Colonus, stare like him, blind and far-seeing like him, like all human beings, look backward, forward, inside, outside, 360 degrees all around, recapitulating, rehearsing, naming my story, our story, where it's been, where it seems to be going, I perceive the same demons and furies that pillaged one kingdom—the Old World civilizations of Africa—pursuing us still, wreaking more havoc in these new, famished hives of steel and glass and plastic where the progeny of those ancient African societies struggle to create meaningful lives. We've been divided from each other and from ourselves, and the divisions within have come closer to conquering us than any invading oppressor. The years in the prisonhouse of race mount, exact their toll. Yet here we are, still strong. Hope's strong. Evil continues to dog us, but we won't surrender to it. Tomorrow we'll knock down the walls. Tomorrow in Jerusalem.

At the gate there's a quiet moment when the horrors of the past are also the road, the only road, our road, our intimate history, our loves and losses bringing us to this moment, a moment when we can decide to go forward or not, and we must realize that choice is still in our hands despite and because of everything we have survived. And as I look back at my life I understand in a flash that recovering the past is claiming the past and survival is always a complex fugue of rising and falling, of good and bad, and that's the music of anyone's life, there is no other way, so in this moment of dreaming in an instant the story of what brought us here to the city gate, dreaming and naming, I can't help both smiling and almost tearing up at the same time as I recall the whole long crazy road, remember what the passage cost. Both then, yes and no, poised at the entrance to the city where once again we'll seek sanctuary, gather strength so we're ready for the next step and next and next, the way forward blurred by a mix of grief and joy, the anguish and astonishment at being spared to reach this moment, the surprising, not quite unhappy tears. *How shall we see thee.*

What inventor/industrialist George Westinghouse thought of people of African descent, I do not know, and largely do not care, except if he was a man of his times (1846–1914) or for that matter a man of these times, his attitudes toward African Americans would have been at best contradictory and vexed, at worst appalling, so the existence of a park and basketball court still freighted with his name in a contemporary African-American community presents problems. Some credit, honor, and gratitude are due to Mr. Westinghouse, since he philanthropically bequeathed a parcel of land (once the site of his private train stop) to the city of Pittsburgh for a public park. For simplicity's sake and perhaps for the sake of Mr. Westinghouse's reputation and posterity, we won't attempt to explore his opinions about race or ask how the land he generously donated to the city came to be his in the first place. We'll leave those matters to other inquiries, let them slumber on a while longer as we sleep the deep sleep of denial that continues to insulate us from the unpleasant facts of our history, the predatory capitalism, apartheid, the hierarchies based on class and gender and ethnicity, the gradual turning away from the founding ideals of a Declaration of Independence, a Constitution, and a Bill of Rights toward governmental institutions and practices that empower the rich at the expense of the poor, protect the interests of the haves by disenfranchising, marginalizing, the have-nots.

I'm not suggesting we should return the park or the nation to sender. Even if the idea appeals to me, there's no place, no way really to send them, except up in smoke, and we've tried that before, in the sixties, and found fire's often satisfying but no solution. Point is the court's here, it's been ours a long while, we shouldn't have much difficulty finding a name more appropriate, less challenging than George Westinghouse's for it. Let's simply assume the prerogatives of Homewood's earliest European settlers. Once they'd arrived and occupied a place, as far as they were concerned, the place possessed no name, no name they were required to learn or respect anyway. They borrowed or made up new names, tagged everything willy-nilly as if the land were virgin territory, uninhabited by history, language, culture until their arrival. Since we've displaced them as the land's latest squatters and become what at first they never were, an overwhelming numerical majority, we don't have to depend on anyone's approval of what we decide to call the park. We'll call it what we wish to call it, and the park will answer to what comes out of our mouths. We've always cultivated a special way of saying things that empowers us by altering what words mean. With our systematic, culturally devised pronunciations and rhythming of standard English words and phrases, we've been renaming, rebaptizing, giving birth to ourselves and alternative realities since we were kidnapped to these shores five hundred years ago, kidnapped and dispossessed of our ancient lands and languages. The struggle continues. We're still formulating new and better names for things, for ourselves, and, more significantly, learning to make them stick. Teaching others to listen. Teaching others it's in their best interest to pay attention to what we're saying, hear what we call ourselves, call our world in our stories. Hear the names they need to know us by. Unlike the names given to us to silence our voices, the names we give ourselves will open the possibility of conversations across so-called racial lines by dynamiting the lines.

Anyway, here's a new name for the park and hoop court behind the school, up by the tracks in Homewood: *Maurice Stokes Memorial Playground*. It's not the entire name I'm going to suggest, but let's begin here, with this portion of the name, the easy part, since Mr. Stokes, "Big Mo," is unobjectionable on most counts anybody sane would count. Maurice Stokes a Homewood boy, college All-American, NBA Rookie of the Year, and three-time All-Star, league-leading rebounder ('56–'57), a player whose talent and gifts were so prodigious it seemed the racist sea of the recently "integrated" (a handful) NBA might just sneak open for this negro man's passage to the promised land of super-stardom. In that era, Stokes, at six-foot-eight, 260 pounds, was a legitimate big man and so good, so overpowering, that watch-ing him play could change your idea of the kind of game basket-ball could become if lots of men his size and even bigger played the sport seriously—quick, smart, graceful men who could shoot, rebound, dribble, pass, control a game from their for-ward or center position by utilizing the skills, hoop knowledge, and instincts seemingly, up to that point in the game's progress, monopolized by small, flashy back-court specialists. The ap-pearance of big men like Stokes offered a glimpse of basketball's bright future, upped the ante of the new NBA venture. Like box-ing's larger-than-life heavyweights, wouldn't agile, mobile, thor-oughbred giants battling on the hoop court attract fans in droves, wouldn't big men with their thunder, power, and intimi-dating presence, like boxing's kings, earn enormous purses and accumulate fame, glamour, notoriety.

Clearly Maurice Stokes, star of the Cincinnati Royals, was the future. Unfortunately, on the last night of the 1957–1958 regular season, in an away game against the Minneapolis Lak-ers, somebody got tangled up in Maurice Stokes's legs while Stokes was airborne. Big Mo, suddenly, helplessly out of con-trol, landed hard, very hard, and lay prostrate on the floor sev-eral minutes until other players assisted him to the bench.

Pro basketball a meaner, rawer sport then, still partly proud of, partly embarrassed by its roughhouse, bare-knuckle origins in the 1920s when rope netting or steel cages segregated fans from players, an often futile measure to prevent bloody melees on the court from migrating into the stands or vice versa. (Though the practice of caging games gradually disappeared, *cagers* as a name for basketball players has stuck.) A cursory examination of old-timers' reminiscences from the fifties would establish the physical, no-holds-barred nature of the pro game.

Racism also more vicious and blatant. Fans and players knew the St. Louis Hawks, the NBA franchise located geographically farthest south, prided itself as the South's team, with all the bad news that title portended for players of color, but throughout the entire league, and this fact again readily verifiable in recorded narratives of former players and coaches, racism inflicted its heavy toll.

Just exactly what happened to Maurice Stokes that winter night in Minneapolis, how it happened, why it happened, whether the accident was purely accidental, whether it was motivated by any conscious desire to maim him or punish his color, his talent, his growing dominance of the league, who can say, except maybe the one who cut Maurice Stokes's legs out from under him. Was it a single person or many bodies colliding. And would any player understand the deep, complex roots of the ancient animosities motivating a split-second decision. If a Laker purposely undercut Stokes, could he have meant to inflict lifelong paralysis. Or was the hit intended only as a warning, a little nudging forget-me-not. Or maybe a hard hit not to permanently injure, just to remind Stokes who's in charge, a not-so-gentle, scary, intentionally intimidating message at the end of one season to be carried over into the next, letting this high-flying black stud know that his well-being and livelihood depend on the good will, the good graces, restraint, and tolerance of the most pedestrian white player. Maybe the attacker changed his mind halfway through the assault but couldn't stop, couldn't reverse direction, so became a victim also of the accident. Acutely aware of his own vulnerability second by second every game, would any sane player, out on the court where anyone might witness the act, dare to assault and risk seriously harming another player.

According to others it was a rough game that night. How rough. Weren't they all rough, physical games, and given prevailing attitudes in the culture at large and in the subculture of sport, games would have been predictably, measurably harder on players of color. On any night, a ball game, like weather, can quickly, drastically deteriorate, assume an ugly, threatening, lethal mood. Long-standing grudges, the fatigue of constant travel, old wounds and body aches, a personal slump, a team's jaunty winning or miserable losing streak, difficulties off court, a meager crowd, an overflow, rowdy, hostile crowd, too much partying with teammates the night before, dissension, not being paid on time or enough when you are paid, the grumps and whining self-centeredness, selfishness, and disdain for less talented others endemic to pampered pro athletes, their competitive fire, pride, anger, jealousy, insecurity, the general disillusionment when the incentive is pay not play—any or all of these can ferment into a toxic brew as thick and pungent as the funk of the other teams' unwashed uniforms smacking you in the face when you step onto the hardwood.

Was it that kind of night, predictable at the end of the season when all the promise of starting out fresh has soured, when reality for most players is a tacky, mediocre stat sheet irreversibly, unforgivingly inscribed in black and white, box scores recording as many defeats as wins. A night when the coach's exhortation to give up your battered body one more time rings hollow. For what. What's at stake. Third place. A tie for first place in the second division. Number two when preseason everybody touted you as number one. One more outing, one more grueling combat mission when your body's running on empty and the enemy you're about to engage has proven on many previous occasions capable of seriously kicking your ass.

One of those nights people get lynched. And what was the guy thinking, if you can call it thinking, as he tackled Maurice Stokes in midair. Was it a coincidence that this large, darker presence, this man who rebound by rebound, point by point, game by game exerted his will over other men, demonstrating unequivocally his superiority in the sport of basketball over white men whose equal he could not claim to be, according to the laws and customs of his country, in almost any arena other than a sports arena, was it just a matter of luck, bad karma, that this man Maurice Stokes wound up unconscious, flat on his back, dramatically, violently cut down to size.

I'd heard it was an accidental fall that ended Maurice Stokes's career. The fall and encephalitis (brain fever) developing as a result of the fall. Or heard a mosquito blamed. A family affair—one displaced African immigrant, the tsetse fly, catching up with another displaced African, transmitting with bite and suck the African scourge "sleeping sickness."

Here are some of the undisputed facts. Still groggy and out of sorts, Maurice Stokes traveled by train from Minneapolis to Detroit the day after the fall for a first-round playoff game. He participated (twelve points, fifteen rebounds) in a losing effort but not with his usual commanding presence and fire. On the flight home to Cincinnati he complained to teammate Dick Ricketts—Ricketts, along with Sihugo Green and Jim Tucker, boyhood heroes of mine from the glory days of Pittsburgh's Duquesne University Dukes, whose games I listened to at night, my ear as close to inside the radio as I could lean—*Dick, every bone in my body pains me. I feel like I'm going to die.* Sicker and sicker during the flight, Stokes finally lost consciousness. Though an ambulance rushed him from the airport to a hospital, he never recovered. He lay in a coma for six days, regained consciousness, but spent the remainder of his life bedridden, unable to speak, languishing for twelve years till he died on April 6, 1970. His family and friends attest to Maurice Stokes's courage, dignity, his good humor and determination to make the best of an impossible situation, his refusal till the day he died to allow the terrible night in Minnesota to crush his spirit totally. Jack Twyman, a fellow Royal and Pittsburgher who'd driven with Ed Fleming and Maurice Stokes from Pittsburgh to upstate New York when all three were embarking on their rookie seasons in the NBA, became his friend's financial guardian and steady supporter, raising money, generously devoting time and energy throughout the course of Maurice Stokes's ordeal.

I'd encountered the general outline of the story above in a variety of sources, including a movie (*Maurie*, 1973), then *Big Mo* on TV, starring Bernie Casey as Stokes and Bo Swenson as Twyman, in a sentimentalized version of the relationship between the two teammates. Not until 1999 when I chatted with Ed Fleming outside a jitney station on Bruston Avenue in Homewood did I learn another set of facts. A different story.

According to Ed Fleming, one of Stokes's oldest and best buddies since those mornings they'd meet and walk down the hill together to Baxter Elementary School, Maurice Stokes had been bothered by a painful lump on his neck for weeks preceding the fall. He'd confided to Fleming his growing concern about the swelling, told Fleming the Royals' doctor had promised that the lump or abscess or whatever would gradually be reabsorbed and disappear. Nothing to worry about, the doctor had reassured him. Think of it as an oversized pimple. But it hurts, Stokes said during a phone call to his friend. Hurts lots. Kind of hot to the touch. He wondered if the headaches he was experiencing might be connected to the lump. And the general rundown feeling, the unfamiliar lethargy. It's really bothering me, man, he said. He'd decided first chance he got he'd do something about it on his own. Maybe see another doctor. How much could Stokes tell a team doctor anyway. A white doctor, of course, paid by the team's owner. Could Stokes trust him to keep what he says private, or will it go on his confidential rap sheet, his colored credentials, and affect his credibility, his contract. Black marks against him, franchise player though he'd proved himself to be.

Everybody nursing injuries by playoff time. What would Stokes look like, complaining about a pimple. Doc said playing won't hurt. Play. Playing's not going to make it worse. The team needs you. Especially now. No point in speaking to the coach.

Coaches expect you to suit up, one leg, half a leg, bloody stumps, no legs at all, unless you want to be labeled a malcontent or malingerer or *soft,* epithets your color disposes you to anyway in the wisdom of the league, the wisdom of the times. So you gut it up, bandage, wrap, and play.

One night in the heat of a very physical game somebody slammed an elbow into the mass beneath his skin and Stokes saw stars. Nearly cried. Involuntary tears did sting his eyes and a nauseating clenching of his stomach and yes it hurt so bad he wanted to sit down right there on the court and cry, but of course you don't do that, you shake it off, let on you're not hurt, grit your teeth and go extra hard after the next board. The next point. Next and next.

Then on another night, from a blow or from the force of the collision after you lose control and hurtle down out of the sky smack against the hardwood floor, the sac under your skin, an abscess full of pus, bursts, and infected fluid courses through your system. For several minutes you can't rise. Then you do and you're back on your feet next day for another game, another rebound, another score, then you're down again, overcome by the poison that's been busy, busy circulating inside you, wrecking you, finishing its work, spreading efficiently, speedily, while you pumped blood flying up and down the court. You go down once more, down and out six days, and when you awaken, never rise, never speak in the twelve years it takes your stricken body to die.

Today a similar case would trigger accusations of medical malpractice perhaps suits against management and league for millions and billions of dollars. Doc said, Nothing to worry about. *Play. Lots at stake. Play. Play at any cost. Bop till you drop.*

No league insurance covered Stokes's hospital bills. But for years the league patted itself on the back for sponsoring an annual *charity* game for his benefit. Maurice Stokes's paralysis, his hospitalization, and his financial debts treated as *his* problems the result of bad luck, an accident. His story, his name easy for many of us to sentimentalize, to translate into the fictions of racialized thinking. Easy to see him as one more example of a poor black boy blessed with unusual size and extraordinary talent, a boy given an opportunity to tear up the NBA, make a name for himself. Then fate stepped in and *boom*, that was that. Too bad, too sad. But don't they all fall one way or another. Doomed, maybe. Maybe they're *doomed*, these large black kids so spectacular at hoop, then everything comes crashing down. Except for the rare extra-extra lucky one, don't all of them wind up falling. Nobody's fault. Or nobody's but their own. Gold and drugs. Fast women, big cars. If not one thing, another brings them down. Down. Crushed. Like *Big Mo* Maurice Stokes. Like *L.D.* Eldon Lawson. Word.

The first time I recall Maurice Stokes's name being spoken, I was in love, deep, hopeless puppy love, with my ninth-grade English teacher. Though I probably knew about Stokes from hoop talk and vaguely recall seeing both him and Chuck Cooper, the first African American signed by the NBA, alive and well on the Homewood court, it's Miss Helen DeFrance saying Maurice Stokes's name to me that I remember. She'd assigned an essay in which we were supposed to write what we wanted to be when we grew up.

In her critique of my essay, Miss DeFrance spoke Maurice Stokes's name, dropping it on me with a twinkle in her eyes that said she might be in love too, maybe, maybe a tiny bit with me, but surely with the *perfect gentleman*, tall, neat, well-mannered, softspoken, unassuming, the intelligent, conscientious, hard worker in the classroom and very good sportsman she'd taught at Westinghouse High, a young man who'd gone on to attend St. Francis College thanks to a basketball scholarship he'd earned by being a perfect negro boy. Before people employed or argued about the phrase *role model*, Miss DeFrance had chosen one for me, described him in admiring detail, defined a future for me whether I became doctor, lawyer, or indian chief, a future in which I knew I must emulate those qualities in Maurice Stokes that had wooed Miss DeFrance, earned her soft, approving smile, the shy green dance of her eyes behind gold wire-rimmed spectacles, the sheen of her thick bun of whitish hair tightly coiled atop her head, earned the caress of her pale, long-fingered hands as they shaped elegantly in the air the big, strong body of a good boy, a good man, her man I couldn't help desiring to be.

Maurice Stokes Memorial Playground, then. For a start anyway. Okay. Now what's next may be less palatable, more controversial, but I hope just as obviously compelling and appropriate. I want the park to carry the name of another large brown man. Another player whose physical dimensions withered after he was struck down and confined. One player coming along too early in the pro game to be a spokesperson, then muted by illness, forced to let his actions speak for him, the other severely compromised by his environment and the acts he chose to commit, forced to let talk be his action. The arc of one man's bad story parallels, crosses, merges with the other's good story in many discomforting ways, sad ways, perplexing, sobering ways, the differences between the men stark, obvious, but also striking because they preserve the truth of much sameness, much shared, prepare us for unexpected similarities, dark and illuminating too. If we wish to make sense of either we need the other. Like Magic and Byrd. Female and male. Rich and poor. Black and white. So it's the *Maurice Stokes/Eldon L.D. Lawson Memorial Playground.*

Maurice Stokes's achievements confirm the promise, the loss of Eldon Lawson. L.D.'s failures confirm the loss, the promise of Maurice Stokes. The cruel denouement of each man's life, how both were crippled but salvaged a part of themselves to hold on to, to save themselves, to share, each man surviving, bearing the stamp of Homewood, the place where both grew up, where both learned a game that shaped them, carrying it with them through very different circumstances, yet circumstances, because saturated by our society's racist attitudes and practices, with more in common the more carefully we scrutinize them. Both men winners, stars in their worlds, on top for a short, bright turn on very different stages, one stage admirable, the other disreputable you could say if you're sure finally of the meaning of any or all of it, the rising, the falling, the careers we suffer, the brief turn that ends for all of us where it begins, in darkness, behind a curtain, so how can we be sure, every life mysterious, and face to face with the unpredictable twists of any life what can we do besides wonder and say, Yes. It too is a life. My son's. My brother's. My sister's. Mine. Submit to the judgment it passes upon other lives.

The Eldon L.D. Lawson/Maurice Stokes Memorial Playground. Does it matter whose name comes first. L.D. the shadow proving the substance of Big Mo. The shadow of Maurice Stokes's fall solidifies his brotherhood with L.D. L.D. Lawson the fire burning around the edges of Maurice Stokes's public image, eating away at it, tempering it, illuminating new shapes, changing shapes, other stories that remind us of the heat, the crucible both men, all of us, must pass through, transforming us, bonding us.

I don't recall anyone in particular saying L.D.'s birth name, Eldon Lawson, before he died, and I'm not sure when I learned he possessed more than initials to serve as a name, though at some point a good long while ago I understood L.D. was King Lawson's son. King Lawson who resided in the corner rowhouse at Susquehanna and Albion, "a large man who, if you get too close, you know he doesn't bathe often" I heard my mom signify to somebody once. Mr. Lawson a hulking yellow man my cousin Kip and I would observe sitting on his porch, sleeping sometimes, often barechested in warm weather, sometimes waving or hollering, calling us over or ignoring us on our way to and from Homewood Elementary by way of the invariable route minimizing busy street crossings my mother had taken me by the hand and taught me and I taught Kip when it was his turn to begin school, demanding, as I'd been told I should, that he take my hand crossing streets till I realized I liked this hand-holding even less than Kip did, and stopped.

L.D.'s daddy seldom combed the longish, bushy hair on his head. His wild chest hair looked like it could stand some grooming too, and even as kids minding our own kid business Kip and I were aware of the stories about the big man on a wrinkle-boarded, needs-paint-badly, one-rail porch that appeared way too small and frail to contain his sprawling body, asleep or awake, moving about or sitting. We knew about his nasty temper. His frequent high-octane, bloody fights. How much he liked his wine. How he hung out behind Tioga Street with our grandfather, John French, and his old-head cronies, gambling, drinking, doing whatever they shouldn't be doing back there in the alley. King Lawson's legend part of Homewood so a part of me as I grew up, but it would be years before I figured out the connection between the King on the raggedy porch I used to pass twice a day coming and going to grade school and the King of the Court L.D. fancied himself to be in the legends he spun for his fellow inmates in the Western Penitentiary yard. (Till this very moment in the writing I hadn't noticed another connection — my father's middle name is Lawson. Would another Homewood tale I don't know make more of this than coincidence.)

Anyway, first there was this oversized, soft, clumsy-footed kid who started showing up at the various playground courts where the best players (including me then) migrated day to day, a regular rotation recycling each week so those in the know could tell you, if you were deemed worthy, the answer to the question it was necessary to pose just so: *where they at.* L.D. wanted to be one of the *they.* Where *they* at, man. So it was him, the man-scale boy people called L.D., delivering himself for the steady pounding, humiliation, and verbal abuse served up by everybody, including and especially players half his size, homage to a youngblood blessed with the height everybody wished they'd been born with, the up-and-coming big man who if he paid his dues and survived would one day be knocking heads, bouncing bodies around, jamming, blocking shots, dominating games, monopolizing precious court time because of the God-given advantage of height and girth. But first he'd have to pay.

Like a younger brother who never exactly sheds the awe and fear of an older brother whose seniority seems to grant him un-catchable head starts in any activity pitting younger brother against older brother, a competitive edge for the older brother often lasting way past its time, maybe forever in the younger sibling's mind, even if the kid brother grows bigger, stronger, smarter, whatever, the big brother can still win by psyching out the younger one, making the kid remember he's always outper-formed him in the past and always will in the future—that's how L.D. related to me. Since I'd been one of the older guys whipping unmercifully on his tender, chubby body and playing games with the boy's head when that didn't work, on the court L.D. always cut me plenty of slack, respected me, deferred to me, even feared me a little because he couldn't help (with a little sly assistance from me now and then) flashing back on those early, hard lessons we'd instilled.

L.D. kept growing bigger, stronger, tougher, became a huge bear of a young man, and his skills dramatically improved. Nu-merous colleges recruited him despite his sorry high school grades. One aspect of his game, however, didn't change much. L.D. was soft his first day on the court and stayed soft. *Soft* meaning he didn't sufficiently assert or engage his physical en-dowments. Wasn't rough or tough enough. *Soft* also meaning he didn't respect the game enough, wasn't willing to work hard and diligently to rachet his natural advantages to a higher level, to shoot for greatness, an unforgivable sin in playground eyes, eyes trained to coldly, accurately calculate an opponent's weak-nesses and strengths, eyes bitterly aware of shortages, the scarcity of opportunities and resources besetting their commu-nity, eyes more angry than envious when they saw a large hunk of raw talent wasted. Uncompromising eyes demanding that a player meet the game's unrelenting demands with his best.

People would say, L.D.'s lazy. Nag and rag on him during games. Say on the sidelines, Well, L.D. ain't bad, but the boy could be lots better, real good if he pulled his knucklehead out his ass. Say, L.D. needs to get serious. Damn. Can you imagine the nigger if he really got in shape. Needs to play hard every day and keep his big behind out the street. Leave them wineheads and potheads alone. L.D. knew what they said because some days the knock-down, drag-out fervor of his play would be his answer. For a few days or a week it seemed he might be listening, might care. His game would rise. Most of the time he'd respond with, You best g-g-g-g-gwan out my face, m-m-man. Or Fuck you. You ain't nothing. W-W-What you know about s-s-s-shit, nigger, and go on about his business at an L.D. pace, with an L.D. intensity, with a soft, mocking, knowing, ironic L.D. smile on his face. He liked to have fun and do it his way and that was L.D., a big, lazy, easygoing kid, years after he'd grown way past kid age. Lil bro backing up, backing off when the action got too intense, when I leaned on him real heavy, when I glared, the kid brother taking low when he could have kicked my ass. Everybody's ass. A damned shame, people said.

When L.D. came back to Homewood after a semester in college, Robby said, Dude's sporting a long duster and a white cowboy hat, big-timing it, and nigger wouldn't sell me no dope neither. Huh-uh. Fronted on me. Calling me little brother, youngblood, cause this other wannabe standing there profiling in his fly red leather shit and L.D.'s showing out in his big Stetson hat and long coat, you know. Pimp timing. King of Homewood Avenue and shit, fronting cause L.D. ain't but a couple years or so older den me. Been knowing L.D. my whole life but he's fronting me for this other dude, you know. Said, Sorry youngblood, can't be turning on no n-n-n-neophytes. Don't w-w-w-wanna be the one start no kid in trouble. It's mean out here, R-R-Rob. You don't want to be messing with this s-s-stuff.

Uh-huh. Steady fronting. Didn't take long before Mr. All-World college boy doing his first little bit over to Western. Treat people like dirt, sure as hell one these rats gon rat you out. Come back home singing a different tune this time. He knows who I am. Me and him straight from then on. Got down together many a time.

L.D. always wanted to be a player. Big time. Living large. And he did. For a minute. Had it going. King L.D. Till it got too good to him. Party hearty and not enough taking care of business. Same ole shit. He start spending more time in the slam than out. Never busted for nothing real bad. Penny-ante crimes. L.D. never was mean. He's like your brother, brother. Just liked them good times too much. Caught little bits for stealing and whatnot. Nothing violent. Just seemed like whatever little shit L.D. did, cops would nab his overgrown ass. Maybe cause he was so big. Seemed like poor L.D. couldn't get away with nothing, man.

Big old guy out there in Homewood strutting around in his long coat and big white hat. Always carried a pocketful of candy. Hard candy he'd suck on. It ain't true but I know you heard how people say you get sugar diabetes from too much sugar. Like from eating too much candy. Well, it's bullshit, but L.D. a perfect case to prove it ain't. Never see him without a big bag of sourballs or LifeSavers or Red Hots. Hey Farouk, he'd say after he learned my Muslim name in the slam. Wanna p-p-p-piece of candy, F-F-F-Farouk. Me and him straight. My man. He's a funny guy, really. I mean like a comic. Bad as he stuttered sometimes, L.D. could rap. Had a quick mind. Very quick, and smart too. Once L.D. got going on a good lie, stutter gone. He'd relax. One funny story after another. Keep me laughing. Dope-hustling stories, and chasing women and cops chasing him and dumbass scams and weirdo dope fiends.

Rob tells me even when the sugar got so bad in prison they start chopping off pieces of L.D.'s legs, L.D. still want Rob to roll him into the prison yard after chow or after lineup when there was an hour set aside in the day for doing nothing, same goddamn nothing you be doing round here twenty-four seven when you spozed to be doing something, roll him out in the sun and let old L.D. talk that talk.

Uh-huh. Like I said, me and L.D. go way, way back, Bro, long before both us wound up lifers in this godforsaken hole. L.D.'s a couple years older, maybe he was in Tish, our sister's, class, Rob guesses. Yeah. Big old nutty L.D. My man. Pretty good ballplayer, I heard. Seen him hobbling and scuffling with them bad knees on the court in here. You could tell he once had game. All-Universe, you ask him. Had that bad stutter, you know. Hardly could get a word out his mouth sometimes. F-F-F-F-Farouk. On a good day, though, after I'd go over to his block and wheel him back to the yard, old L.D. hold forth like a king on a throne. Know what I mean. Sit there talking, cracking everybody up. Making damn good sense too, when he wanted to make sense. A knowledgeable guy. Read all the newspapers and magazines, the few we get anyway in the jive library or borrow from one another. He could hold forth on any subject. You'd be surprised. All the fellows gather round to listen to what he's putting down. On a good day L.D. wouldn't stutter one bit. Lean back in his wheelchair with that fat bag of candy in his lap and tell lies for days. Got to give the boy credit. Bad off as he was, and by the end L.D. was sick, sick, very sick, big Bro, he'd ask me to roll him out there so he could give the fellas an earful. Goofy as he was sometimes, L.D. could preach, make damn good sense when he wanted to. Or keep you crackin up. Everybody standing round his wheelchair and L.D. the king of Homewood Avenue again.

So both names then. The *Maurice Stokes/Eldon L.D. Lawson Memorial Playground*. I realize it's a long name. Long like those many-segmented praise names, glittering strings of bright beads, the *entitles* our ancestors improvised—Lincoln Washington Abraham Marcellus Cudjo Jones—when emancipation entitled former slaves to rename themselves. So there's nothing wrong with a long name, in fact long names have a history with us, going way back beyond freedom days and slavery days, back to the Old World where names were sacred dispensations, wishes, promises, vessels for containing small, shining bits of our familiars, fragments of beings from a world elsewhere that we hoped would animate, guide, and preserve us when we called down these spirits' names.

Anyway, given our people's propensity for combining baroque elaboration with the pithiness of blues, our ability to stuff in a tightly wrapped, highly portable package everything we need for the longest, unknown journey, our spirit bundles capable of holding earth sea sky blood, given the mallet-stroke beat of our music that seems to be one hard, quick shiny thing repeated over and over but is many things contained in the one, always changing, growing, doubling back, flying way ahead, and with all the practice we'd had mashing a few good times down into the sackful of bad times and then pulling out the good times still miraculously intact, creases straight, clean, dap, and waving them around *hallelujah,* strutting in them even through storms of sorrow and tears and pain, given all the above and more, I expect our habit of nicknaming, capturing in a short, sweet riff—*Mo L.D. Magic Pearl Doc Dip*—those long, complicated names carefully chosen and lavishly bestowed on people we love, that habit of ours will prevail and produce a shorthand handle for the court. We'll call it by that abbreviated version most of the time, its ordinary, daily clothes, know it by that easy-sounding sound without forgetting, I hope, how decked-out, how splendiferous it can sound when the whole rest of its name's on display, as it would be on occasion, like Sunday mornings for example when we gather and utter the names, keep them alive. One in the many. Many in one.

Say it with me now, please. Loud and proud. *The Maurice Big Mo Stokes/Eldon L.D. Lawson Memorial Playground.*

One More Time

Forgive me. For losing you. I was afraid I could not bring
you back from the dead so I let go. Though I watched
and watched and dreamed your return, I wasn't strong
enough. I thought your dying betrayed me. I doubted you.
Doubted myself. I ran away from the loving space you
always kept open for me. Ran to find a father, ran to
escape loneliness and shame. To be free of you, of him,
of death, I ran. Now here I am again, asking again for
the loving space deep inside you. Asking again for your
arms. Is it different now. Too late now. How does
anyone ever know.

DEAR FREED:

I am older now than you were when you lost John French and a stroke put you to sleep for a year. I feel kind of foolish saying lots has happened since the summer my job was watching you die. Fifty years of things happening reduced to the word *lots*, lots, lots, lots, Freed, lots a kind of stutter to get me started, an apology for what I'll leave out, an admission of defeat and guilt because it's such an obvious fact, you know as well as I do, the *lots* goes without saying but must be said here at the beginning to acknowledge how much has been lost, how much irrecoverable whether I write ten words or ten million, no stopping, no going back, and said also to acknowledge the *lots* as nothing; we can let it go, squeeze the past into a single word and let it go, it's a film when the projector stops and lights come on and the wall in front of us is blank again. Have we budged an inch since that first day, you in your bed, me in the folding chair, dreaming our separate dreams, each waiting for the other to awaken, to speak at last.

And I'm still waiting. That's what these words in the guise of a letter are about. About finding out what I need to know so I'm able to take my next step. And next. There must have been times when I was a baby learning to walk and you clasped both my hands in yours, me stretching my short arms above my big head, if they reached that far, gripping your thumbs, dangling from your hands suspended just high enough so my bare feet brush the floor and I can learn the future of my body, push one foot then the other forward, practice bearing my weight, balancing it, you smiling, guiding my slow-motion, Frankenstein shuffle across the living room floor and maybe John French, maybe my mother in the room, too, cheering, thinking any day now that boy will be walking, standing on his own two feet and walking, walking away from here. Any day. Ain't he something. And all the days between then and now passing as quickly as that thought through their minds.

Nothing has changed. I need the steady support of your hands. Your encouragement. The thought we have a good long way to go together and we'll make it fine, just fine. I need you listening, reading what's in my mind. Need your voice. Touch. Need you to stay alive.

When I deserted you every afternoon that summer for the basketball court in Westinghouse Park, I'd feel myself growing larger as I bopped along the tracks, kicking the rocky gravel, getting away with something, wondering if a train would catch me before I clambered down from the tracks, knowing it might if I left 7415 at the usual time, just a matter of where, the days were so alike, and trains kept a tight schedule, I could almost count on the moment I'd be overtaken and wiped from the face of the earth by the sound of a train just a few yards away, dropping like a sack over my head. A tunnel of sound. A bone-rattling fist of sound. Black inside it. Shaken till nothing's left, just the shattering, smothering noise and how it feels to be shaken apart and lost to myself, all in less than an instant, before I can catch a breath or gather my thoughts. I know it's coming but nothing I can do to curb the fear, the awful exhilaration taking me over, then dumping me drained, whipped, still trembling from the force of the train's grip, being let go as much a shock as being seized, afraid as I stand there trying to regain my bearings that I might have played this game once too often, I couldn't let a diesel engine swallow me and chew and spit me out and not be changed, not bruised or emptied or doomed when I land wobbly kneed, ears ringing, eyes burning. I might have gotten away with it for a while, my head in the lion's mouth, but one day, sooner or later, just a matter of time. Knowing I'd be punished didn't stop me; knowing the train shaking me apart was only a taste of what could happen if I walked or ran on the forbidden rails didn't slow me down either. The moment I was free and clear of the glove of earth-shattering sound I'd start anticipating my next chance to tempt the tracks.

The possibility of extinction part of the excitement of growing larger. A sweet wind in my face, shadow at my back as I hustled along the tracks. *Can't catch me, I'm the Gingerbread Man.* Wondering if I'd get caught. Or certain I would. Pretty sure I could survive the train's best punch. Bigger, stronger, each step I took away from 7415, toward the ball court, into the roaring, hot breath that might overtake me, test me, devour me before I reached the path down the hillside, through the Bum's Forest to the rabbit hole in the outfield fence.

I know you loved me. I know you warned me away from the tracks out of love. Now I need you to understand that the out-of-bounds, beeline shortcut I sneaked each summer day through Homewood was love too. Though I fled each afternoon, I also carried you with me—your fear and silence, your trembling, your deathsleep, your love—and pitched those parts of you into the fire of the train roaring past so they'd do us no harm. So I could play ball. Grow large. Leave you without losing you.

It's always been less than pleasant to recall the little fame, the little while I was a high school all-city, all-state hoop star and you in the same city, Freed, and not once seeing me play. No one in the family attended my games. Sports a boys' thing, man thing, *play*, so the women had no interest and no time anyway if they were interested, and where were the men of our clan. If not out in the street playing their own kinds of games, then busy working or if no work, then busy in that all-consuming limbo of hyperinactivity, the pressure cooker of indolence, excruciating, helpless waiting between jobs, or the dramatized denial of powerlessness in a thousand devastating little performances daily of power, of ego and worth they could not display anywhere except in these performances, could not document in any context besides the scenarios they staged together for one another's benefit on streetcorners, in barbershops and poolrooms, on ball courts and fields, acting out a style of being in the world that broadcasts to each other and to their people, Hey, things may look pretty bad, I may look like a worthless piece of shit, but there's more to it than that. Always. Keep your eye on me, listen for the unplayed notes at the center of this awkward, gangly syncopation, the counterpoint to this apparent cacophony and chaos of my being, and you will discover there's always more than meets the eye, the ear, an invisible core holds the warring parts together, *my sunshine, my only sunshine,* unsounded notes that if recognized and loved, *and you should, yes, you should recognize them cause you've been there too,* give what you see and hear a certain rhythm, a harmony mirroring the struggle of keeping a life together, holding your own in this vale of tears where each of us must strive by any means necessary to maintain self-respect. Each sung word, stylized gesture the men refine, their double-takes, jokes, handshakes, hats, dance steps, prayers, haircuts, curses, kisses, the explosive casts of dice or cards slammed down, moans, whoops, baroque drives to the hoop, is a refusal to count for nothing.

These exhausting rituals of survival left the men, the ones not sick or dead, the ones who had not yet abandoned their families altogether, no more time than the women to break away, change their routines, and check out kids playing kid games at the high school gym.

Anyway, once most of us escaped high school, why in the world would we ever dream of returning. A person got out, meaning usually dropped out, and that was that. Good riddance. Gone for good. No regrets. Tired of being treated like a child. Black kids, white teachers. They never let us forget who's in charge. Who's just passing through, going nowhere, and deserves no respect unless you're one of their rare pets, sucking up, puckering up, on your knees. The main lessons in high school: Bow your head when told. Be quiet and ready to follow white people's orders no questions asked. Preparation for a world students and teachers knew was coming because it's already there in the segregated textbooks and school buildings, the scheme of rewards and punishments doled out by those in charge, the discipline of bells, the school's power to crack our hours, days, years, our lives, into segments, no questions asked, teaching us that everything worthwhile in the world already spoken for, already grabbed and guarded and hoodooed by white people to hurt us if we sidle too close, so we'd better learn to be satisfied with the meager portion set aside for us, the drab secondhand shit we saw when we walked out the school door into the world, a broken-down, half-ass, no-connect, dark shadow of the bright world the high school books waved in our faces eight hours a day, the world we were taught we could, if we were really good, goody good, a whole lot better than every other grubby little nigger around us, aspire to but never truly claim as ours.

The beatings they absorb in this society evilly disposed against them does not excuse the men's absence. Didn't make me miss them any less at my games. Waking up each morning to play the hand dealt them does not leave the men without choices, even though most of those choices turn out to be straitened, uninspiring, shameful, or dangerous. I remember sitting high up in the stands of the University of Pittsburgh fieldhouse watching Calvin Fowler's father dash out on the basketball court, toss a handful of money at his son's feet after Calvin's Oliver High team (black) beat South Hills (white) for the city championship and Calvin no doubt the MVP. My team,

Peabody High (integrated—me and Carl K), had blown our chance to compete for the title two nights before, losing to South Hills, so I was still upset, still twisted up inside because my lousy performance in the semifinals was one of the biggest reasons my team was watching, not playing, the championship game. I can't say the bitterness and disappointment of losing the semifinal game has ever gone away—how does anyone ever forget such a public, humiliating, irreversible failure. I've never forgiven myself for the loss to South Hills but the bite, the sting, has lessened over the years. Not so the stinging image of Mr. Fowler, followed by a couple buddies, high-stepping onto the brightly lit court, performing a victory dance, tossing good green money to the gods cause I think Calvin was too excited to stoop and gather it up. An image not about envying Calvin's moment of glory, though of course I did, and not as simple as wanting to be Calvin either, nor coveting his daddy. If my father had cut monkeyshines in front of white folks, celebrating my team's victory with a buck and wing and a trashy throwing of cash on the sacred court, I probably never would have forgiven him.

When Mr. Fowler and his buddies busted the cordon of white ushers and cops and pranced onto the gleaming hardwood floor, I wanted the clock to turn back to the beginning of the season with all my games still to be played and my father on a seat behind our bench cheering at every one. The sudden appearance of black men down on the court confirmed missed opportunities, emptied the arena. No crowd roaring and clapping its approval or muttering, frowning its disapproval of the Oliver High win. The whole scene erased just like the trains snatch away a world that seems solid, unquestionable a moment before. No one, nothing left in the Pitt fieldhouse, just me bolted to my seat hearing a voice from the past *Where's John French, Where's John French*. Those words playing silently inside my head, those exact words or different words bearing the same meaning, the same sad music that's always present, waiting to be heard, as you are, Freed, hovering above me, your invisible hands laced into mine, keeping me standing, balanced step by step, before you vanish in the thought that passes through the minds of my mother and grandfather, the thought of me walking alone on my own two feet, a future with no room for you because the clock doesn't turn back, we must go our separate ways.

I'm growing larger sure enough when I escape 7415 and sneak up the hillside to the tracks, a haunted, hollowed-out larger on my way to the court in Westinghouse Park, hurrying to forget you, deny you so I could believe I stood alone. Hustling solo down the tracks toward the lonely person I became. The star.

You never saw me play basketball. During my time in high school, I'm ashamed to say, it seldom if ever occurred to me that you should. I was learning to compartmentalize. Ignore obligations to people when such obligations, or rather the effort and emotion they required, sidetracked me from where I believed I was headed—being better than anyone else on the court, in the classroom, in the stories I needed to hear about myself. *Self-absorbed, tunnel vision, denial* are some of the kinder words I can offer to describe the habit of mind I cultivated toward the old woman dying in a room at the top of the stairs, toward what was left of her when she didn't die and was carried downstairs again to take up residence tucked into a corner of the couch under the front room window, across from the overstuffed chair where John French once had reigned, or sleeping wrapped in a blanket in the ladderback rocking chair beside the fake fireplace, the bars of its little electric heater aglow to keep her feet warm.

After my mom, my siblings, and I moved away from Homewood, after the summer tending you, after it became clear that the stroke had crippled you and stolen your tongue, I never imagined you anywhere outside 7415—not in familiar places where I'd seen you countless times: on Homewood Avenue shopping in the A&P and Murphy's Five and Dime or tending your patch of rosebushes in 7415's tiny fenced-in front yard—let alone visualized room for you in my new world of school and ball. I remember only a few moments of being slightly ashamed of myself for how I treated you. For years I didn't let myself think there was anything wrong about escaping 7415 as fast, as far, as once and for all as I could. I didn't think *escape*, just hurry up, hurry up, don't be late for the game. Except every once in a while I'd sense more. Like the time I sniffed my fingers as I humped along the tracks to the court, worried that the smell of the room, your invisible presence might still be clinging and give me away, worried as soon as I dropped my hand from my face that someone might have observed what I'd been doing and had read my mind and told God.

Not once the whole summer of my twelfth year did I dare ask anyone about the smell in 7415, if they smelled it too, or what they smelled if anything at all. Now I wish I had asked and someone had begun to explain to me that fear and love and guilt can compound and rise like odor from a sweaty, ill body, can spread their weather over distance, from the house on Finance to Westinghouse Park, spread over years. Fear, guilt, love not bodies at all but carry the mystery of things immaterial, absent things strongly present though nothing's tangible to touch or see or smell or hear. Presences so real, so intrusive and demanding, they unsettle what you ordinarily believe is real. *Real* means suddenly less or more, suddenly nothing compared to what you're calling, for want of better words, memories of music, memories of a smell, because you don't know how else to express the fact that an absent thing no one's aware of except you can reshuffle, refashion your understanding of what counts in the world.

Whether or not anyone else notices or shares it, when an absent thing descends and possesses you, you're mounted, ridden, your body a spirit horse.

I didn't ask and no one offered to explain this business to me. I kept quiet about what I didn't know. Unasked questions and the worries they might have addressed I stored deeper and deeper in a numb, mute region where the seeds of a secret life lay dying, waiting to be born. If I had asked, Freed, if you could have listened then and spoken then, perhaps I'd be better equipped now, attempting to explain that summer to myself and not doing a very satisfactory job.

It may be too late. Too much may be past explaining. But I'm writing to you anyway as if these words are a letter and it might reach you, wherever you are. What's to lose.

I'm marching again along the railroad tracks above Finance Street, one of a crew of men in chain-gang coveralls, hammers like John Henry's slung over our shoulders. I'd be singing along with the others and you'd hear us passing up on the hillside and I bet you'd hurry to the front window to watch, so I wave my free hand, and you hurt awhile, the striped suits, shackles, and mounted white men with shotguns, but by the time our song fades you'll be better, remembering our voices, remembering that the miles of shiny rails we're laying will curve back your way one bright morning soon, the circle unbroken, remembering my free hand waving, the fist it raises. I'm growing larger and larger. Too large, I once thought, to need a father, a mother. Large enough to claim a spot in the game you've never seen me play, and since I chanced your life and so much else learning to play it, I want you to come along this time, if it's not too late.

You remember Westinghouse Park, of course (by the way, very soon we'll change its name). Mom told me about the Sunday afternoon treks with you when she was a kid. Summer and long white dresses and permission to sit in the green grass but you better not come home with a mark on you, young lady. Homewood people strolling, picnicking, sitting on the green wooden slats of iron benches. Most everybody still sporting their church clothes except the heathen boys roughnecking ball games and tag games in the hollow around whose rim good citizens promenade. No basketball court in this section of the park, over a footbridge on the far side of the tracks from Finance, on land donated to the city by industrialist George Westinghouse, where Homewood gossiped and courted and politicked and beheld itself in the mirror of its faces, people every shade of brown from coffee without a drop of cream to cream whose drop of coffee is rumored but unseen. Menfolk in starched collars, women in their best dresses, everybody's shoes shined or polished white as snow, ladies all topped by veiled hats, flowered, ribboned, curved like the prows of pirate ships, or snappy, military-looking pillboxes and brimless caps.

I don't know it yet but intend to find the date when the basketball court that borrows its name from Westinghouse Park, though it's not part of the original park, was constructed next to the swimming pool behind Homewood Elementary School. My guess is the men and boys started hooping there in the 1920s, early '30s at the latest.

I have a photo of you from that period, Freed. Someone has penciled *1923* in a little trapezoid of open sky near the top right-hand corner of the picture. Since you were born in 1900, it's always easy to figure your age. Now with the century rolling over again, I wonder how you feel, one hundred years old and counting in this new millennium. The photo's browned by age. Sepia an apter word than brown for the monochrome tint of the approximately three-by-five snapshot still pasted to a fragment of thick, stiff album paper that edges it in black. Without the black-as-coal border I'd probably perceive the darkest portions of the photo—a low passageway opening in the wall behind you, your shadow, your right ankle—as black. The black frame also mellows various deep shades of brown or sepia so they don't contrast too sharply with lighter portions of the picture. Even your long dress, its closest edge nearly dissolving into glare as it's pushed to the front of the picture plane by your extended right leg, a booted foot elegantly pointing at the viewer, retains a creamy, subdued glow, depth, and texture instead of the flat, stark contrast an image printed in black and white would convey.

As I study the photo and try to bring back the time, the place, the spirit of the moment when it was taken, you standing outside what must be the old family house on Cassina Way or maybe the older one on Albion Street with my mother straddling your hip and my father a boy wherever he is in Homewood that day learning whatever skills he will need to join the older guys on the court who are inventing the game they'll pass on to him and he'll pass to a first generation of NBA players, including Maurice Stokes and Ed Fleming and Chuck Cooper, and they'll pass to me and I've passed to my sons and daughter, I worry the precious photo is being damaged by light, by my hard scrutiny. If a photograph could steal a person's soul, couldn't a person's stare pilfer the soul of a photo.

The black backing holds another snapshot on its opposite side—two men I don't recognize posed shoulder to shoulder, smiling at the camera, a sturdy tree trunk growing straight out the top of one's head, both men for some reason poking out their pregnant-looking bellies so that's the portion of their anatomy foregrounded, bumping me away, drawing me into their frozen, fading image.

Each time I handle this relic of you, some of the old backing dissolves to dust. Things can only bear so many touches before they're gone, so I'm concerned about the weight of my touch, of my eyes, the buzz of the overhead fluorescent light. Should I shield the photo when I'm not studying it. Stop studying it, period. Will it lose its integrity. Will I glance away one time and find a blank three-by-five card when I glance back.

You stand not quite centered in the picture's foreground. At first my eyes see only you. You're large, dominate the frame. Then I notice how little of the picture space you actually occupy. The crown of your head doesn't quite reach the middle of the photo's vertical axis and your pointed toe is a good half inch from the picture's bottom edge. The image recomposes itself, scale shifts, your pale, not quite centered figure submits to being an element in a larger design.

Why am I so engaged, so moved by this image of you. As striking as its fragility and vulnerability, its capacity to transform itself, is the photo's artfulness, the simple beauty and uniqueness securing it outside time, beyond accident. Accounting for the impact, the art of the snapshot, there's more at stake than determining what's pretty and what's not. Art is someone speaking, making a case for survival. The art in our styles of playing hoop as eloquent as our styles of playing music. Art is speech in as many forms as we can invent to communicate what we experience, how we feel about being alive. Art's a medium for expressing what's crucial and worthy of being preserved, passed on. What works and doesn't. A culture's art shouts and whispers secrets the culture couldn't exist without, unveils its reason for being. Creates representations of what must stay alive in the lives of those who choose to suffer the vision of the world the culture imagines. Our African-American history and culture emerge in a New World oceans of time and space from older civilizations, but these civilizations are still vibrant in us, if we teach ourselves how to look and listen, how to speak their primal, engendering languages that discipline desire. Through arts of mind and body and media, art flexible, responsive to its immediate spiritual and material environment, but also playful, mindful, bodyful of its ancient origins—aren't we, after all, *sweet children of original darkness*—we continue to challenge new dispossessions in a land rife with powerful enemies who demean us, deny our capacities to produce art, except when what we do, the ways we use our bodies and minds to play and work and speak can be appropriated, commodified, bought and sold to profit others.

> *I hate to hear that engine blow, boo-hoo, boo-hoo*
> *I hate to hear that engine blow, boo-hoo*
> *Everytime I hear it blowin, I feel like ridin too*
>
> *When a woman gets the blues, she goes to her*
>   *room and hides*

When a woman gets the blues, she goes to her
room and hides
When a man gets the blues, he catch the freight
train and rides

To help myself get down and be clearer about what I mean by art, the art of this photo I'm regarding, the art of playground hoop, of African-American music and dance, etc., I'm listening to "Freight Train Blues," a tune first recorded by Clara Smith in 1924, a year after the one penciled in the photo's sky. Clara Smith seizes my attention. After she lays down only a phrase or two, I realize I've never heard anyone sing quite like this Clara Smith, and know there's a special signature in her voice I won't ever hear again unless I listen again to her. Though she's singing a traditional number in a familiar blues idiom, no way I could have anticipated what she brings to the performance, how she personalizes and changes the form, confirms and challenges gender roles. Yet she's chanting my song, *mine*, even as her voice's singularity, its one-of-a-kind peculiarity and edge surprise and unsettle me.

When I'm observing a playground game of basketball or looking at a photo of you two, my grandmother and mother, nothing more or less mysterious goes on than what transpires as I listen to "Freight Train Blues." Once upon a time, a million billion particles of light, ripples of sound vibrating, dancing, converging, created a picture, a song, a game, then rushed away into stillness and darkness, an unfathomable void, except, except when I put on Clara Smith's record or study this snapshot or attend to the chorus of old-timers' bragging on long-gone hoop games, connecting those games to the best players of the moment who are kicking up the action way past the point most of us can go, each of these representations—each in its own way a finely crafted artifact—creates a story. Once upon a time something happened, was seen and heard and felt by somebody who spoke it into art, and what happened can still speak, dances still.

The photo's art, like the art of hoop, is deceptively simple. What you see is what you get and it seems to end there, if you don't penetrate past the surface. Like the best naturalistic paintings, the photo, the game are layered. What appears to be an ordinary, familiar slice of life the painter has observed through a window and spontaneously rendered on canvas is just that, a scene the viewer is able to identify immediately with those snapshots of the world the eyes continuously consume every waking day. Just that but then more if we are paying attention, because we'll also hear the artist saying, Stop. Let's think about what's in front of our eyes. Maybe it's not so simple, so familiar. Or more familiar, more intimately familiar and revelatory than you'd ever guess at first glance.

Beneath the scene that immediately catches my attention — guys running up and down the court or you, a young woman, my grandmother holding my mom on your hip — countless other scenes glide and shimmer. I can pick at them, skins of an onion, scabs, a damp caul, attempt to make more sense of them the way I try to make sense of myself when I pretend I'm able to stand outside the flow of experience and be in it too, reading a composition of transparent, flickering screens with changing messages, stories within stories, unresolvable, but always the tease they may blend, harmonize, and rock church like the many-pitched, many-toned voices of Homewood AME Zion's congregation.

On the canvas of empty court in Westinghouse Park the game waits to be inscribed, shining, imminent, its see-through, multiple layers shivering in August heat. Homewood court offering its shabby self one more time, ready for the game to be contested here again, ready for one more layer to be painted on thin air, like the flashes of myself in action I imagine when I step through the hole in the wire fence, afterimages of stars who've played here before hovering in those crinkles of heat rising off the asphalt, the best players ever, waiting to get it on, ready and waiting to hoop again when they descend and fill the bodies of men and boys who arrive at the court today. *Next.*

You stand, Freed, right leg extended, toe pointed at the camera, your firstborn astride your far, cocked hip. A warm day because your dress is short-sleeved or maybe you've cuffed the sleeves neatly above your elbows, because a bare forearm crosses your body and supports the child on your hip, bisecting you like a sash. The hand of that bare arm, your only arm visible, is tucked into the softness behind my mother's dark-stockinged knee. Maybe because I'm looking for it, I discover you possess a basketball player's trim, broad-shouldered, long-limbed body.

As in those quirky Escher drawings or the geometric designs of dyed African gourds, figure and ground cavort promiscuously, exchange places, bird becomes fish becomes bird, different pictures, different spaces represented, near and far not fixed, everything shapeshifting, changing position and meaning depending on when, where, how I look, how the design looks at me. Which questions we ask each other. You are small, Freed, then large. You're all I see, then you shrink, recede, the subject of the photo becomes the helter-skelter pattern of clapboard walls lining the street behind you. Alongside the doorway to your right, two dark windows, tall enough to swallow you — one on the ground floor, in full view, the other above it, chopped in half by the photo's top edge — peer like blind eyes. Almost black, horizontal seams running between the clapboards are stripes that pull the background forward. Where does the dark, low passageway to your left, between one house and the next, lead.

You stand on what looks to be a wooden sidewalk or platform, sun-splashed, some of its planks curled up at the corners, others missing. You and your daughter posed to provide scale for a sepia study of urban poverty, a still life of jerry-rigged, ramshackle, dilapidated, slightly askew structures on Albion

Street or Cassina Way, a portrait of forms bred by the lives of poor folk in the city's margins, folks temporarily making do, always, forms simultaneously ephemeral and monumental.

Hoop isn't me. But I'm the game. There is no game unless I play. I'm lost without the game. Whose game is it. Do I play it or does it play me. Why is its work play. And play work. Why is it time out and the time that matters most. The game rolls on with me or without me. One monkey don't stop no show.

Your dress's round collar is ornamented with twin half-moon yokes that lie on your chest. A full skirt hemmed to float just above your ankles, belted so its flair emphasizes your slim waist. No way of telling the dress's color. White I assumed at first since it seemed lighter than anything else in the photo except the sun-dazzled boards under your feet, the patch of sky above the building behind you where the date's penciled. Less white if I look more carefully. A rippling brightness definitely not white even though the dress's edge closest to the camera is almost consumed by sunlight it gathers and reflects. The dress's skirt deeply pleated by one long wedge of shadow from hem to waist where the cotton material is gathered and pinched up by my mother's knee jammed into your ribs.

Is it art or accident when things in the photo feel arranged, composed, impelling me to ponder what I see. A drainpipe edging the corner of a clapboard wall is the truest vertical, running straight down from the top of the photo to a point almost exactly halfway from the bottom, marking the picture's middle, dividing it into nearly equal quadrants, if you imagine the four arms of a cross whose eye is this point. The drainpipe, before it disappears behind your shoulders, neatly separates Mom's head from your's and is continued, narrowed to a line, in the deep brown seam of your bodies pressing close together.

When I can't fall asleep and play a lost game over and over in my head, the pieces of the game gradually come together, fit perfectly, but not until I'm on the outside looking in do I see the design, the unforgiving logic, precision, and fierce economy of the game's inevitable unfolding once it begins. How the smallest detail—an opponent's careless pass I anticipated being thrown but for some reason didn't make the effort to intercept—doomed our team's chances of winning no matter how much energy we expended after I'd missed that opportunity to steal the ball in the opening seconds.

The two large windows occupying most of the photo's left half, their dimensions exactly proportional to the dimensions of the snapshot, could be developing negatives hung out to dry. Would the blurred, wet reflections rippling their dark panes gradually resolve into duplicates of the scene I'm gazing at or would different pictures appear.

Is it coincidence that the patch of pale earth exposed by boards uprooted from the wooden sidewalk mirrors in shape, tint, and size the section of open sky directly above it, the space in which somebody has penciled *1923*.

Perhaps to avoid the sun's glare, that harsh, telltale light I associate with summers on the court, your eyes are averted from the camera. My mother's face also turns slightly to the side, but she's peeping at the lens. Her hair floats, a burning bush. Yours parted, brushed, and oiled, pasted tight to your skull, gleams like tar. The camera has caught you both in three-quarter profile, the right side of your faces flooded by light that erases detail, the other side heavily shadowed so only a generalized hint of features available. Still I discover your great-granddaughter, my niece Monique's face in yours, yours in my mom's, hers in yours.

C'mon out here and get some of this, youngblood. You think you're ready, boy. You think you got something for this, old man. Well, bring it on, son. And don't start to whining when it gets hot out here. Bring it on, bad boy. Won't take me but a minute to sit your youngblood ass back down.

Who snapped the picture. Do you remember. Do you recall the day. Somebody's birthday, maybe. Aunt Geral thinks John French probably behind the camera. Mama wouldn't let nobody else touch it, Aunt Geral said. Rummaging one day in the deep bottom drawer of the dining room china cabinet in the house on Finance Street, I dug out a big, boxy Kodak that opened like an accordion. I remember somebody saying, probably Aunt Geral again, That's Mama's camera, boy. You better put it back quick before she catches you with it. I remember wondering what was so special about the clunky, dusty old contraption, and because it was forbidden, I sneaked looks at it, handled it every chance I got from then on.

Let's say it's 1923, '24 again. In about three years in Chicago the Harlem Globetrotters, who won't make it to Harlem till the early 1960s, will drive from Chicago to Hinckley, Illinois, population 3,100, Abe Saperstein, owner, coach, and pitch man at the wheel, embarking on their first road trip. The Renaissance hoop squad out of the Savoy Ballroom on Lennox Avenue, coached by Bob Douglass, who lit victory cigars on the bench long before Red Auerbach of the Celtics became famous for the same habit, is already cooking in Harlem, taking on and defeating just about always all comers, including hard-fought victories over the legendary original Celtics, the generally acknowledged best (noncolored) team in the hoop universe. Probably around this time the other snapshot of you I have, the one with you and your cousins in flapper outfits, was also taken. Anyway, at that glamour-girl time you're also a new mother, still young, fine, and out there styling for the stylish people, though old John French must have suited you just right from what I've heard, him and your fresh baby and the Tobacco Road–looking shack on Cassina Way or Albion whose clapboards reign so dramatically in the background then foreground of the photo I'm attempting to describe to bring you forward in time, to take you back.

I think there was a Center Avenue YMCA Big Five basketball team in Pittsburgh then. And a team sponsored by the Loendi Social Club. I know Pittsburgh sports entrepreneur extraordinaire Mr. Cumberland Posey, who founded a legendary baseball team, the Homestead Grays, managed a hoop squad that challenged the New York Rens to a shootout for the Negro National Championship somewhere around in there. In other words an African-American variety of basketball already prospering, proliferating, in the early twenties, outdoor court or no court up behind the swimming pool back of Homewood school. Hoop flourishing in Pittsburgh. Saturday night live entertainment in African-American communities there and everywhere across the country. Double dips. Hoop and dancing. Dancing and hoop. Wouldn't it be something if you and the girls in the photo were all dressed up for a ball game and dance at the Y.

Did you ever catch a game in those days, Freed. Ever in your life attend one. Did you ever go dancing when a dance was the second attraction of a double-header: hot hoop contest, then hot swing band, all for a quarter. Did you jump and spin and glide and fly on the shiny wooden boards with the players after they'd cleaned up and shined up and smelled aftershave-lotion good.

Nineteen twenty-three. You're a beautiful, athletic-looking young woman with my mom slung on your cocked hip in a sun-dazzled, striped, sepia photo I slip back into its protective folder, the folder into an envelope, envelope into a brown paper bag whose edges I fold over to seal, and we could begin there in 1923, with you looking ready to play ball yourself, the coat-hanger shoulders, long lanky limbs, big hands, we could stroll the long way to Westinghouse Park or hustle along the tracks if you promise not to tell, and you could watch me play or I could watch you play in another era that's coming seventy years or so later when your great-granddaughter, my girl Jamila, competes for money in the WNBA. We could start there, but the game's much older, thousands of years old by 1923, and since it's taken this long for us to find time to go to the court together, let's start closer to the beginning.

The way there is not by counting backward year by year as if we'll discover a particular year when the first ball's tossed up at center court or the first jump shot's launched. That's not the way. Instead, remember my description of how I learned to play in Westinghouse Park, joining other brown boys playing one on one on one, half court, every man for himself, one player with the ball, another guarding him, everybody else waiting for a shot, a rebound, possession of the ball, a chance to score, boys in a kind of line dance, shuffling side to side, up and back, with our eyes focused on the bouncing ball. Well, concentrate on those eyes, our feet, the heating up of our limbs, the fast thumping of our hearts perhaps in synch with the dribbler drumming the ball. Feel our attention sharpening, our bodies revving up in anticipation of the tremendous outpouring of energy the game's about to require, anticipating flight, a prodigious, sky-high leap and maybe we won't ever come back down to earth. Let the familiar geography, the drab features of Homewood court you must have noticed out of the corner of your eye Sundays while passing by on the way to the park, let them fade—the droopy fence, scabby poles, rusty, perforated metal backboard, bent hoops, intermittent traces of sideline and foul lines that have barely survived being tramped on since the city painted the asphalt last—let that stuff go and the rest of Homewood go and let all of Pittsburgh vanish too and just concentrate on the brown boys crouching, shuffling, hearts beating faster and faster as the spirit of the game descends. The details of the court I'm asking you to let go, gone already for the boys. They could be in Detroit, Los Angeles, Milwaukee, Memphis in Tennessee, Memphis in Egypt, under wooden backboards or glass or no backboard or just a peach basket or crooked, netless rim tacked high enough on a wall so only the ones with the best hops can leap up and touch it. Asphalt or dirt or concrete underfoot, it doesn't matter to us, the ball's the center of attention, and the hole where it's supposed to end up almost arbitrary. What matters is how ferociously, loyally, the other boys will battle to prevent any one of the group from getting there and doing what each wants to do, be the first and only to do. But the game's not exactly about accomplishing that solo triumph either, not yet anyway. Not about winning yet. It's about the shuffle, the dance, the space, the drive to excel, to fly. That's what this chosen space manifests and creates for all the participants, and all the participants have a stake in raising the ante, pumping up the action they've come together to conjure and can't achieve without each other so there is a good, demanding, respectful period of communal preparation before each soul goes off on its own, its journey, its quest, its rising and separation from the others. We need this mellow getting-ready time together when what matters is shared space, shared aspirations, the shared shuffling dance, the depth and weight and heat of the shared spirit we are fabricating from nothing, creating it brand-new again as you watch.

You've let go the gray, broken asphalt surface of the court next to the swimming pool behind Homewood school, right, Freed, and let go Homewood too, remember, so now instead of asphalt, think green grass, tamped down flat by dancing feet. Not feet in outrageously, insultingly expensive sneakers, peacock sneakers for show as much as go; think bare brown country-boy feet whose pale bottoms are waffled by calluses tougher than the soles of autographed, autopilot, autocratic, autodestruct tennies. We've lost the fenced rectangle of court and these tough bare feet circle a ring, are the ring, ring-bearers, ring-givers, each step forming one more time what's been outlined by other feet shuffling round and round in the grass and hard mud patches where grass has been rubbed away, a ring also of circles upon circles in the air above the ones written on the earth, under the earth, the bare feet follow these visible and invisible tracks, each stepper, shuffler in concert with the others round and round, eyes fixed not on a basketball but dreaming a shiny point at the center of this ring they animate as they go round, a pinpoint tinier than a needle's eye, so small its dimensions can be expressed only as an idea, the idea that somewhere, somehow, the quick and the dead, past, present, and future, gods and humans must issue from the same infinitesimally small hole that's not a hole but the idea of a crossroads, an intersection where heaven and earth, spirit and matter simultaneously come together and separate, an idea accounting for nothingness and plenitude, for the moment that is not life, not death, but both, neither, nothing, everything we can be, will be, and cease to be and are again. Or something like that at the center of the ring dance, ring shout, something bobbing there in the middle, weaving, doing its steps counterpoint to the counterclockwise-circling boys. Whatever it is, this unseen thing that sometimes takes the shape of a basketball, it moves the boys and draws them together and accounts also for their nearly trancelike focus, the strange cries and howls the players emit, the moans, sweat, tears, and sometimes blood they leak onto this threshing floor, this grassy, stomped-down clearing in a forest older than slavery days, as old as Africa, and maybe Africa its vexed old self still not ancient enough to get us to the game's origins. But it will do for a start.

First let there be the primeval forest and then the game plan (surely it involved discovering, deploying the ability of our bodies to dance with one another in all the modes we now take for granted and plenty we've forgotten and some still to be reinvented), the blueprint our ancestors choreographed for escaping wooded night and chancing the danger of leaving behind the sheltering trees, venturing into the daylight of clan and village. Next comes the ring shout to commemorate the game plan, the escape from loneliness and fear, the ring shout ritual as it was conceived in Africa and practiced in the New World when the Old World's light was snuffed out and we were uprooted, transplanted brutally by people ignorant of our ways, strangers with no concern about whether we'd prosper or survive in Babylon, just that we'd help our captors get over, conquer the land, conquer nature, assist their dreamy ascendancy to the status of gods reigning on the throne of our labor, our corpses, the corpses of nature. The ring shout a means of stepping away, stepping around our captors' plans for us, transforming our captivity, summoning, freeing the spirits we'd secretly transported inside us across the waters, praying that the ancient watchers like Damballah would rescue our captive flesh from bondage.

Ring shouts an archetypal emancipatory ritual for kidnapped Africans in a New World. *You put your left foot in / You take your right foot out / You do the hokey-pokey / then you shake it all about.* Sounds too simple, doesn't it. But no more or less simple than stealing human beings, forcing them to work for you, growing fat from the profits of buying and selling them, exploiting their labor till one crop of slaves dies off and needs to be replaced and the cycle starts over again. That simple idea worked for a while. Founded the incalculable fortunes still pumping out more wealth today. So why not the equally simple, radical expedient of shuffling, dancing out of our chains. Dividing ourselves, hiding ourselves, stealing the parts of ourselves we really need, leaving enough behind so ole Massa doesn't notice we're gone. Performing the ring shout we taught ourselves to shapeshift, conduct our spirits to a region where they could heal themselves, grow strong again, recall and enact their rootedness elsewhere in a far, far different place, a better place, remind ourselves to serve our own interests and destinies but also to assume responsibility for others who shared our color and/or plight, others designated by the obscene lies of race to be eternal servants when in fact race and bondage both mirages, evil figments of our enemies' self-serving imagination, a miasma, a fog the ring shout could penetrate and dispel. *Could dance away.* Once the spirits got to working on all this and we'd learned to allow dancing room for more such work, such *play,* and disciplined the parts of ourselves we could counterfeit and leave behind, leave in the so-called master's service, or seem to leave anyway, why wouldn't we, you, once the lesson of the ring shout connected us to a freer past, protected us from a gruesome present, why wouldn't we invent and perfect a thousand other rituals, public and private, imitating the ring shout model, not only to hasten but to begin to experience in the here and now of Babylon that great day of freedom we're sure is on its way.

The glow at the ring's core a beacon and witness, assurance the great day is coming. On time. One morning soon. The time our bare feet beat in the ring shout on southern plantations, tapped on the boards of Catherine Street wharf in New York City after we'd sold our oysters and figured out more money was to be made, more space liberated by vending the mesmerizing charms of our flying feet, the tune drummed just yesterday by the dribbler's measured patting of the basketball as he jooks, spins, scoots over the asphalt of the court in the Village, over the court in Westinghouse Park, the park reappearing right on time now after we've played at losing it, Freed, on time because it's okay to go there now, it's time to rename it, reclaim it, to let the thought of it materialize again, every detail clear, ready, and shining as we hump down the tracks or down Finance, Freed, to catch a run.